CORPORATE ENVIRONMENTALISM IN A GLOBAL ECONOMY

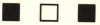

CORPORATE ENVIRONMENTALISM IN A GLOBAL ECONOMY

Societal Values in International Technology Transfer

Halina Szejnwald Brown
Patrick Derr, Ortwin Renn, Allen L. White

with a chapter by
Jeanne X. Kasperson and Roger E. Kasperson

Q Quorum Books
Westport, Connecticut • London

Library of Congress Cataloging-in-Publication Data

Corporate environmentalism in a global economy : societal values in international
   technology transfer / Halina Szejnwald Brown . . . [et al.].
        p. cm.
      Includes bibliographical references and index.
      ISBN 0–89930–802–3
      1. Social responsibility of business—Developing countries.
   2. International business enterprises—Developing countries.
   3. Technology transfer—Economic aspects—Developing countries.
   4. Economic development—Environmental aspects.   I. Brown, Halina Szejnwald.
   HD60.5.D44C67   1993
   658.4—dc20   92–19851

British Library Cataloguing in Publication Data is available.

Library of Congress Catalog Card Number: 92–19851
ISBN: 0–89930–802–3

First published in 1993

Quorum Books, 88 Post Road West, Westport, Connecticut 06881
An imprint of Greenwood Publishing Group, Inc.

Printed in the United States of America

∞™

The paper used in this book complies with the
Permanent Paper Standard issued by the National
Information Standards Organization (Z39.48—1984).

10 9 8 7 6 5 4 3 2 1

Figure 3.5 taken from *Transnational Corporations in a Developing Country: The
Indian Experience,* © 1988 by John Martinussen. Reprinted by permission of Sage
Publications, Inc.

Contents

Acknowledgments

This book reflects a melding of several streams of research. Nearly two decades ago, researchers at Clark University's Center for Technology, Environment, and Development (CENTED) engaged the problem of classifying, comparing, and managing technological hazards. This early work kindled an interest in the ethical and value issues attendant in societal management of hazards, and the group took on studies of equity issues in the management of radioactive wastes and of the management of differential susceptibility and exposures to hazards in the workplace and the general environment.

A focus on the corporate sector flowed naturally from that earlier work at CENTED, and its first chapter came to fruition in a 1988 volume on the corporate management of health and safety. This book can be viewed as the second chapter. It focuses on the international aspects of hazard management at manufacturing facilities and extends the analytical perspective to include all the key actors in international technology transfer: host countries, multinational corporations, and host country joint venture partners.

The National Science Foundation provided financial support for this research project through its Program in Ethics and Values Studies. Our thanks to the program director, Dr. Rachelle Hollander, who encouraged us to submit the consecutive versions of the proposal.

Many individuals and institutions made this project possible and left their mark on the final product. The vision and healthy scientific curiosity of Bruce Karrh, vice president for safety, health, and environment at E.I. du Pont de Nemours and Company; Frank Friedman, vice president for health, environment, and safety at Occidental Petroleum Corporation; and James MacKenzie, corporate director for environmental health and safety at Xerox Corporation, allowed us to enlist the participation of these three corporations. Their colleagues at the U.S. and overseas operations generously contributed time, ideas, and constructive criticism and patiently responded to our voracious appetite for documents and meetings with key corporate managers. Key among these individuals at Du Pont were Jess Stuart, Peter Meyers, Bill Mottel, and Richard Haden; at Du Pont Far East: Scott Gray; at Du Pont Thailand: S. Malin and S. Chalat; at Occidental Chemical: Stan Szymanski, Roger Corwin, and James Miller; at Thai Occidental: Kevin Smith; at Xerox: James O'Brien, Robert Mermelstein, and Carroll Lovett; at Rank Xerox: Donald Baker and Andrew Smith; at Modi Xerox: J. W. van Eerde, R. S. Yadav, and U. R. Saha.

The contribution of our collaborators in India and Thailand was equally pivotal. Professor B. Bowonder and Mr. S. S. Arvind at the Administrative Staff College of India; and Professor Mathuros Ruchirawat, Professor Jutamaad Satayavivad, Dr. Skorn Mongolsuk, and Dr. Udom Chantharaksri of Mahidol University in Bangkok provided key insights into development policies and histories of their countries; focused our field investigations; provided access to the key documents, institutions, and individuals in their countries; and showered us with hospitality during the field research.

The research was further enriched by the constructive criticism offered by the members of the project advisory panel, Paul Shrivastava of Bucknell University, Douglas McLean of the University of Maryland, Karim Ahmed of Environ Corp., Morris Morris of Brown University, and Anthony Marcil of the World Environment Center.

At Clark University, Jeffery Himmelberger worked on the project in partial fulfillment of the requirements for his doctoral degree. His tireless and creative analysis of field data, insightful critique of the many drafts of the manuscript, and significant contributions to Chapters 3, 4, and 5 are deeply appreciated. We also gratefully acknowledge the contributions of Clark University administrative staff members Marcia V. Szugda, program assistant, Environment, Technology and Society Program, and Lu Ann Pacenka, coordinator, Hazard Assessment Group (CENTED), whose meticulous preparation of the final manuscript was a fitting end to a fascinating research journey spanning nearly three years.

CORPORATE
ENVIRONMENTALISM IN
A GLOBAL ECONOMY

CHAPTER 1

Introduction

Considering how much has been said and written on the subject of industrial facilities of multinational corporations (MNCs) in developing countries, it is astonishing how little is known (outside perhaps the corporate circle) about the actual events leading to establishment of such enterprises and about the forces that shape the environment, health, and safety (EH&S) performance at such facilities. How is it that some industrial plants perform better in EH&S than others? To what extent does a corporation influence that outcome and how much can be attributed to a host country or other forces? What motivates and constrains these key actors in their interactions during negotiations, construction, and start-up of the facility-siting process? What trade-offs are made during that process to accommodate the tension among desirable yet competing objectives?

Underlying these questions is a fundamental issue of values related to host country development, to environmental and health protection, and to corporate development. Even a cursory exploration of international development and MNC experience during the last decade suggests that concurrent pursuit of growth, social and political development, and EH&S is laden with potential conflicts and the necessity of making trade-offs, the reconciliation of which is neither self-evident nor automatic. Acting in their best interests, both MNCs and host countries face a plethora of competing demands and priorities originating from internal and external sources. Value conflicts arise because multiple desirable ends cannot be simultaneously achieved in a a world of finite resources. Consider these typical compromises:

- increased automation, designed and adapted to promote safety and environmental protection, may be incompatible with labor-intensive practices designed to promote local employment or to increase profitability;

- location in a densely populated area, intended to improve access for a large number of employees and to facilitate the transportation of materials and products, may be incompatible with community safety;
- location in a poorly developed region, intended to increase employment and equitable sharing of economic gains, may impede efficient mobilization of resources, reduce corporate growth and profitability, and deter response to emergencies;
- reliance on foreign experts, intended to increase safety and environmental performance, may be incompatible with the desire for local control and with the technology assimilation objectives;
- adoption by the MNC of parent country's occupational and environmental standards, motivated by a desire to promote safety and equivalence in protection, may be incompatible with the notion of host country self-determination and with the development of host country regulatory capacity.

Some conflicts may compete in the short term but prove amenable to medium-term reconciliation. Others may be problematic even in medium-term, though compatible in the context of long-run sustainability. Some may be reduced or eliminated through redesign of technology, social arrangements, or institutional changes. Yet others may require substantial trade-offs between competing goods. Although recognition of the value conflicts is the first necessary step in achieving reconciliation or trade-offs, in the normal conduct of business firms and host countries rarely recognize, much less articulate, them, preferring instead to preserve the notion for themselves and the outside world that all desirable objectives may be jointly pursued without sacrificing one for the other. In the post-Bhopal atmosphere of intense international activities aimed at prevention or mitigation of such tragedies in the future, these value issues clearly need to be better understood if substantial international gains are to be made.

It is these questions about values and value trade-offs that are the theme of this book. The book is based on a three-year study focusing on the experience of three large U.S.-based multinational corporations—Du Pont Agricultural Products, Occidental Chemical, and Xerox—in establishing hazardous industrial facilities in two developing countries, India and Thailand, in the 1980s. These are stories of success. The study departed from the familiar impulse to learn from disasters and problems and concentrated on corporations that claim to be socially responsible in business ventures and that pride themselves in being profitable, safe, and environmentally sound.

The project was based on the assumption that both the host countries and the corporations have, as one of their key objectives, an environmentally and occupationally sound facility, and that both share two sets of values: those related to environment, health, and safety (EH&S) goals and those related to development, equity, and independence (DE&I) goals. Further, it was assumed that these two sets of values manifest themselves through country- and corporation-specific policies in relation to siting of MNC foreign affiliates. The study examines the influence and interaction of these two clusters of values upon decisions and activities of the key actors, including any value conflicts and trade-offs that may occur in the course of facility development.

The book has three broad objectives:

1. to examine the entry of the two value sets in the decision-making process and their recognition by corporate and host country officials;
2. to assess the degree to which these values are compatible or in conflict (distinguishing between apparent and real conflicts, and between the conflicts), within and between the two sets; and
3. to elucidate how value interactions contribute to EH&S outcomes on a facility level.

MULTINATIONAL CORPORATIONS, DEVELOPING COUNTRIES, AND EH&S

The emergence of MNCs as the dominant force in post-World War II international capital markets is a much studied and often controversial phenomenon. From their pre-war involvement in extractive activities in the agricultural and mineral sectors, MNCs aggressively entered the manufacturing sector in developing countries in the 1950s and 1960s, led initially by U.S. firms but soon joined by European and Japanese enterprises. Facilitated by rapid advances in transport and telecommunications technologies, and induced by import-substitution policies of developing countries, industrial countries continue to move manufacturing operations into developing countries to gain access to new markets, cheap labor, and raw materials.

Data compiled by the United Nations Centre on Transnational Corporations (UNCTC 1991) show that the average ratio of foreign to domestic investment among developing countries is approximately twice the ratio in Western nations. An estimated 60 percent of all industrial investment in developing nations originates outside such countries, with Western MNCs representing a large proportion of that figure (United Nations Environmental Programme [UNEP] 1984, cited in Covello and Frey 1990). Some 500 MNCs accounted for 80 percent of all direct foreign investment (Stopford and Dunning 1983, cited in Jenkins 1987). MNCs remain the principal source of technologies in the most dynamic industrial sectors. With the globalization of product production and marketing, and attendant expansion of intra-firm transfer of capital and technology, the role of MNCs in the next decade will become even more pivotal in shaping the nature and pace of technology transfer to developing countries.

During the post-war years, the multinational-host country dynamics underwent fundamental changes, driven by both economic and political shifts in North-South relations. The end of de jure colonialism, which had lasted well into the 1960s, together with the rapid industrialization in certain Latin American and Asian nations, spawned aggressive efforts to take control of development and to fashion new strategies for retaining the fruits of such development within host countries. These changes manifested themselves throughout the 1960s and 1970s in a gradual tightening of controls on ownership and management of MNC operations which, until then, had operated largely unfettered by host country controls. In free market and socialist countries alike, MNCs entered in a period of high visibility, the subject of a growing array of legal and economic instruments aimed at appropriating a portion of the MNC surplus for the benefit of host country development. What had once been a relatively invisible presence evolved into a more scrutinized and public activity.

In a parallel development, the replacement of extractive activities with manufacturing activities as the dominant form of MNC investments in developing countries introduced a wave of technological hazards in the form of occupational exposures to hazardous materials, air and water pollution, and the risk of large-scale industrial accidents. In many developing countries, the pace of industrialization outstripped the capacity of host governments to properly regulate the hazards imported by MNCs, whether or not such hazards were inherently greater than those present in parent country operations. For some firms, the absence of a regulatory infrastructure was an invitation to cut corners, import obsolete equipment, and expose workers, communities, and the environment to increased pollution. For other firms committed to achieving greater equality or equivalence with parent country operations, their mere status as foreign-owned enterprises made every mishap, large or small, vulnerable to stigmatization of the corporation as a symbol of Western control and domination.

Collectively, by the 1970s these trends had helped shape the relationship of developing countries and MNCs into one characterized by a mixture of caution, mistrust, and political ideology. The notion that MNCs were a distinctive breed of economic enterprise requiring both international and domestic scrutiny and controls was a position that gained substantial currency among those responsible for fostering Third World development. Underlying this view was a perception that hosting MNCs involved certain unavoidable trade-offs stemming from the intrinsic conflict between corporate and host country development objectives. These views are evident, for example, in the United Nations' Code of Conduct for Transnational Corporations, initiated in the early 1970s (UNCTC 1976), and its contemporary, Organization for Economic Co-operation and Development (OECD) *Guidelines for Multinational Enterprises* (OECD 1976). Both documents clearly assume an inherent conflict of MNC business objectives and host country development and EH&S objectives. These voluntary codes, although designed to guide MNCs in dealing with their hosts, also sent an unmistakeable message of caution to those targeted for MNC investment.

By the 1980s, the theme of conflict and competition had run its course and had given way to a more pragmatic approach built on the notion of long-term shared interest. The realization that access to global capital and consumers is requisite to sustained economic growth has been reinforced by greater sophistication and experience on the part of host countries in negotiating with MNCs. In a remarkable contrast to the 1976 Codes of Conduct, the 1988 United Nations document on transnational corporations and world development stressed cooperation between MNCs and host countries, the need for flexibility on the part of host countries to accommodate the MNCs' business objectives, and need for greater self-regulation by MNCs themselves. The language of the discussion mirrors this shift toward accommodation, mutuality, and compromise: "corporate environmentalism," "public-private partnership," and "product stewardship" exemplify this conciliatory tone (UNCTC 1988; International Chamber of Commerce 1990). At the same time, many Western MNCs have altered their view of environmental protection as a mandated burden to one in which environment and safety are good business from a product, productivity, and public profile standpoint. Thus, without diminishing the need for the developing countries to maintain an active role in influencing the activities of MNCs, the growing consensus in the 1980s and 1990s has been to view all the key players as partners, mutually and fundamentally dependent on each other, and having shared responsibilities for the direction of the development of the Third World.

As this new view of MNC-host country interdependence and co-responsibility has emerged, so has a new large-scale vision of sustainable development, in essence the global and national scale counterpart to the firm-level model described earlier. Starting with the seminal *Founex Report* (Ozorio del Almeida et al. 1971) and Stockholm Conference (UNCESI 1972), gathering momentum with the *World Conservation Strategy* (International Union for Conservation of Nature [IUCN] 1980), *Brandt Commission Report* (Independent Commission on International Development Issues [ICIDI] 1980), and World Industry Conference on Environmental Management (United Nations Environmental Programme [UNEP] 1984), and culminating with the landmark *Our Common Future* report (World Commission on Environment and Development [WCED] 1987), the concept of the long-term compatibility of the environment and economic and social development has replaced the presumption of conflict and incompatibility.

Notwithstanding the conciliatory tone of the last decade, translating earnest intentions into working procedures, especially with regard to exports of hazardous products and processes, remains an unfinished task. Developing countries in particular are vulnerable to technology-related risks because of limited financial resources, inadequate access to data and technical expertise, inadequate regulatory infrastructure, and limited public participation in hazard management (Ashford and Ayers 1985; Covello and Frey 1990).

Among the exported hazardous products, international trade in medicines, pesticides, consumer products, and hazardous wastes, has been the focus of much adverse publicity and lingering concern over the responsibilities of MNC in developing countries. Partly in response to these concerns, during the past two decades multiple legal constraints have been imposed in the United States on the export of hazardous products to the developing world. Some of these took the form of special provisions in laws otherwise primarily applicable to the domestic management of these hazards, such as the Federal Insecticide, Fungicide, and Rodenticide Act (FIFRA), the Resource Conservation and Recovery Act (RCRA), the Toxic Substance Control Act (TSCA), the Food and Drug Act, the Public Health Service Act, and the Consumer Product Safety Act. Others, such as the Export Administration Act, were more general. In the area of hazardous waste trade, perhaps the most volatile of all exports issues, the 1988 Basel Convention, set forth a framework for regulating transboundary movements of such substances.

To varying degrees, the core principles behind these laws and conventions is prior informed consent. Under this principle, each country is entitled to make its own decisions about risks and the seller has a responsibility to inform the trade partner about the risks according to its best knowledge. Thus, proper labeling, information dissemination, notification of the appropriate U.S. agencies, and informed consent by the receiving country are the primary policy tools for protecting the developing nations from adverse effects of these technological hazards. In practice, these requirements translate into a shared responsibility for hazardous product exports between the host country government, which may directly accept or reject these materials, and the parent country government, through its role in monitoring and enforcing its own domestic laws and regulations.

The export of hazardous processes has also been the subject of a flurry of international activity, especially in the aftermath of the 1984 Bhopal tragedy. Industrial trade organizations, governments, corporations, and various national and international governmental and nongovernmental organizations have since announced codes of conduct, policies, guidelines, protocols, and international agreements. The legal liability laws of many countries also underwent major changes after Bhopal, creating powerful disincentives to careless management of hazardous technologies by MNCs.

While these activities will no doubt lead to further risk reduction, in contrast to hazardous product exports (including wastes), the management of EH&S at foreign subsidiaries of MNC is primarily in the hands of the corporation and the host country, with other organizations and governments playing only indirect roles. In principle, this responsibility can be exercised by both parties at all stages of facility establishment and operation. The licensing-and-permitting process allows a host country to influence the design and operating conditions of an MNC facility or to reject it altogether if serious incompatibility occurs. Once established, a facility may be monitored through inspections and licence renewals. The corporation, for its part, may develop formal policies regarding hazard management at foreign subsidiaries, including design, construction, management, training and education, and may respond to the host country's requirements through adaptation or withdrawal.

EARLIER STUDIES

The complex issues related to the export of hazardous manufacturing facilities—driving forces, trends, implications, and prognosis—have been the object of extensive research. The resulting literature can be divided into three broad categories, each deserving of notice.

The first category of studies is corporation-centered and examines the role of firms as agents of EH&S technology transfer through their foreign affiliates. This literature includes analyses of corporate policies and management systems for implementing EH&S in their international facilities (Flaherty and Rappaport 1991; Gladwin 1977; Rappaport and Flaherty 1991; Morrison 1991, pp. 16–17; UNCTC 1991b); studies of organizational behavior of MNCs in the context of host country regulatory climates (Gladwin and Walter 1976; Gladwin and Wells 1976); and studies of implementation of international safety and health guidelines at foreign affiliates of MNCs (International Labour Office [ILO] 1984).

The second category of studies focuses on the role of the host country in shaping the technology transfer decisions and effects of MNCs. This research often gives particular attention to the evolution of regulations and policies relative to environmental and industrial safety, both in general and in relation to MNC facilities. The work of Leonard and Morrell (1981), Morell and Poznanski (1985), Pimenta (1987), Ural (1987) and White (1991) exemplify this cluster.

The third category of research explores the dynamics and interdependencies of the MNC behavior vis-à-vis the developing country's laws, regulations, and political climate. Five lines of inquiry may be distinguished here:

1. the question of "pollution havens"—the flight of hazardous industrial enterprises from developed to developing countries to avoid domestic regulations and standards (Castleman 1987; Duerksen 1983; Gladwin and Wells 1976; Knogden 1979; Leonard 1987; Leonard 1988; Pearson and Pryor 1978; Richardson and Mutti 1976; Walter 1982);

2. analyses of large-scale technological failures and pollution episodes at the MNCs' Third World facilities (Bowonder, Kasperson, and Kasperson 1985; Bowonder and Linstone 1987; Castleman and Purkavastha 1985; Gladwin 1985; Gladwin 1987; Lagadec 1987; Morrell and Poznanski 1985; Shrivastava 1987; Weir 1987);

3. comparative analysis of environment, health, and safety performance of MNC affiliates in industrial versus developing countries (Hassan 1981; Ives 1985; Knodgen 1979; ILO 1984; Royston 1979);

4. comparative analysis of environment, health, and safety performance of domestically owned versus MNC-owned facilities in developing countries (Castleman 1987, ILO 1984; Pimenta 1987; and Royston 1985). Notably, recent work of

the United Nations (United Nations Economic and Social Commission for Asia and the Pacific 1988 and 1990) addresses the latter four lines of inquiry; and

5. negotiations between host countries and multinational corporations over the environmental aspects of industrial enterprises (Leonard 1985; Pinz 1987; Leonard 1988).

Collectively, these studies mirror the evolution of MNC-host country relations during the last three decades. The initially dominant interests were in the goods and bads of corporate behavior and in the balance of power between host countries and multinational corporations. These have been gradually enriched by inquiries into the complexities of achieving environmentally sound and safe facilities, into the most appropriate roles for the key actors in pursuing that objective, and into the actual negotiation process over the foreign subsidiaries. At the same time, the reality emerging from this body of research is one that defies simple characterization and generalization. Time has tended to blur, rather than resolve, the debate about pollution havens and double standards, in part because aggregate trends do not automatically translate into measurable outcomes and in part because of the paucity of on-the-ground performance data to assess how facilities actually perform in home versus host countries. The occasionally inevitable major accidents at MNCs' overseas facilities only polarize the debate further.

In the area most akin to our study, the case studies of Pinz (1987) and Leonard (1988) explore the environmental negotiations between host country and multinational corporation. However, their focus on select countries (Papua, New Guinea, and Mexico, Ireland, and Spain, respectively) and on visibly polluting industries (mostly mining, energy generation, and large chemical complexes), as well as their limited interest in the *process* of negotiation and in the actual performance of the new enterprises, leaves many unanswered questions at the nexus of MNC-host country interactions. At this juncture, we have few explanations as to the underlying values that motivate the principal actors in their mutual interactions and how such interactions translate into different levels of facility performance. Between the initial steps in MNC strategic planning for overseas expansion and the final stage of facility operation lies a largely unexplored domain in which negotiation, trade-offs, and reconciliation of competing objectives shape the terms, conditions, and performance of foreign affiliates.

Despite the intense interest in MNCs in developing countries, EH&S aspects of MNC facilities continue to be treated generally as a black box within which these interactions occur. Our study provides a glimpse inside this box in an attempt to unravel some of its content.

SCOPE AND RESEARCH DECISION

This study explores the influence of two crucial sets of values—development, equity, and independence, and environment, health, and safety—upon the decisions, negotiations, and policies that ultimately determine the EH&S performance of MNC facilities in developing countries. We stress at the outset that the study is not directed at comparing the domestic and foreign facilities of MNCs. Neither does it attempt to document or refute the case for corporate misconduct. Instead, we direct our attention to the dynamics of MNC-host country interactions in the course of facility development as the two parties put into practice their respective pursuits of DE&I and EH&S values.

The vehicle for achieving this is a chronicle of decisions and events that, in turn, are interpreted by referring to the underlying values, trade-offs, and compromises. This chronicle includes negotiations, licensing, construction, and start-up of each facility. The analysis of sustained performance of each facility is conducted only to the extent necessary to understand the effects on performance of the decisions made during siting. Similarly, the analysis of the DE&I and EH&S-related policies of the host countries and the corporations is conducted primarily for the purpose of interpreting the events and decisions that occurred in each case.

Case study, rather than survey, research was the chosen methodology since it afforded a close-up view of the actors and nuances of each case. It also enabled us to undertake the study with a relatively "soft" working hypothesis— that value conflicts occur in multiple, diverse, and unanticipated forms in the course of facility siting (Yin 1988). At the same time, the small sample size severely limits the capacity to generalize our findings, in the end leaving as many issues discovered as resolved. We examine these limitations again in the final chapter.

The data for analysis were collected by way of interviews, discussions, site visits, and review of key documents. Each of the three stories was reconstructed by tapping the key participants: the host country authorities, the U.S.-based corporate officers and management, and the management and workers of each facility. Unfortunately, in two cases that were jointly owned, we did not succeed in reaching the joint venture partners. Many hours of unstructured interviews were conducted at Clark University, at the corporate headquarters of the corporations, and on the premises of the three facilities. The documents studied include official corporate and national policy statements, facility permit and license records, and such internal corporate documents as joint venture agreements, facility blueprints, internal memoranda, and letters. Some of the corporate documents were confidential; they were used as sources of information but not quoted verbatim. In addition, performance data for the three facilities under study, as well as other facilities of the three corporations, were analyzed.

Three teams of investigators participated in the study: the U.S. team provided the overall direction to the project, while the teams from Mahidol University in Thailand and from Administrative Staff College in India concentrated on providing the host country perspectives and on providing the U.S. team with access to high officials in each country.

Securing the participation of the corporations was difficult. The reluctance of any large organization, including corporations, to submit to external inquiry was not unexpected, particularly in the sensitive area of EH&S. Extensive and critical publicity surrounding corporate mismanagement is well known to any executive who deals with hazardous materials, processes, and products. Furthermore, to conduct the study as we designed it required a major commitment of staff time and resources at both headquarters and foreign affiliates. This was essential to understanding the processes and interactions that lie at the heart of the research questions and the reconstruction of the stories behind each facility's development. Not surprisingly, the three corporations that agreed to participate, of the approximately fifty approached, are large, rich in resources, and eager to share their strong policies and commitment to EH&S. This self-selection, which we fully recognize, further restricts the ability to generalize findings.

VOLUME PREVIEW

The volume is organized into eight chapters. Following this introduction, Chapter 2 defines the terminology and conceptual framework used throughout the study. Chapter 3 sets the stage for the three case studies by profiling the host countries and the corporations, emphasizing EH&S policies and procedures governing the siting of foreign MNC facilities. Chapter 4 details the stories of the three facilities, the paths, diversions, obstacles, and ultimate success in siting in India and Thailand. From these stories emerge three themes that help explain the processes and outcomes attendant to each facility: the host country's DE&I values, corporate culture, and the nature of business arrangements between parent and partner. Each of these themes is explored in detail in Chapters 5, 6, and 7, respectively.

Chapter 8 synthesizes the team's findings. It presents a revised model of facility development; offers our conclusions regarding the value of trade-offs, corporate environmentalism, the key determinants of facility performance, and the roles played by the key participants; and offers recommendations for improving the negotiating process.

REFERENCES

Ashford, Nicholas A., and Christine Ayers. "Policy Issues for Consideration in Transferring Technology to Developing Countries." *Ecology Law Quarterly* 12:4 (1985): 871–905.

Bowonder, B., Jeanne X. Kasperson, and Roger E. Kasperson. "Avoiding Future Bhopals." *Environment* 27 (1985): 6–13, 31–37.

Bowonder, B., and H. A. Linstone. "Notes on the Bhopal Accident: Risk Analysis and Multiple Perspectives." *Technological Forecasting and Social Change* 32 (1987): 183–202.

Castleman, Barry. "Workplace Health in Developing Countries." Pages 149–174 in Charles S. Pearson (ed.), *Multinational Corporations, Environment, and Third World: Business Matters*. Durham, NC: Duke University Press, 1987.

Castleman, Barry, and Purkavastha Prabir. "The Bhopal Disaster as a Case Study in Double Standards." Pages 213–221 in Jane H. Ives (ed.), *The Export of Hazard: Transnational Corporations and Environmental Control Issues*. Boston, MA: Routledge and Kegan Paul, 1985.

Covello, Vincent T., and R. Scott Frey. "Technology-Based Environmental Health Risks in Developing Nations." *Technological Forecasting and Social Change* 37 (1990): 159–179.

Duerksen, Christopher. *Environmental Regulations of Plant Siting: How to Make It Work Better*. Washington, DC: The Conservation Foundation, 1983.

Flaherty, Margaret, and Ann Rappaport. *Multinational Corporations and the Environment: A Survey of Global Practices*. Medford, MA: Tufts University, The Center for Environmental Management, 1991.

Gladwin, Thomas, N. *Environment, Planning, and The Multinational Corporation*. Greenwich, CN: JAI Press, 1977.

Gladwin, Thomas N. "The Bhopal Tragedy: Lessons for Management." *NYU Business* 5:1 (1985): 17–21.

——. "A Case Study of the Bhopal Tragedy." Pages 223–239 in Charles S. Pearson (ed.), *Multinational Corporations, Environment, and Third World: Business Matters*. Durham, NC: Duke University Press, 1987.

Gladwin, Thomas N., and Ingo Walter. "Multinational Enterprise, Social Responsiveness, and Pollution Control." *Journal of International Business Studies* 7 (Fall– Winter, 1976): 57–74.

Gladwin, Thomas N., and John G. Wells. "Multinational Corporations and Environmental Protection: Patterns of Organizational Adaptation." *International Studies of Management and Organization* 6 (1976): 160–184.

Hassan, Amin, Eliana Velasquez, Roberto Belmar, Molly Coye, Ernest Drucker, Phillip Landrigan, David J. Michaels, and Devin B. Sidel. "Mercury Poisoning in Nicaragua: A Case Study of the Export of Environment and Occupational Health Hazards by Multinational Corporations." *International Journal of Health Services*. 11 (1981): 221–226.

Independent Commission on International Development Issues. *North–South: A Programme for Survival*. Cambridge, MA: MIT Press, 1980.

International Chamber of Commerce. *Papers presented at the Industry Forum on Environment: A Meeting for Industry Leaders in Connection with the 1990 Bergen Conference "Action for a Common Future."* Bergen, Norway, 8–16 May, 1990.

International Labour Office. *Safety and Health Practices of Multinational Enterprises*. Geneva, 1984.

International Union for Conservation of Nature and Natural Resources. *World Conservation Strategy: Living Resource Conservation for Sustainable Development*, International Union for Conservation of Nature-United Nations Environmental Programme-WWF 1980.

Ives, Jane H. "The Health Effects of the Transfer of Technology to the Developing World: Report and Case Studies." Pages 172–191 in Jane H. Ives (ed.), *The*

Export of Hazard: Transnational Corporations and Environmental Control Issues. Boston MA: Routledge and Kegan Paul, 1985.

Jenkins, Rhys. *Transnational Corporations and Uneven Development: The Internationalization of Capital and the Third World.* London and New York: Metheun, 1987, page 8.

Knogden, Gabriele. "Environment and Industrial Siting: Results of an Empirical Survey of Investment by West German Industry in Developing Countries." *Zeitschrift fur Umweltpolitik* 2 (1979): 407.

Lagadec, Patrick. "From Seveso to Mexico and Bhopal: Learning to Cope with Crisis." Pages 13–46 in P. Kleindorfer and H. Kunreuther (eds.), *Insuring and Managing Hazardous Risks: From Seveso to Bhopal and Beyond.* Berlin: Springer-Verlag, 1987.

Leonard, H. Jeffrey. "Confronting Industrial Pollution in Rapidly Industrializing Countries: Myths, Pitfalls, and Opportunities." *Ecology Law Quarterly* 12 (1985a): 779–816.

———. "Politics and Pollution from Urban and Industrial Development." Pages 263–291 in H. Jeffrey Leonard (ed.), *Divesting Nature's Capital: The Political Economy of Environmental Abuse in the Third World.* New York: Holmens and Meier, 1985.

———. *Are Environmental Regulations Driving U.S. Industry Overseas?* Washington, DC: Conservation Foundation, 1987.

———. *Pollution and the Struggle for World Product.* Cambridge: Cambridge University Press, 1988.

Leonard, H. Jeffrey, and David Morell. "The Emergence of Environmental Concern in Developing Countries: A Political Perspective." *Stanford Journal of International Law* 17:2 (1981), 281–313.

Morrell, David, and Joanna Poznanski. "Rhetoric and Reality: Environmental Politics and Environmental Administration in Developing Countries." Pages 137–176 in H. Jeffrey Leonard (ed.), *Divesting Nature's Capital: The Political Economy of Environmental Abuse in the Third World.* New York: Holmens and Meier, 1985.

Morrison, Catherine. *Managing Environmental Affairs: Corporate Practices in the U.S., Canada and Europe.* New York: The Conference Board, 1991.

Organization for Economic Co-operation and Development. *Guidelines for Multinational Enterprises,* Paris, 1976.

Ozorio del Almeida, M., W. Beckerman, I. Sackhs, and G. Corea. *Environment and Development: The Founex Report.* Carnegie Endowment for International Peace, No. 586: 1972.

Pearson, Charles S., and Anthony Pryor. *Environment: North and South.* New York: John Wiley, 1978.

Pimenta, Joao Carlos P. "Multinational Corporations and Industrial Pollution Control in Sao Paulo, Brazil." Pages 198–220 in Charles S. Pearson (ed.), *Multinational Corporations, Environment, and Third World: Business Matters.* Durham, NC: Duke University Press, 1987.

Pintz, William. "Environmental Negotiations in the Ok Tedi Mine in Papua New Guinea." Pages 35–63 in Charles S. Pearson (ed.), *Multinational Corporations, Environment, and Third World: Business Matters.* Durham, NC: Duke University Press, 1987.

Richardson, David J., and John Mutti. "Industrial Displacement Through Environmental Controls." Pages 57–102 in Ingo Walter (ed.), *Studies in International Environmental Economics*. New York: John Wiley, 1976.

Rappaport, Ann, and Margaret Flaherty. "Multinational Corporations and the Environment: Context and Challenges." *International Environment Reporter* 14:9 (1991): 261–267.

Royston, Michael G. "Control by Multinational Corporations: The Environmental Case for Scenario 4." *Ambio* 8 (1979): 84–89.

——. "Local and Multinational Corporations: Reappraising Environmental Management." *Environment* 27:1 (1985): 12–20, 39–43.

Shrivastava, Paul. *Bhopal: Anatomy of a Crisis,* Cambridge, MA: Ballinger, 1987.

Stopford, J., and J. Dunning. *Multinationals: Company Performance and Global Trends*. London: Macmillan, 1983.

United Nations Centre for Economic and Social Information. *Environment: Stockholm*. New York: United Nations, 1972.

United Nations Centre on Transnational Corporations. *Transnational Corporations: Issues Involved in the Formulation of a Code of Conduct*. New York: United Nations, 1976.

——. *Environmental Aspects of the Activities of Transnational Corporations: A Survey*. New York: United Nations, 1985.

——. *Transnational Corporations in World Development: Trends and Prospects*. New York: United Nations, 1988.

——. *World Investment Report 1991: The Triad in Foreign Direct Investment*. New York: United Nations, 1991a.

——. *Benchmark Corporate Environmental Survey: First Statistical Results, Management Systems and Methodology*. New York: United Nations, 1991b.

United Nations Economic and Social Commission for Asia and the Pacific/United Nations Centre on Transnational Corporations Joint Unit on Transnational Corporations. *Transnational Corporations and Environmental Management in Selected Asian and Pacific Developing Countries*. Bangkok: United Nations, 1988.

——. *Environmental Aspects of Transnational Corporation Activities in Pollution-Intensive Industries in Selected Asian and Pacific Developing Countries*. Bangkok: United Nations, 1990.

United Nations Environment Programme. "World Industry Conference on Environmental Management: Outcome and Reactions." *Industry and Environment*. 5 (1984): 1–41.

Ural, Engin. "Environmental Protection and Foreign Private Investment in Turkey." Pages 175–197 in Charles S. Pearson (ed.), *Multinational Corporations, Environment, and Third World: Business Matters*. Durham, NC: Duke University Press, 1987.

Walter, Ingo. "Environmentally Induced Industrial Relocations to Developing Countries." Pages 127–151 in Seymore Rubin and Thomas Graham (eds.), *Environment and Trade*. Totowa, NJ: Allenheld, Osmon and Co., 1982.

Weir, David. *The Bhopal Syndrome: Pesticides, Environment, and Health*. San Francisco: Sierra Club Publications, 1987.

White, Allen L. "Venezuela's Organic Law: Regulating Pollution in an Industrializing Country." *Environment* 33:7 (1991): 16–20, 37–42.

World Commission on Environment and Development. *Our Common Future*. Oxford: Oxford University Press, 1987.

Yin, Robert, K. *Case Study Research: Design and Methods*. Newberry Park, CA: Sage Publications, 1988.

CHAPTER 2

Values and Culture in Technology Transfer

This study deals with the influence and interaction of two clusters of values upon decisions concerning the transfer to and siting of hazardous technological facilities in less developed countries. The study's design was influenced by a range of initial assumptions (both normative and empirical) and models (both substantive and heuristic), which helped to define the project, to direct the field work, and to guide the interpretation of empirical results. This chapter endeavors to identify and clarify these assumptions and models in sufficient detail to render them vulnerable to rational criticism, evaluation, and refinement.

The first section of this chapter characterizes the EH&S (environment, health, and safety) and DE&I (development, equity, and independence) value clusters, which are treated as independent variables in our study of hazardous technology transfer decisions. The second part explicates a number of concepts that are central to research reported here. These include the concepts of *value, value conflict, value trade-off, technology, culture, actor, policy,* and others. Most of these have widely varied meanings in different scholarly disciplines, and their interdisciplinary use requires special care. The third part considers some of the peculiar methodological problems posed by research aimed at the discovery and reconstruction of value-laden decision-making processes. The fourth section articulates the structural and developmental models of technology transfer that guided our research.

THE EH&S AND DE&I VALUE CLUSTERS

Environment, Health, and Safety Values

This cluster includes values relating to occupational health and safety and the protection of the public against disease, environmental hazards, and technological disasters. These values treat human health and safety as fundamental goods and consider environmental effects to the extent that these will in turn affect human health, safety, and well-being. Concern about the impact of industrial activities on sacred land or on highly valued landscapes, both of which are of special importance to many developing nations, are examples of such values.

But the EH&S cluster also includes values relating to environmental protection that are not derived simply from concern for human health and safety, that is, values that treat the environment as an intrinsic (and not merely an instrumental) good. The preservation of biotopes, for example, may be regarded as an important goal independent of its consequences for human beings. (For representative arguments in support of the view that the environment is an intrinsic good, see Hargrove 1989.)

These EH&S values are commonly held by nearly all parties involved and are broadly reflected in policy, legislation, and regulatory practice of host countries and corporations alike. Many nations have developed legislative and regulatory policies that reflect their EH&S values. In the highly developed nations that serve as MNC parent countries, these rules and policies may be so detailed that one can calculate the implicit value of saving a human life as a function of the individual's occupational status, the nature of the hazard, and the victim's involvement in the creation of the hazard. There is a rich literature discussing such calculations (see Berman 1978; Thaler and Rosen 1976; Shakow 1983). Using methods of contingent evaluation or replacement costs, one can calculate the implicit value (in terms of subjective utility losses or jobs or production lost) of saving a particular species (such as the snail darter) or biosphere (such as the Arctic wilderness reserve).

There is broad support for three sets of values we include in the EH&S value cluster. These are:

1. *Health and safety*—understood as referring to the protection of human life from avoidable risk or harm, and manifested as, for example, efforts to reduce or avoid occupational injury or illness; concern for the protection of specially vulnerable people and groups; and prevention or remediation of adverse public health effects from environmental or industrial sources.

2. *Consent and compensation*—understood as referring to the belief that human beings deserve information about the occupational and environmental hazards to which they may be exposed, have the capacity and right to make choices about accepting such risks, and deserve compensation for harms. These beliefs are man-

ifested in, for example, labeling and right-to-know regulations; workers' compensation systems; tort liability for consumer products; and legally mandated reporting of environmental releases and occupational accidents.

3. *Environmental protection*—understood as referring to a concern for the protection and preservation of nonhuman species and biotopes and diverse ecological domains, whether for their own sake or because of their consequences for human health, safety, and welfare. These values are manifested in, for example, legal protection of endangered species and habitats; creation of national wildlife and wilderness reserves; and regulation of destructive environmental discharges.

General acceptance of these EH&S values obviously does not entail any homogeneity of policy or practice between different nations: Different cultural and environmental circumstances can lead to very different national strategies for accomplishing similarly cherished EH&S goals. A nation convinced that "wealth is health" may prefer less stringent EH&S regulation in the short-term in order to accelerate development and maximize EH&S protection in the long-term (see Wildavsky 1990); a nation traumatized by a Bhopal-like catastrophe might be more concerned with implementing stringent EH&S standards from the outset, regardless of their effect on the pace of development.

Development, Equity, and Independence Values

The DE&I value cluster includes economic goods such as national wealth, standard of living, productive capacity, and balanced trade, equity values related to the socially acceptable distribution of these economic goods, and political values such as national political stability, preferences for particular forms of government, independence from other nations, and international reputation and influence.

Like the EH&S values, these values are commonly held by nearly all parties involved and are broadly reflected in the policy, legislation, and regulatory practice of host countries and corporations alike. We distinguish three sets of values within the DE&I cluster:

1. *Growth*—understood as expansion of national productive capacity and manifested as an increase in, for example, national production, worker productivity, savings, fraction of labor force engaged in wage economy, and basic infrastructure development.

2. *Equity*—understood as referring to the more equal distribution of the benefits of growth among different national regions, sub-populations, and generations, and manifested as, for example, reduction of skewed land and resource ownership and income differentials; broadened access to basic social, educational, and health services; and equality of economic opportunity.

3. *Independence and self-determination* — understood as referring to the capacity to autonomously make and enforce decisions concerning the shape, pace, and direction of economic growth, and manifested as, for example, national political stability and relative freedom from foreign control, national planning capacity, participatory planning structures, regional development blocks that effectively buffer industrial nation hegemony, and preservation of historically rooted values and social structures.

Even within the academic discipline of development theory, which has been characterized since World War II by intense polemics and controversy, it is apparent that there is broad support for these three sets of values. For example, Killick (1981) identifies three categories of values: efficiency-related values (concerned with maximizing total welfare accruing to the economy); social justice values (concerned with the most satisfactory distribution of total wealth among people); and national cohesion values (concerned with national self-determination). Hughes (1981) develops a similar taxonomy, distinguishing three value clusters: growth and efficiency, equity and welfare, and national independence. Kirkpatrick, Lee, and Nixson (1984) propose a taxonomy of two clusters: efficiency-related values and distribution-related values.

The policy and planning strategies adopted in pursuit of these generally accepted development-related values can vary dramatically between different nations and cultures: One nation may view strict self-sufficiency as critical to its development or independence and accordingly pursue such self-sufficiency even at the expense of reduced foreign trade or investment. Another nation may regard full integration into the global economy as critical to its development or independence and therefore accept economic dependence on foreign trade and increased international influence upon national economic policy. Similar strategic differences are apparent in different nations' attitudes toward the pursuit of growth and equity: Indian policies generally seem to attach more immediate importance to equity (e.g., between different regions), even if the result is slowed growth; Thai policies seem generally to attach more immediate importance to growth. These significant differences are discussed in detail in the chapters that follow.

Development, equity, and independence are corporate, as well as national, values. Similarly, corporations face the same general trade-off decisions regarding these values as do nations with the same diversity of strategic approaches. Some corporations, like Du Pont, place a high emphasis on independence, and will in certain circumstances decline growth opportunities, however apparently lucrative, that would compromise corporate control of the subsidiary operation. Other corporations are more willing to accept national or financial arrangements that involve diminished corporate control but provide significant corporate growth.

In situations matching corporations and nations that have similar DE&I priorities (for example, both Thailand and Occidental Chemical appear to give growth relatively greater emphasis than independence or equity), one might expect negotiations to proceed relatively smoothly. In situations matching corporations and nations that have significantly different DE&I priorities (for example, Xerox and India seem to order corporate independence, national independence, growth, and equity very differently), one might expect negotiations be more protracted.

CONCEPTUAL AND DISCIPLINARY ISSUES ABOUT VALUES

Values, Conflicts, and Trade-offs

The noted philosopher and value theorist William Frankena has observed (1967) that:

The terms "value" and "valuation" and their cognates and compounds are used in a confused and confusing but widespread way in our contemporary culture, not only in economics and philosophy, but also and especially in other social sciences and humanities . . . In using the terms, one should choose a clear and systematic scheme and use it consistently. Because of the ambiguity and looseness that the terms often engender, it would seem advisable to use them in their narrower senses or not at all, keeping to more traditional terms like "good" and "right," which are better English, whenever possible.

Here and in the chapters to follow, our analysis adopts Frankena's advice. This section presents a clear and systematic usage of the term *value;* the several chapters which that follow will use *value* and its cognates and compounds in the sense explicated. As far as possible, the many other usages attached to the term *value* in contemporary intellectual culture are avoided.

For the purposes of this discussion, assume that some person, P, holds a set of beliefs to the effect that some set of objects and states-of-affairs are good and that the term *good* includes, but is not necessarily limited to, *desirable.* Many social scientists and some philosophers have held that *good* simply means *desirable,* so that whatever is desired is ipso facto good. Many other scholars, including Aristotle and the majority of philosophers since, have held that whatever is desired must be desired as good, but that what is desired as good can fail to be good; on this view, whatever is desired is believed (perhaps wrongly) to be (in some way) good. Other scholars have promoted other views. We intend our usage and analysis to be neutral on this fundamental philosophical issue.

Assume also, for the purposes of this discussion, that this person P has some set of evaluative norms, that is, a system of value-related rules, categories, and concepts, which (in combination with relevant empirical information) he or she uses as justifying grounds for his or her beliefs that certain objects and states-of-affairs are good. For most individuals, evaluative norms include moral and ethical commitments (typically of religious or philosophical origin), social and cultural mores, preferences of individual taste, and so forth. Strictly speaking, one can distinguish first-order beliefs (that is, beliefs to the effect that objects or states-of-affairs are good) from second-order beliefs (that is, the evaluative norms used to justify first-order beliefs). The former might then be called *values* (in a narrower sense) and the latter *evaluative norms*. Although this distinction is important in other contexts, it is unnecessary for the purposes of the research reported here. Accordingly, we use the term *values* to include both first- and second-order beliefs of the kinds mentioned previously.

Given these assumptions, we can propose the following pattern of usage for the term *value* and its cognates:

1. The phrase "P's values" can be used to denote, inclusively, both P's beliefs to the effect that certain objects and states-of-affairs *as they are conceived* (whether correctly or not) *by P* are good, and P's evaluative norms (that is, the system of value-related rules, categories, and concepts that function as justifying grounds for the beliefs that these objects and states-of-affairs are good).

2. The cognate phrase "P values X" can be used to mean that P has a belief to the effect that X (as she or he conceives it) is good.

   These usages make it clear that to refer to X as a value is to refer to X *as it is conceived as a good by some person.* That P values X does *not* entail that X is realizeable for P, or even that X exists: Thus, some environmentalists may value zero-risk conditions despite the fact that no human activity can be without risk.

   Similarly, on these usages, the fact that P values X does *not* guarantee that X is "good for P" in the everyday sense of the phrase, or even that X is simply "good": A drug addict may value narcotic intoxication despite the fact that, in common usage, it is neither "good for him" nor simply "good."

3. The term "goods" can be used to denote the extra-mental objects and states-of-affairs to which P's beliefs (more or less accurately) refer.

   As conceived by a narcotics addict, whether accurately or not, a gram of heroin (and its anticipated intoxicating effect) is a value. But the "good" to which this value refers is not the addict's concept, but the actual bag of heroin (and its effects) in his hand. The good shares many properties with the value (e.g., color and texture); the good may have properties that are not a part of the value (e.g., diluent contamination); and the good may lack properties that are part of the value (e.g., the ability to prevent frostbite).

   This example displays the typical relationship between a *value* and its associated good: When sought-after objects and states-of-affairs (values) are actually obtained (goods), they are usually more complex, and often somewhat different, than their conceptions. This distinction between goods and values enables us to speak of "shared values" in two senses.

4. We can say that two people share a certain value *in the strong sense* if they have identical beliefs to the effect that some object or state of affairs is good. (This requires that they have identical conceptions of the object or state-of-affairs.)

5. We can say that two people share a certain value *in the weak sense* if each has a similar belief to the effect that some object or state-of-affairs is good. (This requires only that they have similar conceptions of the object or state-of-affairs.)

Obviously, values that are shared in the strong sense are a *fortiori* shared in the weak sense. But shared values in the strong sense, which require identical conceptualizations of their object, are very rare. Here and later in this chapter, we use the phrase "shared values" in the weak sense, which requires only that all those who share a given value have sufficiently similar conceptions of that value to pick out the same good. It is in this weak sense, for example, that *health* and *development* can be called *widely shared values,* despite the fact that no nations or corporations that share these values may have precisely the same concept of the states-of-affairs to which they refer.

Diverse understandings of important values are common even in narrow academic specialties: Few topics in bioethics are as hotly disputed as the meaning of the concept of *health.* Scholars almost unanimously reject the World Health Organization's definition of health (W.H.O. 1946): Health is a state of complete physical, mental, and social well-being and not merely the absence of disease of infirmity. But there is no consensus for any alternative definition, and outside academia, the dispute is even sharper. Consider the status of three conditions (political dissent, 'excess' fertility [defined as more than one child], and homosexuality) in four nations (the United States, Saudi Arabia, Indonesia, and China): Whether one is "diseased," "criminal," "a cultural hero," or none of the above would seem to be a cultural artifact. Despite all this disagreement, all cultures and peoples agree that "Health is a basic human value and a fundamental good!"

It is worth noting that much social and interpersonal conflict is related to the fact that so many shared values are only weakly shared. Friends or allies who have worked long and hard to attain a (weakly) shared value can be rudely surprised when the state-of-affairs realized by their success fails to match exactly most (or even any) of their individual expectations. Thus it can happen that political movements are divided by electoral success, or marriages strained by the accomplishment of long-sought goals.

Weakly shared values underlie many important conflicts in the area of environmental protection and Third World development. In the National Environmental Policy Act (NEPA) of 1969, for example, human welfare is defined as "wide access to life amenities, aesthetically and culturally pleasing surroundings, important historical, cultural and natural aspects of . . . national heritage, high standard of living, and individual choice." Although human welfare is a value shared by both developed and developing nations, the NEPA definition takes for granted the prior attainment of other shared values (e.g., absence of squalor, adequate food and shelter, education, and political empowerment), which may be missing in developing nations, and the pursuit of which may conflict with the pursuit of NEPA-defined human welfare.

Values, as we have seen, can be shared. They can also conflict. As used in the literature, the phrase "value conflict" seems to have no commonly adopted core usage. This section will indicate how the term will be used in the chapters to follow.

Negatively, to assert that two values "conflict" (in a given context) is *not* to assert that they are in some way intrinsically opposed. Benevolence and malevolence may be intrinsically opposed in this way. Values would be *intrinsically opposed* if there were (and could be) no circumstances in which both could be realized; Mill's "Utility" and Aristotle's "Eudemonia" values, rooted in irreconcilable metaphysical systems, might be opposed in this way. But these are rare examples—and it is notable that even the values at stake in most "zero sum" problems, which typically result from *extrinsic* constraints, are rarely opposed in any *intrinsic* way. Clearly, the values and goods upon which this project is focused (health, safety, development, and national independence, for example) are *not* intrinsically opposed in any way. Accordingly, to speak of a "conflict" between environmental and development values is not to assert any intrinsic opposition between them; rather, it is merely to indicate that, in a given place and process and time, the values are so related that the policy and practice options that would advance one value tend to exclude the policy and practice options that would advance the other value.

In many situations, a value conflict consists simply of the fact that the policy and practice options that would best advance each value must compete for scarce attention and resources. This might be called *weak value conflict.* A government agency endeavoring to balance fast-track approval for a socially beneficial construction project, detailed analysis of the project's environmental effects, and lengthy public participation hearings, finds itself confronted with such weak (but real) conflict. In other situations, the policy and practice options that would advance one value may significantly retard the other. This might be called *strong value conflict.* A marginally profitable corporation that must choose between bearing the costs of more stringent occupational or environmental regulation or moving its operations to countries with less stringent EH&S standards would seem to face a strong conflict involving health and safety, on the one hand, and growth and employment on the other. (This particular conflict is explored in Shue 1981.) Unless noted otherwise, we will use the phrase "value conflict" to include both weak and strong conflicts.

Many individuals believe that EH&S and DE&I strongly conflict with each other. According to the "Crisis Environmentalist" school of thought articulated by Paul Ehrlich's *Population Bomb* (1968) and defended by *Limits to Growth* (Meadows 1972) and the widely cited *Global 2000* (Council on Environmental Quality 1980) report to President Jimmy Carter, our economic system encourages greed, excessive profits, and competition, and therefore inevitably leads to resource depletion and environmental degradation. (These and the opposing arguments are analyzed in Shrader-Frechette 1988, pp. 196–219; and in Dyck 1977, pp. 32–51.) According to the opposing "developmentalist" view advocated by Drucker (1988) and the authors of *The Resourceful Earth* (Simon and Kahn 1984) however, there is no conflict between EH&S and DE&I values; instead, they argue, the financial and human assets necessary to repair and preserve the environment can only be produced by economic growth (see Kahn et al. 1976; and Rich 1973).

The question of conflict between EH&S and DE&I values is particularly difficult in the context of less developed nations, where desperate human poverty can give national economic growth enormous importance. The uncritical assumption of a strong conflict between EH&S and DE&I values powerfully influenced past discussions of the international development agenda. That assumption was evident in the remark of Brazil's then-ambassador to the United States, João Augusto de Araujo Castro, "It is our turn to pollute." (1972) Although the more recent concept of sustainable development views the EH&S and DE&I values as compatible or even mutually supportive, its practical applications are still in the embryonic stage (see *Our Common Future*).

Other scholars have focused attention on weak conflicts within, rather than between, the EH&S and DE&I clusters. For example, Branscomb (1987) points out that host country initiatives that increase foreign economic investment and thus promote development are often perceived as diminishing national independence. (Recent reactions by U.S. society to Asian and European investment suggest that this problem affects developed as well as less developed nations.) Kirkpatrick and colleagues (1984) discuss numerous other conflicts among DE&I values, for example, the adoption of measures that promote more equitable distribution of economic benefits but interfere with the most efficient use of human and natural resources.

It should be clear that value conflicts are not the result of biased reasoning or incoherent value beliefs. Value conflicts are objective features of particular situations. They may be well or poorly understood by some or all of the actors in the situation. In the worst case, real value conflicts may go unnoticed while spurious conflicts are regarded as real (see Coser 1956). The work reported in this volume suggests that some of the value conflicts raised by hazardous technology transfers may not be well understood by all the principal actors and that other conflicts, which are taken for granted by some policy commentators, may be less serious than is presumed.

If the phrase "value conflict" has had no common meaning in the literature, neither has the phrase "value trade-off." In general, the phrase "value trade-off" will be used to denote the resolution of a value conflict by the selection of particular policy or practice options that thereby determine the extent to which each involved value will be satisfied.

Within this general usage, we can distinguish within any value trade-off both a "subjective" and an "objective" component. Subjectively considered, a value trade-off consists essentially of a decision-making or negotiating process *as understood by one or more of the participating actors.* Objectively considered, a value trade-off consists essentially of the objectively determinable *set of (value-laden) consequences* that result from the decision-making or negotiating process. An objective account of a particular trade-off can be inferred from the following information: the initial values of the participants; the actual outcome (value-laden consequences) of the negotiation process; the effect of the outcome on the participants' initial values; and the range of decision options available to the participants. To the extent that a policy or practice option has consequences that do *not* reflect the balance of values aimed at by an actor, we may say that the subjective and objective trade-offs are more or less divergent, an eventuality that is virtually guaranteed by the fact that the actors have imperfect knowledge.

Strictly speaking, there are two different distinctions to be made here. First, *process versus outcome:* There is a distinction to be drawn between the deliberative processes by which a trade-off is adopted and the negotiated trade-off that is in fact finally adopted. Second, *actor versus consequence:* Given a particular policy or practice, there is a distinction to be drawn between the outcomes anticipated by a particular actor and the outcomes actually produced by the adopted policy.

In much of the work that follows, it will not be necessary to consider these distinctions separately. In these contexts, the phrase "subjective component" will be used to call attention to the *process* and *actor* dimensions of a trade-off, and the phrase "objective component" will be used to call attention to the *outcome* and *consequence* dimensions of a trade-off.

Value trade-offs are an inevitable feature of any decision in which multiple values are at stake, not all of which will be best served by any one policy or practice option. This is explicitly recognized by most U.S. legislation regarding EH&S values, which typically includes specific guidelines for balancing the pursuit of EH&S objectives against the cost of their achievement. For example, the Federal Insecticide, Fungicide and Rodenticide Act (FIFRA) of 1972 directs the administrator of the Environmental Protection Agency (EPA) to "prevent any unreasonable risk to man or the environment . . . taking into account economic, social, and environmental costs and benefits of pesticide use." According to the Superfund Amendments and Reauthorization Act (SARA) of 1986, the EPA is to take action that "protects human health and the environment, and is cost-effective and practical."

Most other U.S. environmental statutes dealing with EH&S issues contain similar provisions regarding trade-offs between EH&S values and economic values. Compromises are usually mandated by statutory language indicating that neither cluster of values is to be given overriding priority: qualifiers such as *feasible, available, practical,* and *cost-effective,* for example, are usually attached to statements of EH&S goals. Among notable exceptions is the Endangered Species Act, which gives an almost absolute priority to environmental values if the extinction of a species is demonstrably at stake.

U.S. statutes dealing with EH&S issues also take explicit note of potential conflicts between EH&S values and national security or independence values. In this case, however, the statutory language generally gives national independence values a clear and overriding priority by, for example, granting the government exemptions from EH&S standards when national security is at stake. (Recent disclosures regarding needless environmental destruction at many military facilities suggests that these well-intentioned legislative exemptions may be widely abused.)

A decision-making process involving more than one actor usually will be characterized by multiple trade-off processes at multiple levels: at a minimum, there will be (1) a set of internal trade-offs by which each actor endeavors to reconcile his or her own internal value conflicts; and (2) a set of external trade-offs by which the actors, as a negotiating group, endeavor to reconcile the conflicts between their several value systems.

Because value trade-offs are inevitable in decisions made under value conflict, giving them explicit attention would seem to offer some advantages to the negotiating parties. For example, mutually acceptable compromises might be more easily devised if each party understood the other's values (see Winterfeldt and Edwards 1986). Nevertheless, actors involved in such decision processes often seek to improve their negotiating positions by concealing (or even misrepresenting) their internal value systems or their real trade-off preferences. These behaviors raise important methodological problems, which are discussed later in this chapter.

Culture and Cultural Values

All the value trade-off decisions accompanying a particular technology transfer take place within a complex multicultural environment. Each actor's behavior is influenced by the culture(s) of his or her home nation and his or her home institution (corporate, regulatory agency, and so on). The internal and external value conflicts discussed previously result, in large part, from conflicts between the value elements of these multiple cultural environments. Some discussion of the relationship between culture and values may therefore be helpful.

The term *culture* is sometimes used so broadly that any set of consistent behaviors can be called a culture. In the chapters that follow, the term is construed more narrowly. Within the context of confined social systems (such as corporations, national, or ethnic groups), we will use the term *cul-*

ture to denote the rich matrix of values, roles, and interpretations that underlie the consistency and distinctiveness of group members' behavior and expectations. To a greater or lesser extent, these values, roles and interpretations (including role models and internalized codes of conduct) define the personal and public identities of members of the culture.

Many cultures have at least a peripheral influence upon the value trade-off decisions accompanying a particular technology transfer process, and a thorough consideration of such cultures would need to consider, inter alia, the national culture of the home (technology-exporting) nation, the international or multinational culture of supra-government agencies, the media, and so on. But the three cultures that most profoundly affect such trade-off decisions are the corporate culture of the MNC and the national and institutional cultures of the host nation.

Many corporations consciously endeavor to develop a corporate culture that will motivate employees to internalize corporate rules and perform in predictable ways. Such culture building will succeed only to the extent that the corporation's efforts nurture linkages between corporate values and employee identity and self-esteem. Developing such a corporate culture is a long and sometimes expensive process, but the rewards can be very substantial. A company with a strong corporate culture can expect its employees to promote corporate goals even in absence of immediate supervision or direct external rewards.

Corporate culture is an important variable in technology transfer, particularly for facility transfer. A company with strong corporate culture can reasonably expect that the employees responsible for siting a facility abroad will not compromise fundamental corporate principles nor jeopardize the success or reputation of the company while interacting with the host country. Moreover, employees who have internalized a strong corporate culture will be powerfully motivated to replicate that same culture in the new foreign subsidiary. Thus, to the extent that EH&S and other performance variables are related to basic corporate-cultural values, strong corporate culture will tend to reduce performance differences between home and foreign facilities.

Strong corporate cultures can also ameliorate many short-term value conflicts by providing long-term values under which the short-term conflicts can be subsumed. For example, short-term conflicts between safety and profit may be ameliorated by a corporate-cultural belief that "safety pays off in the long run." Sometimes, this sort of conflict amelioration will require that the culture be sufficiently strong to redefine certain key values, for example, that it be able to redefine *profit* in a long-term perspective.

In addition, this kind of conflict amelioration requires that the individuals within the culture perceive the resolution as consistent with other elements of the overall culture. For example, attempts to create a safety culture must not be undermined by management behavior that is perceived to contradict the cultural safety goals: Such intracultural value inconsistencies effectively taint all proposed conflict resolutions. In the sociological literature, cultural value inconsistencies of this kind are called *intra-cultural paradoxa* (Luhmann 1986, p. 234ff). Cultures that contain many paradoxa will fail to provide effective contexts for the resolution of short-term value conflicts. As noted later in this chapter, this is a problem for host nations as well as for corporations.

With respect to host country culture, it seems obvious that culturally conditioned lifestyle factors can have significant consequences for the pursuit of EH&S and DE&I values. For example, the health and safety of both workers and the public can be affected by local customs regarding dress, diet, and sanitation, or by cultural attitudes toward death, suffering, and risk-taking. Progress toward national development and independence can be influenced by cultural attitudes toward national identity, authority, and trade. It seems clear that culturally conditioned administrative and regulatory factors can have equally important consequences.

These cultural factors are difficult for non-native scholars to assess, and in the case studies presented here, they are considered only to the extent that they were important influences upon the facility siting and negotiating process. Even in this context, only those factors are considered that derive from the institutional and national cultures of the host country; no effort has been made to reconstruct the influences of, for example, regional or ethnic subcultures.

The host country institutions involved with the siting, licensing, and regulating of technology transfer have their own cultures and values. In many developing countries, these institutions have had neither the time nor the resources to develop a strong institutional culture; as a result, linkages of institutional values and employee identity and self-esteem may be weak. Symptoms of such weak linkages include corruption, nepotism, arbitrary decision-making, and subordination of institutional goals to personal ambitions.

Moreover, the values of the institutional culture may embody serious paradoxa that insiders or outsiders perceive as excuses or invitations to bypass the "official" rules. Finally, the values of the institutional culture may conflict with the values of the broader national or regional culture.

All these considerations suggest that officially stated institutional policies are not the sole determinants of the institutional effect on technology transfer decisions. It is also necessary, so far as possible, to consider the many (and perhaps conflicting) individual and social values that may be involved, including, for example, values rooted in the national and local political systems, the business and trade communities, and the key individual actors representing institutions with weak institutional cultures. Some of these cultural considerations have been referred to as *regulatory style* (Renn 1989; O'Riordan and Wynne 1987). But despite efforts to classify regulatory styles, case studies (including those presented in this volume) have repeatedly shown that even within the same host country, regulatory styles vary considerably from one type of hazard to another and from one time to another.

The most complex component of this multicultural milieu is the cultural environment of the host country. National cultural values may be important components of the value conflicts surrounding technology transfers, and other national cultural values may powerfully constrain the kinds of trade-offs that can be adopted to resolve the conflicts. Thomas Donaldson has described several examples of such values and trade-off constraints (1987), for example:

> . . . A citizen of Pakistan may be more eager to preserve her country's Moslem heritage, a heritage with strict sexual differentiation in the division of labor, than to increase the country's economic welfare through integrating women into the workplace. (p. 34)

From a western point of view, the integration of women into the national economy and the general increase of national productivity are both regarded as goods. Moreover, they are seen as complementary and mutually reinforcing values. In a developing nation (e.g., Pakistan), it may be quite the opposite. Thus it is crucial to identify the values of the host culture (and, in some instances, the values of important subcultures) with care.

A comprehensive consideration of the influence of cultural values upon value trade-off decisions would also need to consider the national and institutional cultures of the MNC parent country, the institutional and international culture of various supra-governmental organizations, and perhaps even (as an influence upon the behavior of multinational corporations concerned about their reputation) the institutional culture of the international media. Nevertheless, these additional sets of cultural values are beyond the scope of this book.

Technology and Technology Transfer

This book deals with issues raised by the transfer of potentially hazardous technologies to less developed nations. Unfortunately, the concepts of *hazard, technology* and *technology transfer* are each subject to widely diverse interpretations in the literature.

In the literature, *technology* is often narrowly construed as knowledge necessary to provide means to accomplish certain goals (Brooks 1968, p. 254; von Weizsacker 1990). Other scholars adopt a broader view and then distinguish such components of technology as *hardware* (machinery and facilities), *software* (blueprints or computer programs), and *services* (technical or professional work) (United Nations Centre for Transnational Corporations [UNCTC] 1988, p. 176). We also construe *technology* broadly as including not only knowledge but also (and centrally) knowledge-based facilities, products, and processes.

As Cavusgil has noted, *technology transfer* is a multifaceted, diversified, and constantly changing process subject to variation in industries, product lines, companies, and types of host countries (Cavusgil 1986, p. 219). Given the broad definition of technology adopted here, technology transfer can be understood as the acquisition of technological knowledge or its related facilities and processes from foreign sources (United Nations Centre for Transnational Corporations [UNCTC] 1987, p. 2). And, as Doctors has noted, the acquisition of technological knowledge by less developed nations often involves a creative adaptation of the knowledge in order to facilitate its application within the host country (1969, p. 3).

For the purposes of national development, technology transfer need not always involve ownership of a technology; it may, for example, involve a limited right to use a technology for a certain period, subject to the control of the firm that developed or owns the technology. Host countries may seek or accept technology transfer even subject to such limitations or external controls, in part because they hope thereby to increase their capacity for technology development (for the indigenous generation of technology by the host country).

Technology transfer can be accomplished in many different ways: by the export and import of manufactured products; by the transfer of industrial processes; by the provision of technological services or research and development (R&D) assistance; by the training of host country personnel; or by the construction of industrial facilities (see Ashford and Ayers 1985, p. 875; National Academy of Sciences 1980, pp. 6–7). Technology transfers between advanced nations are commonly accomplished by licensing. Technology transfers from advanced nations to developing nations usually involve a combination of capital, facilities, technical knowledge, and services (Cavasgil 1986, pp. 219–220). Technology transfers from newly developed nations to less developed nations often involve special management methods or industrialization concepts (a so-called role model approach). Technology transfers between developing nations usually involve indigenous technologies such as agricultural practices or seed stocks.

From the perspective of national development, the most common and perhaps most important form of technology transfer has been the direct investment of multinational corporations in developing countries (Tavis 1988, p. 10ff). Our three case studies examine just one variety of this modality of technology transfer: the design, siting, and construction of an industrial manufacturing facility in a developing country by a U.S. multinational corporation. As the studies will show, this kind of facility transfer involves a wide range of supporting technology transfer activities, such as capital, services, management tools, know-how, and R&D efforts. Thus, although the cases described in this volume reflect only one of the many primary varieties of technology transfer processes, they do involve an interesting range of transfer activities.

Actors and Policies

The focus of our study is on the decision-making process of the principal actors involved in the technology transfer projects represented by our cases: (1) the developing host country that receives the technology, (2) the MNC that transfers it, and (3) the local joint venture partner. We have included the joint venture partners because they are often influential parties in the decision-making processes and have goals and interests that may differ from those of the other principal actors (Robinson 1988, p. 193).

The principal actors in each case are just those institutions and individuals who take an integral part in the decision-making process that eventuates in the technology transfer activity. Each case also involves numerous peripheral actors, institutions, and individuals outside the actual decision-making process who influence or determine the set of external constraints within which the principal actors' negotiation process takes place. These peripheral actors include the national government of the MNC's home country, various non-governmental institutions and international organizations, other affected industries, or consumers, workers, and cultural opinion leaders, both internationally and in the host country (see Tavis 1988, p. 11ff). The values of the home country institutions may have a particularly strong influence on the behavior of MNCs at home and abroad. Our research was not focused on these peripheral actors, but has suggested some interesting hypotheses regarding their activities and influence.

The last three concepts needing preliminary clarification are *process, policy,* and *outcome.* These concepts are central to the models and case studies reported here, and are subject to a wide range of usages.

As used here, *policy* will be understood to denote a course of action adopted by an organization (e.g., a corporation or regulatory institution) for the purpose of advancing a particular objective or set of objectives. More particularly, a policy specifies some set of procedures (policy tools), together with the circumstances in which the procedures are to be employed. The procedures are intended to advance the policy objective(s). Policy implementation thus consists of applying the specified procedures in circumstances consistent with policy's specifications. For example, a host country development agency might use licensing procedures as tools to implement a hiring quota policy for MNCs with the objective of increased indigenous employment. For its part, an MNC might use training programs and design standards as tools to implement an EH&S policy with the objectives of protecting both employee health and corporate reputation.

It is through the process of implementation that the working of policy can be best understood (Pressman and Wildavsky 1973). In the context of this book, this implementation process may begin when an MNC notifies a host nation of its intention to acquire or build a facility and may continue for months or years through facility design, construction, and start-up. The implementation process will typically involve all the principal actors: institutional, national, corporate, and (when present) local venture partners.

Finally, following Levy, Meltsner, and Wildavsky (1974), we understand *outcomes,* in this context, to include the consequences of the corporate and the host country policies and of the facility siting negotiation processes during which the two sets of policies come in contact with each other. For the purposes of this project, the most important of such consequences are the negotiated agreements and the physical and social consequences of these agreements. Accordingly, the field studies and models presented here are principally concerned with three kinds of outcomes: (1) the actual agreement(s) arrived at by the principal actors; (2) the accomplishment of host country and MNC policy objectives; and (3) the extent to which EH&S and DE&I values are served by the MNC facility. Management of EH&S at the local facility level is thus a critical outcome and was an important focus of our field work.

METHODOLOGY FOR RECONSTRUCTING VALUE ROLES

Central to all the research reported here are the difficult problems of reconstructing each of the actual decision-making processes, explicating the value conflicts and trade-offs inherent in each, and, finally, teasing out the role and interaction of EH&S and DE&I values in the process and in the decisions of all the principal actors. The analysis of value trade-offs within the context of technology transfer projects has been suggested by a number of authors (Ashford and Ayers 1985, p. 882; Tavis 1988, p. 18; Robinson 1988, p. 192ff; Gladwin and Walter 1980, p. 428). The kind of reconstructions required by such analyses and reported in the chapters that follow, involve several serious methodological problems.

Prioritizing versus Balancing

Following Ackerman and Strong, we can distinguish in the philosophical and scientific/medical literatures two quite different conceptual approaches to the analysis and resolution of value conflicts.

The first approach, which Ackerman and Strong call the *prioritizing approach,* seeks to rank all the competing values at stake in a particular problem. The highest-ranked value then is given priority in the strong sense that "its requirements must be met before acting on other competing values or obligations." (Ackerman and Strong, 1989) In other words, decision options that fail to meet the claims of the highest-ranking value (no matter how excellent their consequences for other values) are eliminated. If the highest-ranking value suffices to determine a unique decision option, the claims of other values will not even be considered. If the highest-ranking value does not suffice to determine a unique decision option, the next-highest ranking value is used to sort out the remaining decision options, and the claims of this second-ranking value then are given strong priority (in the sense explained) over the claims of all the lower-ranking values. This prioritizing approach is called the *lexicographic method* in the decision sciences (Edwards 1954) and is very prominent in contemporary philosophical literature on applied ethics. It appears to be reflected in the adoption by some developing nations, including Thailand, of policies and practices that give an almost absolute priority to development or independence over environmental or safety values.

In contemporary decision theory, several different variations of this general prioritizing approach can be distinguished. The Parieto Optimality Rule provides the most elegant solutions to prioritizing problems, since it selects just the solution that serves every relevant value better than any alternative solution. Unfortunately, few problems have any Parieto-optimal solution. The elimination-by-aspects method sorts options according to a hierarchy of values and selects the one that meets the most values, proceeding from the top to the bottom of the hierarchy (Tversky 1972). The "Satisfying Strategy" method adopts minimal satisfaction criteria for all relevant values and then selects a solution from among only those options that meet all the specified minima (Simon 1976).

The second general conceptual approach, which Ackerman and Strong call the *balancing view,* attempts in each case of value conflict to formulate a resolution that gives at least partial satisfaction to all the competing values. Precisely how each value may be partially satisfied, and which values may be most fully satisfied, can vary from case to case. This balancing approach, which is predominant in contemporary medical and scientific literature on applied ethics, appears to be reflected in the adoption by some developing nations, including India, of policies and practices that endeavor to give at least partial satisfaction to all or most of the competing EH&S and DE&I values.

To the extent that this volume offers policy suggestions dependent upon a choice between these frameworks, it adopts the balancing approach. That is, it does not presume that an absolute priority can be given to any of the competing values that this research considers or that such an absolute priority was assigned to any one value by any of the actors involved in our case studies. Neither do we presume that a strict prioritizing of such values, even if it could be defended for one culture or technology or situation, would necessarily be correct for all cultures, technologies, or situations. Certainly, the cultures involved in our case studies do not exhibit any such monolithic value prioritizing.

Interdisciplinary Issues

Value trade-offs are sometimes conceived as involving, at least implicitly, the assignment of relative weights to the different goods at stake, as though, for example, the weights could be used as coefficients in a simple hedonic equation, the maximization of which could be determined by application of Bentham's hedonic calculus. It remains to be seen whether modern decision theory, armed with mathematical tools that Bentham could not envision, will produce a calculus adequate to the analysis of the complex value trade-off processes involved in international technology transfer. (On the use of sophisticated weighting analyses in contemporary decision theory, see Winterfeldt and Edwards 1986, or Keeney and Raiffa 1976.) We are skeptical of the claim that any one theory or discipline already possesses all the tools necessary for such an analysis. The multidisciplinary analysis presented here draws on the resources of decision theory, geography, environmental chemistry, hazards management, philosophy, sociology, and risk assessment. Nevertheless, it could have been significantly extended by application of the resources of economics, anthropology, management theory, and other disciplines.

The value trade-offs studied in this volume involved the complex interaction of many values and many actors at many levels. An analysis that hopes to illuminate rather than obliterate such a complex, value-laden, deliberative process must reconcile itself to such complexity. As Aristotle noted in the *Nichomachean Ethics,* "The same kind of precision is not to be sought alike in all discussions."

Reconstruction Problems and Strategies

An important component of the research reported here was the discovery and articulation (or "reconstruction") of the value systems of the several principal actors. Without a reasonably accurate reconstruction of these value systems, no analysis of the value-laden trade-off decisions would be possible. Although the research team was given access to extensive (and even confidential) documentary evidence and was able to interview many of the key national and corporate officials, the reconstruction of the principal actors' value systems still involved significant methodological difficulties.

For a number of reasons, including negotiators' use of deception and concealment, it is not possible to reconstruct with confidence any principal actor's value system simply by observing her or his public negotiating behavior. In the cases reported here, fortunately, reconstruction from negotiating behavior alone was not necessary. The research team had access to multiple independent sources of information regarding the value systems of the corporate and national actors, including interviews with multiple key actors, access to extensive written documentation, and field study of actual outcomes. Thus, the principal actors' EH&S and DE&I values were inferred indirectly from multiple independent and mutually cross-corroborating sources. This methodological approach has been used in other empirical investigations of these value clusters by such scholars as Lowrance, Wenk, Strong, McAllister, and Kirkpatrick, Lee, and Nixson.

In the case of the corporations, there is an extensive body of public information regarding corporate history and behavior in the area of environmental and health protection. In addition, the research team was given broad access to key corporate executives and to private corporate records, policy documents, and procedural and training manuals. In some cases, corporate cooperation extended even to generating specially requested data not already collected by any corporate unit.

In the case of the host countries and their regulatory agencies, there was again a substantial body of public information regarding national and institutional development policies and national and institutional behavior relative to implementing those policies. The research team was also given access to high-level officials at key institutions, the activities of which include technology transfer and environmental and health protection.

In some cases, national EH&S legislation can also serve as a key source of information regarding societal EH&S values. For example, the EH&S and, to a lesser extent, DE&I values prevalent in the United States during the golden years of environmental and health legislation of the 1970s and 1980s are reflected in an extensive set of statutory and regulatory acts from that period. The ten most important federal acts regarding EH&S values are the National Environmental Policy Act (NEPA) of 1969; Clean Air Act of 1970; Occupational Safety and Health Act (OSHA) of 1970; Clean Water Act of 1972; Federal Insecticide, Fungicide, and Rodenticide Act (FIFRA) of 1972; Endangered Species Act of 1973; Safe Drinking Water Act of 1975; Toxic Substance Control Act (TSCA) of 1976; Resource Conservation and Recovery Act (RCRA) of 1976; and the Comprehensive Environmental Response, Compensation, and Liability Act (CERCLA) of 1980, including the 1986 amendments. These ten acts mirror the evolution of societal attitudes toward environment and public health; they are national in scope and address human, animal, and plant species and all environmental media (air, water, land, and the workplace); they created major regulatory institutions and triggered the growth of an environmental protection industry. Their value content is not difficult to discover.

Both *human life and health* and *economic prosperity* are treated as intrinsically valued goods by every one of the statutes (excepting the 1973 ESA, which dealt with the value of nonhuman species). In addition, *human welfare*—defined in NEPA as wide access to "life amenities," "aesthetically and culturally pleasing surroundings," "important historical, cultural and natural aspects of . . . natural heritage," "high standards of living," and "individual choice"—is treated as an intrinsic good by all the statutes.

Each statute focuses on a slightly different aspect of human welfare and creates or uses a different set of tools for the purpose of advancing human welfare thus understood. For example, the Clean Air Act considers such entities as livestock, crops, property, and recreation to be instrumental goods that promote public welfare. The Clean Water Act seeks to protect the agricultural, industrial, recreational, and navigational uses of surface waters, while the Safe Drinking Water Act emphasizes aesthetic quality of drinking water. FIFRA stresses the need to increase food production at low cost (hence the need to use pesticides) as a path to greater prosperity, while the Endangered Species Acts lists the recreational value of diverse biological species to human welfare. Taken together, this diverse list of goods suggests an inclusive understanding of the ways in which human welfare can be advanced or undermined. The list includes both basic human goods that serve universal needs (for example, food, potable water, and transportation) and less basic goods instrumentally linked to culturally and socially conditioned needs (for example, aquatic sports and recreational hunting).

The statutes give evidence of a shared desire to protect the *environment* and of a range of different conceptions of environmental values. Generally, the NEPA, Clean Air Act, Clean Water Act, and Safe Drinking Water Act all treat the environment as an instrumental good to be valued for the ways in which it can advance such other human goods as human life, health, welfare, and economic prosperity. Generally, the FIFRA, TSCA, RCRA, and CERCLA all treat the environment as an intrinsic good that ought to be preserved and promoted for its own sake, whether or not this instrumentally advances other human goods. The Endangered Species Act seems to invoke both conceptions of environmental values: It notes that the continued existence of diverse nonhuman species offers aesthetic pleasure, educational resources, historical continuity, and scientific interest. But it also asserts that such species have value apart from their use as recreational, nutritional, or medicinal materials.

Each of the ten statutes also treats *national security* as a vital good, something we find particularly noteworthy in view of the fact that the purposes of these statutes seem far removed from issues of national independence. The NEPA requires that all actions taken to protect the environment must be consistent with essential considerations of national policy. The Clean Air Act, Clean Water Act, Endangered Species Act, Safe Drinking Water Act, TSCA, and CERCLA contain specific language that permits exemptions "in the interest of national security." Even RCRA and OSHA exempt federal occupational and disposal practices from their regulation.

FIFRA, TSCA, and RCRA embody clear *national self-determination* values. These statutes permit U.S. corporations to export to foreign countries hazardous chemicals that have been banned (as threats to health, welfare, or the environment) in the U.S. market. The acts do not appeal to different ethical standards for U.S. and foreign societies; indeed, they articulate a strict obligation to inform the purchaser and the foreign government of the hazardous properties of the agents and to obtain an explicit consent from the trade partner. Rather, the acts seem to rest on the view that each nation is entitled to make its own decisions about risk.

Eight of the ten statutes also acknowledge an obligation to inform those who are at risk of injury, thus invoking a *right to know*. OSHA, FIFRA, TSCA, and RCRA require appropriate labeling to assure that workers (including pesticide applicators and hazardous waste transporters) are, in the words of OSHA, ". . . appraised of all hazards to which they are exposed." In these statutes, the right to know is articulated with reference to occupational hazards. The Clean Air Act and Safe Drinking Water Act extend the right to include the general public's knowledge of hazardous substances in the environment; when exposure standards for air and water pollutants are exceeded (thus creating an unreasonable risk), both laws require notification of the affected publics. SARA, the 1986 amendments to CERCLA, requires that information about hazardous substances used by businesses and institutions (including potential hazards) be made available, on request, to members of neighboring communities.

The OSHA, Clean Air Act, and Safe Drinking Water Act all invoke an ethical obligation to *protect vulnerable members* of the population. OSHA requires that "no worker" suffer adverse effects of technological hazards. In the other two statutes this value is expressed through the criteria by which safety-of-exposure standards for air and water must be judged. The Clean Air Act and Safe Drinking Water Act both require that such standards must provide an "ample" or "adequate" margin of safety to protect (in our interpretation) vulnerable individuals or subpopulations.

Clearly, the U.S. environmental and health laws are a rich source of data on the prevailing national values. Unfortunately, because much of the EH&S legislation in developing nations has been modeled on analogous statutes in developed nations, it cannot be assumed to provide evidence of an established social consensus in those countries. Our analysis therefore attaches less importance to host nation EH&S legislation than to the analysis of institutional behavior, empirical field work, and interviews with key decision makers. In the two case studies in Thailand, the research team was able to interview the key government actors and to consult with native scholars. In the India case study, our efforts to reach key regulatory officials were less uniformly successful; however, this deficiency was substantially ameliorated through collaboration with native academics.

By using multiple sources of data, it was possible for the research team to overcome the shortcomings of any one source as a mirror of any particular principal actor's values. In each of the three cases, the team had access to multiple and varied sources of information regarding the principal actors' value systems and the influence of those values upon their decisions throughout the facility siting process.

Reconstructing the principal actor's value trade-off decisions depends also upon knowledge of the range of options the actor considered, rejected, and adopted. In each of the case studies reported here, sufficient information was available regarding these options and with regard to the negotiated outcomes.

Given the knowledge of the actors' value systems, it was relatively easy to reconstruct the principal actors' EH&S/DE&I trade-off decisions with some confidence. Accordingly, while the case studies and analyses reported here are subject (as noted) to many limitations of scope, the core analysis is offered with some confidence.

The Technology Transfer & Facility Siting Model

Based on the factors enumerated and upon our understanding of how they may influence the decision-making process for siting a facility in a developing country, we have developed a conceptual model of the sequential stages that characterize technology transfer decisions. The focus of the model is on the three-step sequence: (1) negotiations, (2) construction, and (3) start-up. A fourth stage, sustained operations, follows start-up, but is not a focus of our research (see Figure 2.1).

At each of these stages, one can investigate the nature and resolution of value conflicts. Our investigation focused on the questions of how EH&S and DE&I issues were addressed and how potential conflicts between EH&S and DE&I were resolved in the facility siting process. As the model is used in our research, EH&S and DE&I values are treated as independent variables, and the outcomes already enumerated (negotiated agreements, the objectively determined value trade-offs, and actual EH&S- and DE&I-related consequences) are treated as the dependent variables.

Sequential Model of Facility Siting Process

The dynamics of facility siting can be conceptualized as a sequence of events that starts with contract negotiations between the corporation and the government of the host country and ends with an on-line productive facility. The three major stages of this process are negotiations, construction, and start-up. The fourth stage, which follows after the process, is sustained operations.

Interactions between the principal actors may have a significant history before onset of negotiations regarding any particular facility. Du Pont's presence in Thailand, for example, was established by two decades of carefully and deliberately phased growth. This kind of planned, gradual market entry

Figure 2.1
Stages of Facility Siting Process

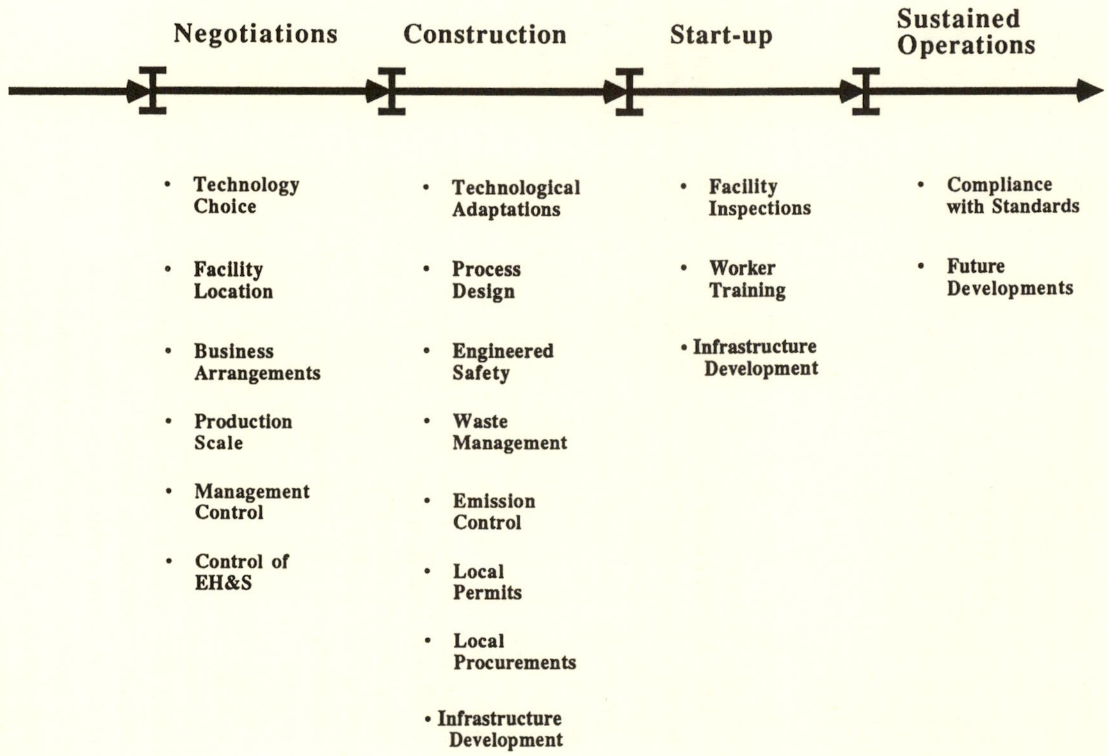

Negotiations	Construction	Start-up	Sustained Operations
• Technology Choice	• Technological Adaptations	• Facility Inspections	• Compliance with Standards
• Facility Location	• Process Design	• Worker Training	• Future Developments
• Business Arrangements	• Engineered Safety	• Infrastructure Development	
• Production Scale	• Waste Management		
• Management Control	• Emission Control		
• Control of EH&S	• Local Permits		
	• Local Procurements		
	• Infrastructure Development		

seems to be the rule, rather than the exception, for MNCs in many industrial sectors (Granger 1979). These preliminary activities, however, are not incorporated in the model that follows.

The *negotiation stage* refers to the process of initial interaction between corporate representatives, host country officials and, where applicable, the various joint venture partners. These negotiations may involve protracted and direct bargaining by the principal actors or may consist of routine administrative processes. In cases that involve a joint venture partner, two parallel sets of interactions may proceed: one set between the host country and the joint venture; another set between the members of the joint venture. In the India case, the joint venture was incorporated and the second set of negotiations far advanced, before any application for host country approval was filed. In the Occidental Chemical case, the order was somewhat different; in the Du Pont case, no joint venture partner was involved.

In this stage, the principal actors must settle issues about location, building requirements, property rights, safety standards, employment, and a range of other matters.

The product of the negotiation phase will be a working agreement between the principal actors regarding the major features of the proposed facility. This agreement will specify basic decisions regarding the location, nature, and scale of the facility, equity participation arrangements, management structure, profit remittance, taxation schedules, export and import permissions, and agreements regarding control of proprietary technology. The agreement may be implemented in different forms in different circumstances, such as industrial licensing, letters of intent, preliminary agreements, binding contracts, permits to export, and so on.

The *construction stage* refers to the design and construction (or, in the Occidental Chemical case, redesign and major modification) of the facility and the associated infrastructure. This stage requires important decisions regarding waste management systems, choices of engineered EH&S control systems, adaptation of standard facility designs to local conditions, and so forth. In this stage, the facility design is completed or modified in compliance with the conditions of the agreement with the host country and in view of the objectives of the parent company. As our field work revealed, the agreement itself is not a perfect predictor for the facility design. Issues that were not discussed during the negotiations may emerge and must be concretely resolved, during this design process.

This stage also includes a range of management and regulatory activities that precede facility start-up—for example, final issuance of any environmental, occupational, import, and export licenses not completed during the negotiations stage; procurement decisions relating to facility construction or modification; preliminary hiring and employee training activities; and development of relevant infrastructure (which may include options as diverse as employee housing, water supply, and local fire-fighting capability).

The *start-up stage* refers to the period in which the facility is tested, put on-line, and brought to full planned operating capacity. In this stage, all the prior facility design, organization, and operation plans are concretely implemented and tested. Typically, new issues arise in the start-up stage that may require modification of the prior agreement or redesign of elements of the plant or process. This seems particularly true with respect to EH&S equipment and regulations, which depend crucially upon the availability of particular materials, local building codes, the quality of workmanship, the cultural background and technical skills of the work force, and so forth.

In this stage, vital management decisions must be made regarding the implementation and cultivation of corporate EH&S culture among the local workers and managers and regarding the joint venture partner's support for EH&S values. Standard safety training programs may need to be modified in order to effectively influence worker behavior.

The *sustained operations stage* refers to the on-going operation of the facility following start-up. It is in this stage that many consequences of the decisions made in the prior stages will become evident. Long-term EH&S performance, although crucially influenced by prior design and management decisions, will depend upon the management policies and practices that evolve throughout the sustained operations phase. As the Bhopal and Chernobyl disasters suggest, poor management in this stage will eventually undermine any EH&S gains made in the design and construction decisions.

The types of decisions generally characteristic of each stage in this sequence are summarized in Figure 2.1. In each of the four stages, the value trade-off process and the final EH&S- and DE&I-related outcomes are largely determined by the principal actors, but peripheral actors may exert important influences. Two sets of factors govern the principal actors' prenegotiation positions: their respective cultural values and their empirical expectations about the potential benefits and risks of undertaking or permitting the desired activity. These factors are interrelated, but not identical. The cultural values provide the rules and standards used to assess and evaluate the benefits and risks; but the quality and magnitude of both the benefits and the risks depend on the concrete situation. For example, corporate EH&S values will influence a company's profit projections, but so, to a larger extent, will empirical assessments of market potential, production costs, and so on.

Peripheral actors may influence the decision process in a wide variety of ways. The international community and the national cultures of the two involved countries influence the process in part by virtue of the fact that many of their values are internalized by the major actors: The MNC may incorporate the values of its home country, the joint venture partner may incorporate the values of the local culture, and so on. Media and interest groups may also exert a control function by commenting on the outcome of the decision-making process or even trying to intervene. They may demand that their specific interest (e.g., protection of endangered species or ecosystems) be taken into account. The extent to which peripheral actors can influence one or more principal actors is widely variable. For example, international reputation may be important to the MNC and the host country, but irrelevant to the local joint venture partner. This differential sensitivity toward international reputation can cause conflict between the MNC and its local partner (Robinson 1988, p. 192ff).

The model described earlier was an exploratory guide for our field work. For example, given the belief that national and institutional culture and expectations would be major factors influencing technology transfer agreement decisions, a major field task was to interview the major actors and learn as much as possible about their values, internal values conflicts, trade-offs, expectations, and areas of compromise. By reconstructing the actual decision process, we expected to discover how these initial factors evolved and how external conflicts between the actors were resolved.

Our analysis juxtaposes the cultural values of the MNC with the institutional values of the host country's licensing and regulating agencies. We also consider the values of the host country's culture, insofar as these differ from the values of its institutions. Our empirical research showed that within the host country, there were significant differences between the values of the different institutions and between the values of institutions and the parent culture. These conflicts between host country institutional values and host country cultural values were sometimes apparent and important in the actual negotiation and permitting process.

Our model is similar to some other models described in the literature. Among these is the model of multiple stake holders and their influence on technology transfer (Tavis 1988, p. 13). Another is the multicultural influence model by Sirgi (1986, p. 186). A third is the model developed by Robinson (1988, p. 54). Like Tavis, we consider multiple actors with differential influence on the decision process; like Sirgi, we emphasize the importance of cultural factors; and like Robinson, we include the situational expectations regarding risks, costs, and benefits.

The model was a useful research tool, but it is not a final theoretical explanation. In chapter 8, we discuss some of the ways in which the model was confirmed or modified by the results of our empirical case studies.

A FINAL NOTE

It is worth emphasizing that the research reported in this volume is not philosophical or ethical but empirical. The chapters that follow constitute an empirical study of how, in certain instances, specified sets of values (or valued outcomes or goods) affected, and resulted from, the complex decision-making process involved in hazardous technology transfer. The point of this work is not to determine what is good or evil (although, of course, our selection of *socially responsible* corporations presumes, at a preliminary level, some ability to distinguish good and evil activity). Rather, the point of this work is to add to our understanding of the process by which *this* set of goods (rather than *that* set of goods) becomes the outcome of a technology transfer process. In sum, the work reported here does not aspire to be empirically informed normative ethics. It aspires to be ethically informed empirical science.

REFERENCES

Ashford, Nicholas A., and Christine Ayers. "Policy Issues for Consideration in Transferring Technology to Developing Countries." *Ecology Law Quarterly* 12 (1985): 871–905.

Araujo Castro, João Augusto de. Environment and Development: The Case of the Less Developed Countries, *International Organization* 2 (Spring 1972), p. 401.

Berman, D. M. "How Cheap is a Life?" *International Journal of Health Sciences* 8 (1978): 79–99.

Branscomb, Lewis M. "National and Corporate Technology Strategies in an Interdependent World Economy." Pages 246–256 in Bruce R. Guile and Harvey Brooks (eds.), *Technology and Global Industry*. Washington, DC: National Academy Press, 1987.

Brooks, Harvey. *The Government of Science*. Cambridge, MA: MIT Press, 1968.

Cavusgil, Tamer S. "Multinational Corporations and the Management of Technology Transfers." Pages 217–229 in A. Coskun Samli (ed.), *Technology Transfer: Geographic, Economic, Cultural, and Technical Dimensions*. Westport, CT: Quorum Books, 1986.

Coser, L. A. *The Function of Social Conflict*. New York: Free Press, 1956.

Council on Environmental Quality and the Department of State, *The Global 2000 Report to the President: Entering the Twenty-First Century*. Washington, DC: Government Printing Office, 1980.

Doctors, Samuel I. *The Role of Federal Agencies in Technology Transfer*. Cambridge, MA: MIT Press, 1969.

Donaldson, Thomas. "The Ethics of Risk in the Global Economy." *Business and Professional Ethics Journal* 5, No's. 3 and 4 (1987): 33–34.

Drucker, P. F. "Saving the Crusade." Pages 200–207 in Kristin Shrader-Frechette (ed.), *Environmental Ethics*. Pacific Grove, CA: Boxwood Press, 1988.

Dyck, Arthur. *On Human Care*. Nashville, TN: Abingdon Press, 1977, pp. 32–51.

Edwards, Ward. "The Theory of Decision Making." *Psychological Bulletin* 51 (1954): 380–417.

Ehrlich, Paul. *The Population Bomb*. New York: Ballantine Books, 1968.

Frankena, William. "Values and Valuation," *The Encyclopedia of Philosophy*, Volume 8. New York: Macmillan, 1967, pp. 229–230.

Gladwin, Thomas N., and Ingo Walter. *Multinationals Under Fire: Lessons in the Management of Conflict*. New York: Wiley, 1980.

Granger, John V. *Technology and International Relations*. San Francisco: W. H. Freeman, 1979.

Hargrove, Eugene. *Foundations of Environmental Ethics*. Englewood Cliffs, NJ: Prentice-Hall, 1989.

Hughes, H. "Achievements and Objectives of Industrialization." Pages 11–37 in John Cody, Helen Hughes, and David Wall (eds.), *Policies for Industrial Progress in Developing Countries*. Oxford University Press for World Bank, 1980.

Jones, Charles. *Clean Air: The Policies and Politics of Pollution Control*. Pittsburgh: University of Pittsburgh Press, 1975.

Kahn, H., W. Brown, L. Martel, and the Judson Institute Staff. *The Next 200 Years*. New York: Morrow, 1976.

Keeney, R., and A. Raiffa. *Decisions with Multiple Objectives*. New York: Wiley, 1976.

Killick, T. *Policy Economics: A Textbook of Applied Economics for Developing Countries*. London: Heinemann, 1981.

Kirkpatrick, C. H., N. Lee, and F. I. Nixson. *Structure and Policy in Less Developed Countries*. London: Allen and Unwin, 1984.

Levy, F., A. J. Meltsner, and A. B. Wildavsky. *Urban Outcomes*. Berkeley, CA: The University of California Press, 1974.

Lowrance, W. W. *Modern Science and Human Values*. Oxford: Oxford University Press, 1985.

Luhmann, N. *Ökologische Kommunikation*. Opladen: Westdeurscher Verlag, 1986.

McAllister, Donald. *Evaluation in Environmental Planning*. Cambridge, MA: MIT Press, 1980.

Meadows, Donella, Dennis L. Meadows, Jorgen Randers and William Behrens III. *The Limits to Growth*. New York: Universe Books, 1972.

National Academy of Sciences. *The International Technology Transfer Process*. Washington, DC: National Academy of Sciences, 1980.

O'Riordan, T. and B. Wynne. "Regulating Environmental Risks: A Comparative Perspective," in: P. R. Kleindorfer und H. C. Kunreuther (Hrg.), *Insuring and Managing Hazardous Risks: From Seveso to Bhopal and Beyond* (Springer: Berlin u.a. 1987), S. 389–410.

Pressman, J. L., and A. B. Wildavsky. *Implementation*. Berkeley, CA: University of California Press, 1973.

Renn, O. "Risk Communication in the Community: European Lessons from the Seveso Directive," *Journal of the Air Pollution Control Association*, 40, No. 9 (October 1989), S. 1301–1308.

Rich, William. *Smaller Families through Social and Economic Progress*. Washington, DC: Overseas Development Council Monograph, no. 7, 1973.

Robinson, Richard D. *The International Transfer of Technology: Theory, Issues, and Practice*. Cambridge, MA: Ballinger, 1988.

Shakow, D. "Market Mechanisms for Compensating Hazardous Work: A Critical Analysis." Pages 277–290 in Roger E. Kasperson (ed.), *Equity Issues in Radioactive Waste Management*. Cambridge, MA: Oelgeschlager, Gunn & Hain, 1983.

Shrader-Frechette, Kristin. (ed.). *Environmental Ethics*. Pacific Grove, CA: Boxwood Press, 1988.

Shue, Henry. "Exporting Hazards." *Ethics* (July 1981): 579–606.

Sirgi, Joseph M., A. C. Samli, and Kenneth D. Bahn. "Personality, Culture, and Technology Transfer: A Parsonian Social System Perspective." Pages 177–191 in A. Coskun Samli (ed.). *Technology Transfer: Geographic, Economic, Cultural, and Technical Dimensions*. Westport, CT: Quorum Books, 1986.

Simon, Julian L., and Herman Kahn. *The Resourceful Earth: A Response to Global 2000.* Oxford: Basil Blackwell, 1984.

Simon, S. *Administrative Behavior.* New York: Basic Books, 1976.

Strong, Douglas, and Elizabeth Rosenfeld. "Ethics or Expediency: an Environmental Question." Pages 5–15 in Kristin Shrader-Frechette (ed.), *Environmental Ethics.* Pacific Grove, CA: Boxwood Press, 1988.

Tavis, Lee A. *Multinational Managers and Host Government Interactions.* South Bend, IN: University of Notre Dame Press, 1988.

Thaler, R. and S. Rosen. "The Value of Saving a Life: Evidence from the Labor Market." Pages 265–298 in N. E. Terleckyj (ed.), *Household Production and Consumption.* New York: National Bureau of Economic Research, 1976.

Tversky, A. "Elimination by Aspects: A Theory of Choice." *Psychological Review* 79 (1972): 281–293.

United Nations Centre on Transnational Corporations. *Transnational Corporations in World Development: Trends and Prospects.* New York: United Nations, 1988.

Transnational Corporations and Technology Transfer: Effects and Policy Issues. New York: United Nations, 1987.

von Weizsäcker, C. F. "Technik und Natur," in: M. Schüz, Risiko und Wagnis. Die Herausforderung der industriellen Welt (Neske: Pfullingen 1990), pp. 14–25.

Wenk, Edward Jr. *Tradeoffs. Imperatives of Choice in a High-Tech World.* Baltimore: Johns Hopkins University Press, 1986.

Wildavsky, Aaron. "No Risk Is the Highest Risk of All." Pages 120–127 in T. S. Glickman and M. Gough (eds.), *Readings in Risk.* Washington, DC: Resources for the Future, 1990.

Winterfeldt, D. von, and W. Edwards. *Decision Analysis and Behavioral Research.* Cambridge, MA: Cambridge University Press, 1986.

World Health Organization. "Preamble to the Constitution of the World Health Organization." *Official Record of the World Health Organization* 2 (July 1946): 100.

CHAPTER 3

Corporate and Host Country Profiles

As stated in Chapter 1, this study attempts to explicate the facility development process in light of the principal actors' pursuit of their respective EH&S and DE&I values. This chapter sets the background for the case studies by outlining the policy and implementation systems adopted by the participating host countries and corporations in order to pursue these two clusters of values.

Our discussion of the corporations focuses on international operations and on EH&S related matters: corporate EH&S policy and philosophy; EH&S organization for domestic and foreign operations; and the international EH&S management attitudes of the executives and managers interviewed during this study. These qualitative data are supplemented by a number of quantitative performance indicators for domestic and international facilities, for example, standardized occupational injury and illness rates, occupational standards compliance records (for Xerox), environmental assessment score records (for Oxychem), and other data provided by the corporations at the research team's request.

These data are not used to compare the EH&S performance of the three corporations with each other: Except for the standardized occupational injury rates, the data is so company specific that inter-company comparisons would be meaningless. Rather, we use the quantitative data to provide an empirical check on our interpretation and analysis of the MNCs' domestic and international EH&S policies.

Following the individual corporate profiles, we offer a brief comparative analysis that highlights those shared characteristics of the three that make them unlikely candidates to represent their industries as a whole, for example, their large size and significant resources; their commitment to EH&S

values and record of EH&S improvements over time; and their experience with hazardous processes. That section also underscores important differences among the three corporations, especially concerning the origins of their respective corporate cultures.

Notably, most of the intra-company analyses of quantitative performance indicators included in this chapter were performed for the first time in the course of this study. Each of the corporations studied maintains good quantitative EH&S performance records and uses those records to set internal goals for each facility, to motivate local personnel to improve facility performance, and to spot significant departures from company averages. But the MNCs display surprisingly little interest in performing their own retrospective and interregional comparisons of their many facilities' performances, despite the fact that such analyses might be useful tools for investigating the relative importance of different management and technological factors.

The survey of host countries presented in this chapter focuses on the administrative structures, policies and procedures they use to regulate the siting and operation of multinational manufacturing facilities. For each country, these policies reflect two sets of considerations, one set related to national DE&I goals, the other related to EH&S goals. Our discussion considers these clusters separately.

THE CORPORATIONS

Xerox: An Overview

Founded in 1906 as the Haloid Company to manufacture and sell photographic paper, this company acquired license to basic xerographic patents from Battelle Development Corporation in 1947. In 1959 it produced the world's first automatic plain-paper copier (the Xerox 914) and subsequently changed its name to Xerox Corporation. In 1961, it became listed on the New York Stock exchange. Since then, Xerox has blossomed into a giant enterprise with over 110,000 employees worldwide and gross revenues exceeding $19 billion for 1990. Figure 3.1 shows the importance of photocopier technology in the company's business equipment operations.

The Americas Operations of Xerox oversee the facilities in North, South, and Central America as well as in the Caribbean, Middle East, and North Africa. Four U.S. manufacturing facilities (including engineering/development operations) are located in California, one in Illinois, two in New York, and one in Oklahoma. Other facilities in the Western hemisphere include two manufacturing facilities in Canada, three in Brazil, and one in Mexico.

In 1959 Xerox extended its international operations by forming a joint venture with the Rank Organization PLC, a British company, under the name of Rank Xerox. Rank Xerox is a majority-owned subsidiary of Xerox Cor-

Figure 3.1
Xerox Organizational Structure

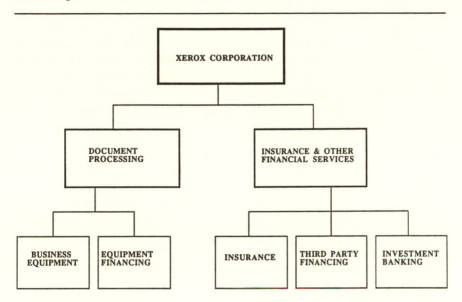

poration. Five Rank Xerox manufacturing facilities for photocopier technology are located in Europe, one in Egypt, one in China, and two in India. The India operations include the Modi Xerox joint venture in Rampur and Indian Xerographic Systems in Bombay. Rank Xerox also holds a 50 percent equity in Fuji Xerox following a 1962 joint venture with Fuji Film Company. The gross revenues of Rank Xerox totalled $4.6 billion in 1989, with almost 98 percent resulting from European operations. Rank Xerox's consolidated operations in Africa, Asia, Australia, the South Pacific, and the Middle East totalled only about 2 percent of the company's 1989 revenues.

The domestic and international Xerox manufacturing facilities associated with photocopier technology are listed in Table 3.1, along with their product lines. The corporation tends to focus each facility on just one or two technologies. The Rampur facility is the most integrated, due to host country insistence rather than corporate preference. (The Chinese facility is almost as integrated, again at the insistence of the host country governments.) The integration of multiple technologies in the Rampur facility is particularly striking because it is one of the smallest facilities operated by Xerox in the world. Also notable in Table 3.1 are the joint venture operations. Nearly one third of Xerox's international facilities are jointly owned.

Rank Xerox pursues three major goals in the conduct of its international market strategy:

Table 3.1
Domestic and International Facilities at Xerox

XEROX	LOCATION	TYPE OF TECHNOLOGY*	JOINT VENTURE (Y/N)
U.S. OPERATIONS			
	California	M ; E	N
	California	E	N
	California	M	N
	California		N
	Illinios	M	N
	New York	M; T; P; D	N
	New York	T	N
	Oklahoma	T; P; D	N
AMERICAS OPERATIONS	Canada	M	N
	Canada	T; D	N
	Brazil	T; D; P	N
	Brazil	M	N
	Brazil	M	N
	Mexico	M	N
RANK XEROX OPERATIONS	U.K.	E; P	N
	U.K.	M	N
	France	M	Y
	Netherlands	M; T; D	N
	Spain	M; T	N
	India (Bombay)	M	Y
	India (Rampur)	M; E; T; P; D	Y
	Egypt	M	Y (with govt)
	China (under construction)	M; T; P; D	Y (with govt)

M, Machines; E, Electronic boards; T, Toner; P, Photoreceptor; D, Developer

1. to make profits, at least in the medium and long term;
2. to diversify markets as a buffer against regional sales variations, an especially important consideration for a company with a monolithic product line and little product diversity; and
3. to be represented in every major market.

In pursuit of these goals, the company will enter joint venture arrangements in developing countries, provided that the arrangements meet these four corporate requirements:

Assurance of quality control. The top priority is that the product manufactured abroad is absolutely identical in quality to the same product in the home facilities.

Assurance of health and safety. Systems equivalent in performance to those in American and European facilities must be achieved.

Assurance of financial control. Key decisions concerning the ratio of reinvestment and distribution to shareholders are to be made by the corporation.

Assurances of management control. All first-line managers have to be appointed or at least approved by Rank Xerox before they are hired.

Other requirements, such as share of stock or production guarantees, are handled in a more flexible manner. Rank Xerox is willing to enter a joint venture with less than 50 percent equity ownership if and only if all four of the listed requirements are met. The second and fourth requirements, equivalency of health and safety systems and management control, give Rank Xerox the major tools needed to implement its EH&S philosophy.

With regard to foreign investment strategies, joint venture requirements, and EH&S management and philosophy, our interviews with top and middle managers at Rank Xerox and Xerox Corporation detected no difference between the two companies' philosophies or operating practices. Accordingly, for the purposes of this study, the Rank Xerox facility at Rampur has been treated as a subsidiary of Xerox and Rank Xerox alike.

Xerox: EH&S Policies, Implementation, and Performance

Historically, EH&S issues became part of Xerox corporate consciousness in the mid-1960s, and significant resources were committed to the area in the late 1970s. The change was prompted by the discovery that one of the toners used by Xerox photocopiers tested positively in a bacterial mutagenicity test. An extensive multidisciplinary investigation conducted by Xerox in collaboration with vendors, consultants, and other parties established that the mutagen was an impurity present in trace amounts in a single type of carbon black (a toner colorant). New procedures and standards promptly reduced the impurity (and other potential mutagens or carcinogens) to an undetectable level in toner extracts, but the events left an enduring corporate legacy: Corporate attention was focused on the importance of effective EH&S management to the company, consumers and workers. Extensive health and safety evaluation procedures, reflecting a greater sensitivity to health and safety issues, were adopted. The corporate EH&S structure currently in place at Xerox was adopted in 1980 as a direct result of these considerations.

Xerox EH&S organization is shown in Figure 3.2. The Xerox Corporation Safety Network maintains a centralized health and safety function, ensures that all manufacturing plants and operations report to the corporate director of environment, health and safety, and facilitates implementation of companywide EH&S policies. Corporate EH&S staff set and enforce worldwide standards and have the authority to shut down a plant if necessary.

Figure 3.2
Safety Network at Xerox Corporation

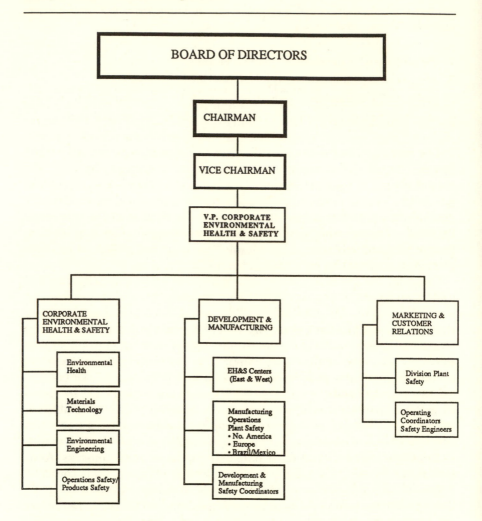

Individual departments have ongoing responsibility for compliance activities, but major issues may also be brought to the attention of corporate authorities. The company's corporate safety/environment office reports directly to the corporate director of EH&S, as do significant safety/environment units located within development and manufacturing, marketing, and customer relations. An official Environmental Health and Safety Policy Committee within the developing and manufacturing unit reviews specific safety/

environment issues, develops action plans to resolve the issues, and oversees implementation of the action plans throughout all industrial operations.

Four principles guide occupational hazard management within the international Xerox organization:

1. the primacy of engineered safety/environment controls;
2. compliance with all laws and regulations of the host country;
3. preference for application of uniform occupational corporate standards worldwide;
4. equivalency in safety and health performance among international facilities.

The first two principles are explicitly articulated in written policy statements. The last two reflect the working practices and shared beliefs of the management. For example, Xerox's *Environmental Health and Safety Manual* states: "Facilities design, including engineering controls, are the primary methods of controlling employee exposure to chemical and physical agents. Personal protective equipment, work practices, and/or administrative controls are utilized only when engineering controls are not feasible or as a supplement to engineering controls (Xerox 1982)."

Based on the research team's discussions and interviews with top and middle managers, it appears that the equivalency criteria is understood at Xerox to require both equivalent compliance with corporate occupational standards and equivalent performance relative to the company's average recordable incidence rates for occupational injuries. Individual facilities may achieve these through different combinations of engineered controls, personal protection, work practices, and administrative controls.

External safety and environmental audits at Xerox facilities are conducted by various insurance carriers, with Marsh & McLennan Protection Consultants serving as broker. The auditing program focused on safety issues when begun in 1970, but has gradually expanded to include environmental concerns. Xerox maintains significant control over the audits by explicitly determining their scope, format, and schedule. The external audits are supplemented by internal audits at both the corporate program level and the local plant level. Plant audits are conducted approximately once a month and reviewed by the plant manager. Auditing procedures at international facilities are the same as at the domestic facilities. Corporate audits take place every one or two years, depending upon the degree of hazard involved and the insured value of the equipment and property.

The occupational exposure standards implemented in the Xerox facilities are listed in Table 3.2, along with the comparable governmental standards (United States, Europe, and India). Dust standards at Xerox are significantly lower than those required by the U.S. Occupational Safety and Health Administration (OSHA). The first corporate standard for total dust, adopted

Table 3.2

Comparison of Xerox and Government Occupational Standards

Standards / Substance/Technology	Government Standards			Xerox
	US	Europe	India	
Total Dust* (toner production, mg/m3)	15	10 (UK)	10	5.0 (1977) 2.5 (1988)
Respirable Dust** (toner production, mg/m3)	5	5 (UK)	None	0.4 (1989)
Respirable Arsenic (photo receptor production, mg/m3)	10	50 (Sweden)	200	10
Respirable Selenium (photo receptor production, mg/m3)	100	100	200	100

* Standard for Total Dust in Thailand is 15 mg/m3.
** Standard for Respirable Dust in Thailand is 5 mg/m3.

in the mid-1970s, was lowered in 1988 following completion of a long-term inhalation bioessay with animals. In 1989, the company also set a standard for respirable dust. Studies conducted by Xerox (not shown here) indicate that as the concentration of total dust in toner facilities decreases, the proportion of respirable dust to total dust increases. Thus, at a total dust level of 10 mg/m^3, the fraction of respirable dust is approximately 3 percent, but at a total dust level of 1 mg/m^3 the fraction is approximately 10 percent. These data suggested that as total dust levels approach the 2.5 mg/m^3 standard, the respirable dust level might not meet the respirable standard. Hence, total and respirable dust requires separate monitoring.

The results of total airborne dust monitoring at all Xerox toner facilities are shown in Figure 3.3. Each point represents an arithmetic mean of 12–100 samples (depending on the facility) collected at random over a 12-month period. The facilities clearly have different performance records, with the Dutch facility lagging behind the rest, but over time there is both an unmistakeable downward trend and a convergence. In 1988, for example, all but one facility were in the 0.5–0.75 mg/m^3 range. The results of airborne

Figure 3.3
Trends in Mean Annual Concentrations of Total Dust at Individual Xerox Toner Facilities

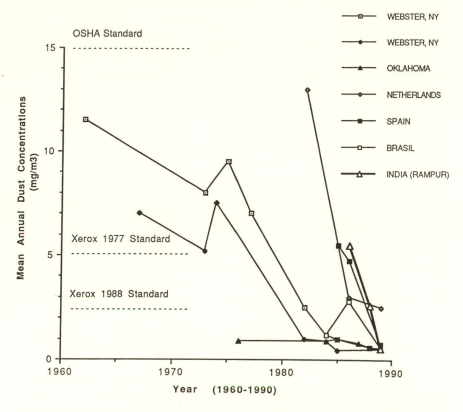

arsenic and selenium monitoring in the photoreceptor plants, shown in Figures 3.4 and 3.5, respectively, indicate that all facilities represented by the data were in compliance with the relevant standards.

In addition to monitoring compliance with airborne standards, the corporation uses routine urinalysis to monitor the biological arsenic and selenium burdens among photoreceptor workers. It is difficult to translate urinalysis data (not shown here) into occupational exposure data because individual biological burdens can be affected by nonoccupational sources, such as ambient air, local diet and drinking water, exposure to local pesticides or rodenticides, and so on. The urinalysis data therefore are used primarily as a warning sign of sudden changes in the work environment and as a general indicator of employees' health.

Comparative analysis of reportable incidence rate data for selected Rank Xerox facilities (Figures 3.6 and 3.7) shows that rates vary substantially by

Figure 3.4
Mean Annual Arsenic (As) Concentrations at Individual Xerox Photoreceptor Facilities

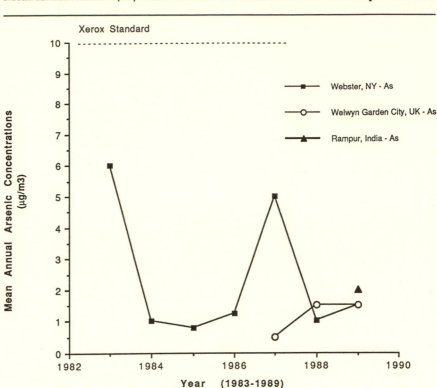

year, facility, and even production area. For example the incidence rate for the Spanish facility is notably higher than all other facilities' (Figure 3.6). The incidence rate for the Dutch facility is 1.18 but the rate for the toner area alone is 5.52; in Spain the analogous rates are 1.58 and 9.07 (Figure 3.7). In the Spanish toner plant the incidence rate varied by an order of magnitude between 1987 and 1988.

As a group, the European facilities had a lower average incidence rate (0.79 in 1988) than the corporation as a whole (3.49 in 1988), and the India facility was consistently much lower than either (average of 0.9 between 1985 and 1988) (Figure 3.6).

The low incidence rate at Modi Xerox may reflect fewer accidents, but the facility managers interviewed by the research team suggested a different explanatory hypothesis, based on their personal experience. Because of local cultural attitudes and concern about lost income, minor accidents that would be reported by almost all U.S. workers and by many European work-

Figure 3.5
Mean Annual Selenium (Se) Concentrations at Individual Xerox Photoreceptor Facilities

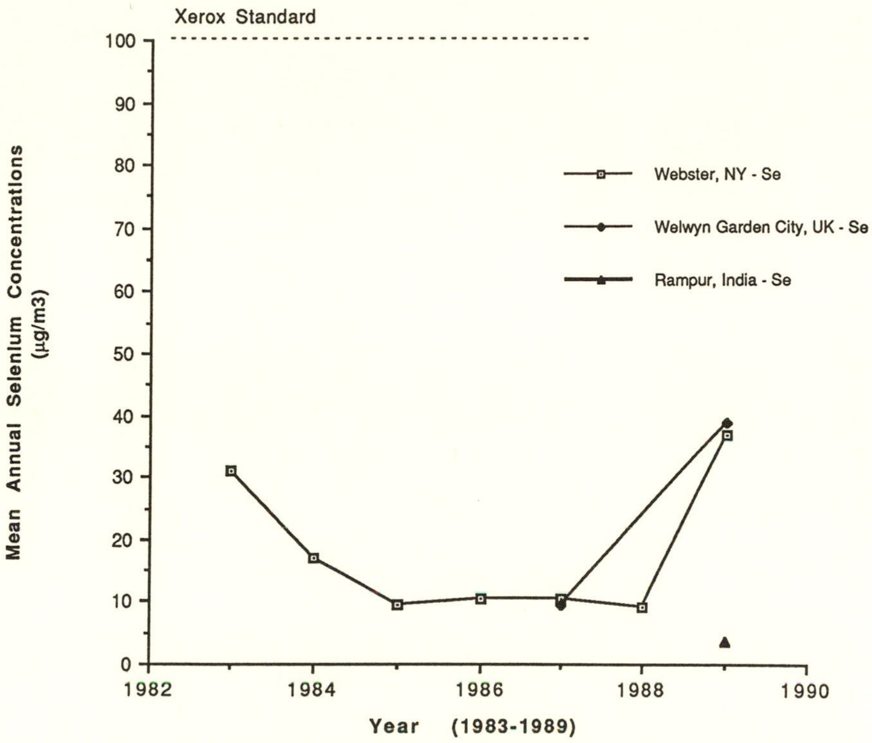

ers are almost never reported by Indian workers. It is therefore important to consider the possibility of under- and over-reporting when comparing RIR statistics across countries and cultures.

Taken together, Figures 3.3 through 3.7 reflect an extensive monitoring and reporting network for occupational health and safety hazards. Although individual facilities do not show equal EH&S performance, all are in full compliance with governmental occupational standards, and most are in compliance with Xerox standards. Health and safety improvements over time are obvious, but there are recent deviations in compliance with the selenium standard and in average occupational injury rates. The data do not demonstrate performance differences between U.S., European, and developing country facilities, but this finding should be interpreted with caution because of the limited time period involved and because of monitoring/reporting differences among individual facilities, countries, and cultures.

Figure 3.6
Reportable Incidence Rates for Individual Xerox Facilities

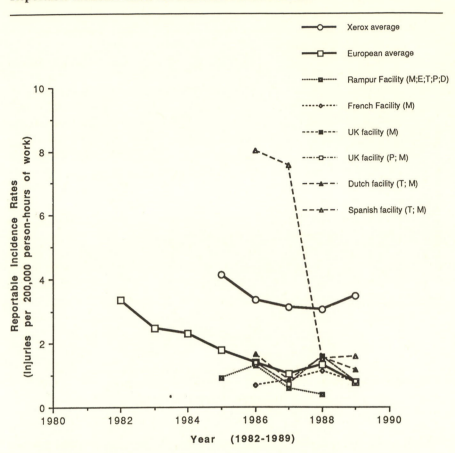

Du Pont Agrichemical Products Division: Overview

The Du Pont de Nemours Corporation began in 1802 as a manufacturer of black powder. Through its first century, it remained essentially an explosives manufacturer and grew by geographic expansion. In 1903 Du Pont became one of the first corporations to launch a formal R&D program, opening of its first research laboratory in New Jersey. Although initially focused on ways to expand the company's explosives business, the research soon extended into chemical processes unrelated to explosives.

Corporate growth and diversification have been principally driven and accomplished by internal Du Pont R&D, with such landmark developments as cellophane (1923), synthetic ammonia (1924), Freon (1931), white pigments

Figure 3.7
Reportable Incidence Rates at Individual Xerox Facilities and Production Areas

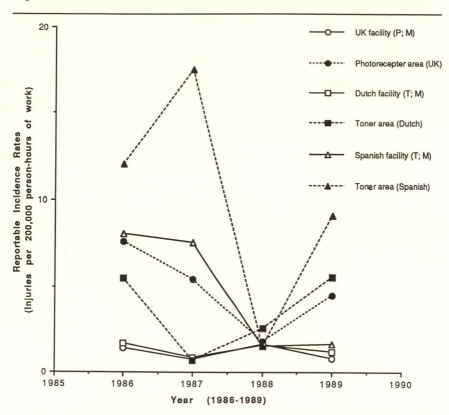

(1935), and Teflon, Nylon, Orlon, and Dacron (1938–50). But diversification has also been advanced by notable acquisitions, including the Fairfield Rubber Company (1916), Endo Pharmaceutical Labs (1969), Berg Electronics (1972), New England Nuclear (1981), Conoco (1981), and Shell Agricultural Products (1986). Today, the science-based company is one of the largest and most diversified industrial corporations in the world.

The key components of Du Pont's organizational structure are shown in Figure 3.8. This study focuses on Du Pont's agrichemical products group, which is one of its ten major manufacturing groups. (The others are imaging systems, medical, fabricated products, petrochemicals, textile fibers, automotive parts, chemicals and pigments, electronics, and polymer products).

The agrichemical products business has 5 domestic and 13 international facilities. Argentina, Australia, Brazil, China, Colombia, France, Italy, Puerto Rico, Taiwan, Thailand, and the Philippines each have one facility; Mexico

Figure 3.8
Du Pont Organizational Structure

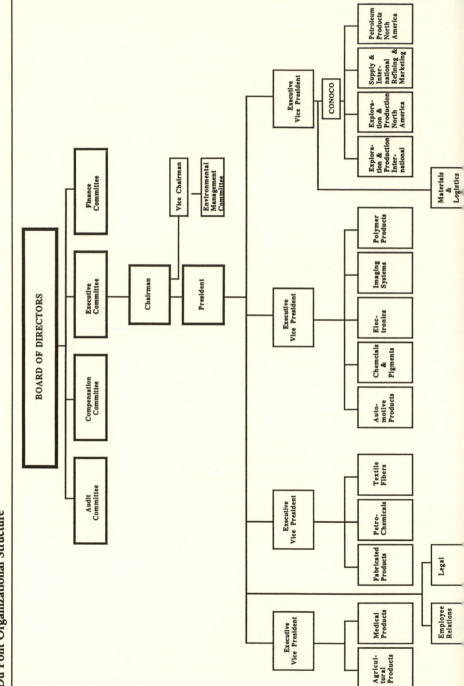

has two. Approximately 70 percent of these agricultural facilities were built by Du Pont. The other 30 percent were acquired as existing plants, and of these, the recently acquired Shell U.S. Agrichemical Products facilities are the largest block. Because the facilities built by Du Pont tend to be larger than the acquired facilities, approximately 85 percent of the total agrichemical products manufacturing capacity is based in company-built plants. Eleven of the 13 international facilities (85 percent) are wholly owned. Du Pont owns 45 percent of the Argentine facility and 80 percent of the facility currently under construction in China. In both cases, local business interests are the joint owners. Because acquired facilities and joint ventures account for such a small part of its overseas agrichemical facilities, Du Pont has been deeply and directly involved in the design, licensing, and operation of its overseas facilities.

Du Pont's primary goal in making foreign investments is the acquisition of new markets. When evaluating potential new investments, the company applies two general criteria: the global business value of the product, as measured by the potential global sales and profit margin, and the strategic value of the host country. The United States, Japan, Europe, China, Australia, and India are strategically valuable countries for agrichemical products because of their large populations, their significant agricultural production, and their commitment to modern agricultural technology.

Du Pont's decision to site a new agrichemical manufacturing facility overseas is made in the context of a planned market entry strategy that spans at least several years. The general chronological model for such market entry is shown in Figure 3.9. Several stages are typical.

Stage 1—Fully formulated and packaged product is imported from the United States. During this stage, the company gets to know the local market, culture, and business conditions as well as the natural conditions and practices that may require changes in the product formulation and/or packaging.

Stage 2—Fully formulated bulk product is imported from the United States and packaged locally.

Stage 3—Active ingredients and formulation ingredients are imported from the United States and formulated and packaged locally. Formulation and packaging may be performed by local contractors, or Du Pont may build its own facility to conduct these operations. The construction of a formulating facility is not a necessary step for the transition to Stage Four to take place.

Stage 4—Synthesis of active ingredient is transferred to the foreign country. At this stage only the last step or steps of the synthesis are conducted abroad. The intermediates are either imported from the United States or purchased locally, depending on the process and economic considerations.

Stage 5—The entire production process, and some of the R&D, is carried out in the foreign country. At this stage, the foreign subsidiary facility carries out complete synthesis, including manufacture of intermediates, using local and imported raw materials and starting substrates. Stage 5 represents full "backward integration" of technology.

Figure 3.9
General Model of Transferring an Agrichemical Product to a Foreign Country at Du
Pont

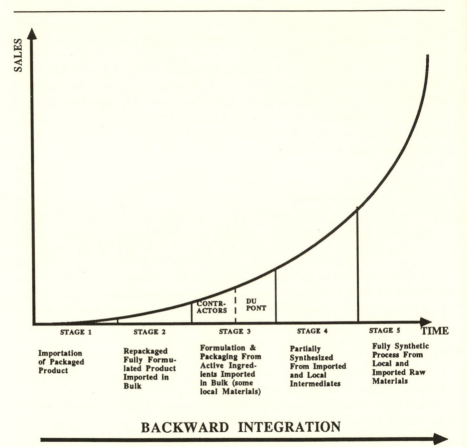

BACKWARD INTEGRATION

The development of the Thai case study conforms to this general chronological model. Stage 1 entry was accomplished in the 1960s. Local repackaging
(Stage 2) was initiated in the early 1970s. The transition to Stage 3 was made
in the mid-1970s and relied upon local contractors until the early 1980s,
when Du Pont constructed its own formulating and packaging facility.

The model shown in Figure 3.9, which focuses on total sales as a variable
in transitions between stages, oversimplifies business reality. It ignores the
political, cultural, economic, and regulatory climate of the host country
(current and projected), and it ignores a range of other circumstances (discussed later) that affect corporate business decisions. The model also over-

simplifies corporate policy. In appropriate circumstances, Du Pont is willing to forgo gradual market entry and enter a host country at an advanced stage, even including the construction of a technologically integrated facility, as evidenced by its current facility construction project in China. In this case, the push toward full backward integration came from the Chinese government, but corporate policy was sufficiently flexible to allow adaptation of the usual development strategy.

Nevertheless, despite these oversimplifications, the model highlights two characteristics of Du Pont agrichemicals overseas activities. First, Du Pont ordinarily does not decide to build a facility in a foreign country until after the company has been in the country for several years, has become familiar with its cultural and business climate, and has established a network of relationships with suppliers, distributors, and host country authorities. Second, Du Pont's planned and staged entry into a foreign market ordinarily involves several decision points at which the interaction of corporate and host country objectives can be observed.

Du Pont: EH&S Policies, Implementation, and Performance

Du Pont's corporate EH&S structure is shown in Figure 3.10. Three key executive committees guide policy-making: the Safety, Health, and Environment Steering Committee; the Environmental Management Committee; and the Environmental Resources Committee. These committees include corporate personnel representing operational departments (petrochemicals, consolidated coal, polymer products, agricultural department, chemicals and pigments department, Conoco), an employee relations department, a central research department, and departments for development, engineering, external affairs, legal issues, and marketing.

In addition to this corporate EH&S structure, the several manufacturing departments (and some subunits within the manufacturing departments) each have their own EH&S specialists. In the Agricultural Products Department, EH&S experts are important resources, continually providing a key liaison with the foreign facilities plant managers and other units within the company, including engineering and research. The number of employees who specialize in EH&S matters at international facilities varies with the size of the facility, the hazards associated with the product, and the local conditions.

The safety culture of Du Pont employees is deeply entrenched and can be traced to the origins of the corporation. Du Pont's first major product was gun powder. The hazards associated with Du Pont's traditional chemical products have helped to promote a singularly intense occupational safety culture, a culture which (although emulated by many other firms) still seems to be the most extensive and deeply rooted in the chemical industry. Over time, Du Pont's occupational safety culture expanded to include product

Figure 3.10
Environment, Health, and Safety Organizational Structure at Du Pont Corporation

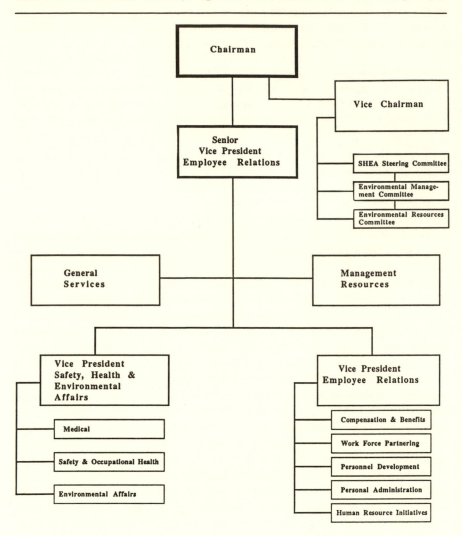

safety and environmental management areas in which Du Pont has again been among the corporate leaders.

The values just mentioned—occupational safety, product safety, and responsible environmental management—are key elements of the corporate image that Du Pont aspires to project to both the industrial community and the general public. But safety culture is not just a public relations issue at Du Pont; it is manifestly a cherished historical tradition, a prerequisite for professional success in the company, and a major source of pride and professional identity among its employees. These excerpts from the introductory paragraph of Du Pont's *Policy Manual for the Bangpoo Plant* and from the introduction to the general information section of Du Pont's *Operating and Procedures Manual for the Bangpoo Plant,* illustrate the culture:

The bedrock principle that governs relationships at Du Pont is that each person will be treated with fairness and respect. Du Pont maintains confidence in its men and women and their honesty in all company related activities, and relies on them to follow specified safety and operating procedures, department and division rules, and supervisory instructions (Policy Manual, Du Pont 1981, p.1).

Control of discharges of liquid and solid wastes to the environment such that there is no potential of injury to personnel or the environment is a requirement of the job and a condition for employment. It is imperative that we control the disposal of all materials that leave the site for safe disposal (*Operating and Procedures Manual,* Du Pont 1982, p. 6200).

The foundations and implementation of Du Pont safety culture are explored in greater depth in Chapter 6.

Du Pont conducts formal corporate EH&S audits every 1.5 to 3 years (depending upon facility size, industrial processes, etc.) for both domestic and international facilities. The audits use a participative survey methodology. Central topics include safety and health management (staff, rules and procedures, communication channels, committees, contractor safety, and health); work practices (compliance with rules and procedures, personal protective equipment, training); and work environment (area and equipment guarding, transportation equipment inspections, material handling and waste disposal, working conditions, preventive maintenance). Some surveys also have a "health emphasis" and add chemical, biological, and physical health hazards to the central topics. Others have a "safety emphasis" and add process safety management and emergency control to the core survey objectives.

Site survey teams consist of site personnel but are led by a survey consultant from the Corporate Safety, Health, and Environmental Affairs Division. In order to avoid "policeman–suspect" relationships between auditors and plant managers, the reports are not sent through the regular agricultural products manufacturing group's reporting channels. Instead, the survey team's report is given to the plant manager for review and, after mutual discussion, is sent directly to the corporate health and safety group.

In addition to these formal surveys, each overseas facility is visited by the U.S. director of manufacturing every two years, by the regional manager (Du Pont Far East in the case of Thailand) every six months, and by the managing director of the local corporation (Du Pont Thailand) every month.

Safety performance indicators used by Du Pont include standardized numbers reported to the U.S. Department of Labor, such as lost workday incidence

Figure 3.11
Lost Workday Injury Cases at U.S. Du Pont Facilities

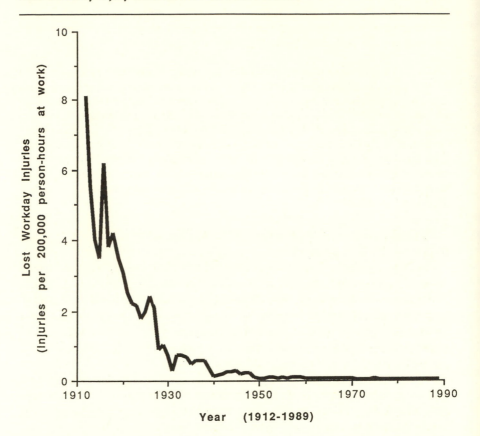

cases and total reportable injury cases. The company also keeps records of non-work related injuries. Figure 3.11 shows the average lost workday incidence cases experienced at U.S. facilities between 1912 and 1989. The dramatic decrease from 1912 to 1930 was followed by modest but consistent decreases in subsequent years, with apparent leveling off at approximately 0.02. Du Pont's reportable injury rates are approximately two orders of magnitude higher than the lost workday rates.

Figure 3.12 shows the injury rates for Du Pont's worldwide chemicals and specialties products (including agrichemicals). Figure 3.12 also shows the off-the-job injury rate for Du Pont's worldwide chemicals and specialties products; the off-the-job injury rate closely parallels the on-the-job rate, suggesting that the same behavioral and attitudinal changes that promote safe working conditions also promote off-the-job safety among the Du Pont employees.

Figure 3.12
Lost Workday and Total Recordable Injury Cases at Du Pont Chemicals and Specialties Facilities

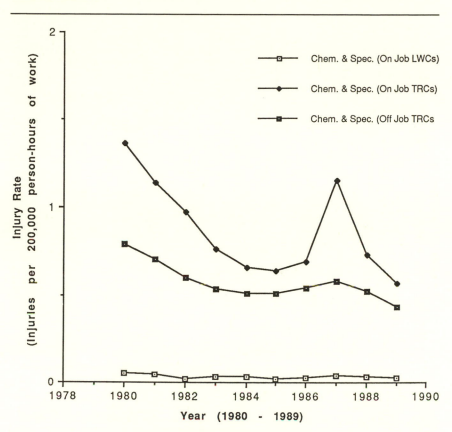

Figures 3.13 and 3.14 compare the injury rate performance of Du Pont agricultural product facilities in the United States to Du Pont facilities in other industrialized countries and in developing countries. The facilities in developing countries rank lowest in both on-the-job and off-the-job injury rates. These comparisons challenge the common belief that facilities in industrialized countries have better safety records than equivalent facilities elsewhere. However, as noted earlier, these data may reflect cultural differences that incline workers in developing nations to underreport occupational incidents.

When compared to Du Pont-owned facilities, the facilities of Du Pont contractors have significantly poorer safety performances. For example, the average standard on-the-job lost workday incident rate among 20 Du Pont agrichemical contractors in the United States was 12.21 per 200,000 person-

Figure 3.13
Average Total Occupational Injury Rates for Du Pont Agrichemical Facilities

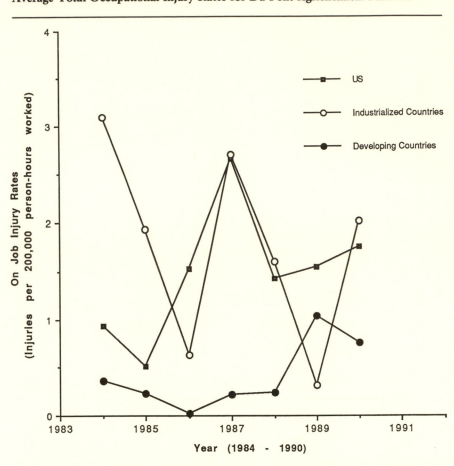

hours in 1988 and 13.6 in 1989, roughly an order of magnitude worse than the record at Du Pont-owned plants.

In summary, Du Pont's occupational injury statistics are consistent with its traditional commitment to safety. The issues related to developing and maintaining the Du Pont safety culture are discussed in detail in Chapter 6.

Occidental Chemical Corporation: Overview

Occidental Chemical Corporation (Oxychem) is a wholly owned subsidiary of Occidental Petroleum Corporation. Initially focused in the fertilizer industry, Oxychem launched a program of substantial growth with its 1968

Figure 3.14
Average Total Off Job Injury Rate for Du Pont Agrichemical Facilities

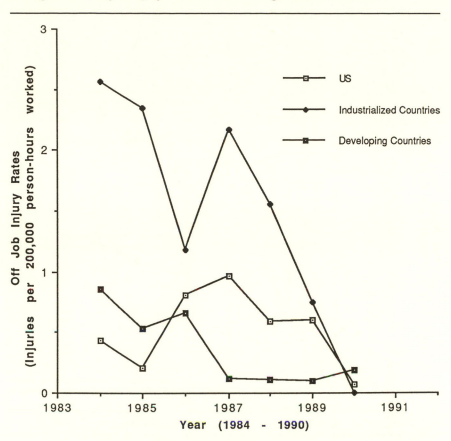

acquisition of Hooker Chemical. Oxychem now has three core business areas: agricultural products, plastics, and industrial and specialty chemicals. Figure 3.15 shows its organizational structure. The general corporate growth strategy calls for acquisitions of the biggest, best quality, and lowest cost manufacturers of commodity chemicals. Since acquiring Hooker, Oxychem also has purchased Tenneco Chemicals (polyvinyl chloride facilities), W. R. Grace's Brazilian facilities, and, most recently, Diamond Shamrock Chemicals and Caine Chemicals in the mid 1980s. These acquisitions doubled Oxychem's size over the last decade.

All of Oxychem's acquisitions over the last two decades were based on mutual consent and were preceded by careful study of the target company's culture. Moreover, foreign or domestic subsidiaries of newly acquired corporations are sold if they do not fit well with Oxychem's corporate strategy.

Figure 3.15
Occidental Chemical Organizational Structure

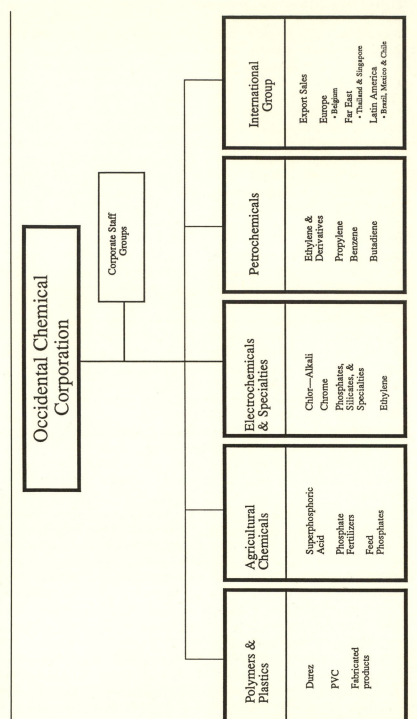

Nevertheless, as a company with a distinct and unified identity, Oxychem has a very short corporate history.

Oxychem is predominantly a U.S. company and aspires to become the largest domestic manufacturer of commodity chemicals. In recent years, it has given increased attention to foreign development. Oxychem's 16 international facilities are located in Belgium (1), Brazil (7), Chile (1), Mexico (4), Singapore (1), and Thailand (2). Only three of these facilities were built by Oxychem (Belgium, Singapore, and Mexico); the other thirteen were acquired.

Oxychem uses several criteria to evaluate potential investments abroad: anticipated profits; market share (the company is determined to be the number one or number two producer in each national market, and, if number two, to have a major market share); past experience with the product, the country, and the local market; adequacy of the local market to support economy of scale; market growth potential; local economic and political climate; and the ability to maintain significant influence on the operation of the facility, including management of environmental health and occupational safety. Some of these variables are largely beyond corporate control, for example, local market size, local economic climate (such as inflation, indebtedness, availability of money, regulations of foreign investment, availability of skilled work force), local political climate, or market share and growth potential. Others are subject to negotiation and trade-off, either within the company or with the company, joint venture partner, and host country, for example, taxation, protection of technology patents and trademarks, epatriation of profits, host country incentives, and maintaining major influence over the operation of a facility.

Ten of the thirteen (77 percent) Oxychem international facilities are joint ventures. The Oxychem manager of the Thai facility viewed the partnership as a local business advantage, provided that the local partner accepts the company's philosophy and key business objectives. A joint venture partner can supply major strengths, including close knowledge of local market conditions, cultural practices, and rules for dealing with local authorities.

Most of Oxychem's international facilities were purchased from other companies: nine from W. R. Grace and three from Diamond Shamrock. Only three were built by Oxychem. Oxychem's decision to grow by acquisition has important consequences for EH&S management at its international subsidiaries. First, newly acquired facilities usually require major EH&S-related upgrading, which can cost as much as 15 percent of the facility's purchase price. Second, Oxychem has repeatedly faced the challenge of imposing its own EH&S philosophy and policies on new groups of workers and managers. Third, because many of the facilities purchased in developing countries were joint ventures, the company has also been confronted with the challenge of dealing with venture partners whose EH&S views may be very different than Oxychem's. These issues are further discussed in Chapter 6.

Figure 3.16
Environment, Health, and Safety Organizational Structure at Occidental Chemical
Corporation

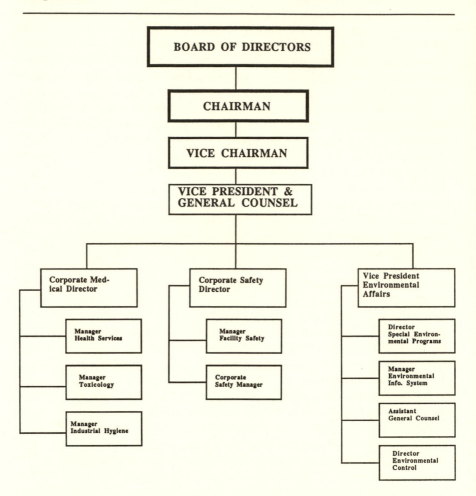

Oxychem: EH&S Policies, Implementation, and Performance

Both Occidental Chemical and Occidental Petroleum have relatively recently embraced the concept of corporate involvement in environment, health,
and safety. As with Xerox Corporation, the occasion for this change was a
serious environmental problem for which Oxychem assumed responsibility.

The corporate EH&S network, shown in Figure 3.16, was created in
1981. The vice president of corporate environmental affairs is responsible
for environmental remediation, environmental control, environmental

information, and legal/regulatory affairs. The corporate medical director is responsible for physical and mental health of employees (medical examinations), while the vice president of safety and hygiene is charged with broader health-related responsibilities (safety assessments, toxicologic studies pertaining to employee health, and industrial hygiene). Because most health hazards associated with Oxychem's processes are well known, long-term epidemiological studies of employees have not been undertaken. Toxicological testing, if needed, is contracted out, and the company rarely sets its own standards.

Oxychem's decision to acquire existing facilities means that the company must be prepared to respond to environmental problems resulting from previous operations. Oxychem calls these remedial activities "special environmental projects." The special fund for remediating past practices is funded by the corporate budget and receives annual contributions from Oxychem's overall gross revenues before corporate profits are calculated. In 1989, special remediation projects judged appropriate by current standards of environmental management and supported by the fund totalled $25 to $30 million. (Oxychem's total environmental expenses, including the fund, were over $90 million in 1989).

Explicit corporate policy calls for the application of uniform occupational standards worldwide and the achievement of "functional equivalency" between domestic and international facilities. *Functional equivalency* is defined by Occidental Petroleum's vice president for health, environment, and safety as "a level of protection of human health and the environment that is compatible with the intended objectives of the U.S. laws and regulations" (Friedman 1988).

Functional equivalency at individual facilities usually calls for the use of site-specific methods to achieve similar levels of EH&S protection. For example, different technologies may be employed at different facilities to achieve compliance with a uniform worldwide occupational standard. Where U.S. law mandates the use of a particular pollution control technology (a so-called best-available technology rule) at domestic facilities, a company may substitute an environmental standard or a pollutant discharge limit in order to achieve equivalent environmental protection at its foreign facilities. In other situations, a company may choose to disregard certain procedural requirements mandated in the United States, such as reporting or community outreach. The last chapter of this book discusses a body of empirical evidence that bears on the question of how Oxychem, Xerox, and Du Pont interpret the concept of functional equivalency.

Oxychem corporate safety assessments at domestic facilities are conducted by a team of safety or environmental specialists from corporate headquarters staff, one or more safety or environmental officers from other Oxychem facilities in the same industry group, and the safety and/or environment administrator from the facility being assessed. Sometimes the team includes

Figure 3.17
Safety Process and Safety Program Implementation at Occidental Chemical Facilities

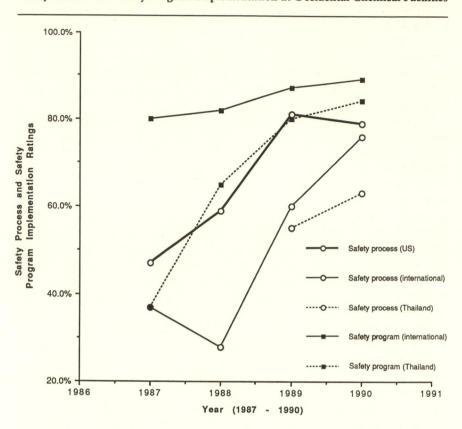

the production manager of the facility. These unannounced assessments are conducted annually at large plants and biannually for small plants.

Corporate safety assessments at international facilities are conducted with the same frequency as at domestic facilities. The assessment teams for international facilities are usually composed of a safety and environmental expert from the divisional headquarters staff, the local facility's program director, and the facility representative responsible for safety and environmental control. The manager of Environment and Safety International participates in most safety assessments of international operations. A representative of the parent company, Occidental Petroleum, participates in approximately half of the assessments.

The results of safety assessments are expressed quantitatively on two scales: a 100-point Index of Safety Program Implementation (derived from quantitative ratings concerning 36 categories), and a 100-point Index of

Figure 3.18
Total Injury Rates for Occidental Chemical Facilities

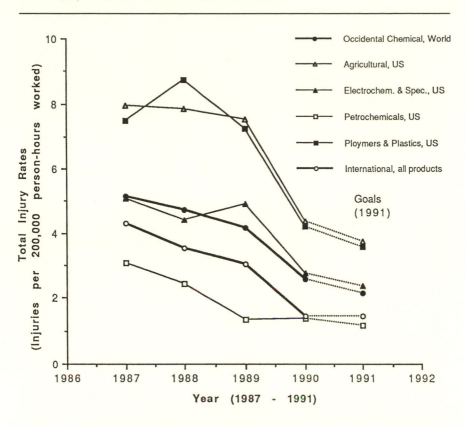

Safety Process Management (derived from the ratings concerning 8 of the 36 categories). Results from 1987 to 1990 for domestic and international facilities and for the Thai facility are summarized in Figure 3.17. Steady improvement over time is obvious in all categories. It appears that domestic U.S. facilities may be performing slightly better than international facilities (all but one of which are in developing countries), and that the Thai facility lags behind both groups. However, these comparative data should be interpreted with caution, because many of the ratings upon which they depend involve an inherently subjective judgment.

Standardized total reportable injury rates for Oxychem and its individual divisions for 1987–1990 and corporate goals for 1991 are shown in Figure 3.18. Statistics for product-based divisions include only domestic U.S. facilities; the international group includes all nondomestic facilities, regardless of product line. Steady improvement over time is evident for each manufacturing group, including the international group. As a group, the international

Figure 3.19
Total Injury and Illness Rates for Occidental Chemical Facilities

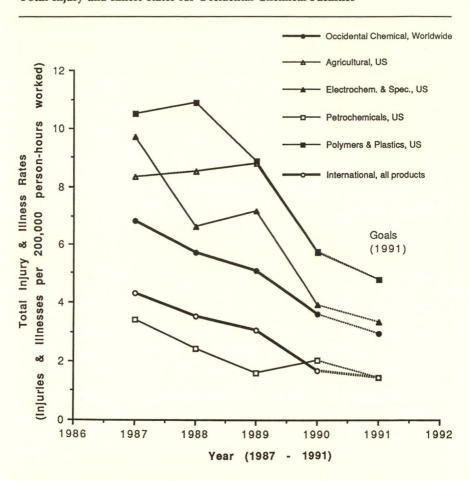

facilities performed slightly better than the company average. This comparison seems to conflict with the international facilities' lower safety/environmental assessment scores, but the apparent discrepancy may result from underreporting of occupational incidents at foreign facilities, although no direct evidence of such underreporting has so far emerged.

Combined injury and occupational illness rates are reported in Figure 3.19. They show essentially the same trends as the injury rates alone.

In summary, Oxychem's numerical facility performance indicators show steady improvement over time in all categories studied here. Interesting and significant differences can be observed among some categories: for example, occupational injury and illness rates vary widely between product line categories. But the gap between these categories has been narrowing over time.

Table 3.3
Vital Statistics of the Corporations

	Du Pont	Occidental Chemical Subsidiary of Occidental Petroleum	Xerox Parent Co. to: Rank-Xerox & Modi Xerox
Year of Establishment	1802	1968*	1959
Unit Under Study	Agrichemical Products	Company	Company
Principal Product • Company Studied	Agrichemicals, Coal, Fibers, Construction, Electronics, Health care, Petroleum	Industrial Chemicals	Photocopiers, Electronics
• Division Studied	Agrichemicals	-------	-------
• Plant Studied	Crop Protection Chemicals	Leather Tanning Chemicals	Photocopying Machines & Chemicals
Number of Corporate Employees Worldwide (1990)	144,000	12,000	111,000
Total Corporate Revenues (1990)	$40,000,000 (44% Foreign)	$2,800,000*** (10% Foreign)	$19,200,000 (42% Foreign)
Number of Plants** (1989) • US	5	42	9
• Other Industrial Countries	3	1	7
• Non-Industrial Countries	8	14	8
Mode of Facility Growth During Past 15 Years**	30% Acquired (20% of manufacturing Capacity)	Primarily via Acquisitions	None Have Been Acquired

   * Previously Hooker Chemical Corporation
  ** Only for Agricultural Products Department of Du Pont; includes only Xerox Americas and Rank Xerox Operations
 *** Assuming that Occidental has 15% of $20 Billion Parent Company assets

COMPARISON OF THE CORPORATIONS

Table 3.3 presents the overall vital statistics for the three companies studied. Although Occidental is significantly smaller than Xerox or Du Pont, all three companies are large corporations with multiple overseas facilities.

The corporations have quite different histories: Du Pont is one of the oldest chemical companies in the United States, with a long and cherished tradition of stability. Its growth has been steady but slow, primarily due to expansion rather than acquisition. Practically all hazardous chemicals produced by the agricultural division are consumer products and thus present uniquely complex safety performance challenges.

Table 3.4
Percent Ownership and Origins at Foreign Manufacturing Affiliates of the Companies
Studied

	Du Pont Agrichemical Products		Occidental Chemical		Xerox*		
Ownership of Foreign Affiliates By Facility							
	Thailand (b)	100%	Thailand (a)	49%	Rampur, India (b)	40%	
	Mexico (b)	100%	Thailand (a)	49%	Bombay, India (b)	40%	
	Mexico (b)	100%	Singapore (b)	50%	Brazil (b)	100%	
	Columbia (b)	100%	Chile (a)	100%	Brazil (b)	100%	
	Brazil (b)	100%	Brazil (a)	50%	Brazil (b)	100%	
	Puerto Rico (b)	100%	Brazil (a)	50%	Mexico (b)	100%	
	Taiwan (b)	100%	Brazil (a)	50%	Egypt (b)	49.99%	
	Philippines (b)	100%	Brazil (a)	100%	China (b)	100%	
	Agentina (b)	45%	Brazil (a)	100%	Canada (b)	100%	
	China (b)	80%	Brazil (a)	100%	Canada (b)	100%	
	Australia (b)	100%	Brazil (a)	100%	U.K. (b)	100%	
	France (a)	100%	Mexico (b)	49%	U.K. (b)	100%	
	Italy (a)	100%	Mexico (a)	49%	France (b)	<100%	
			Mexico (a)	49%	Netherlands (b)	100%	
			Mexico (a)	49%	Spain (b)	100%	
			Belguim (b)	100%			
Percent Wholly Owned	85%		38%		73%		
Percent Built	85%		20%		100%		
Percent Acquired	15%		80%		0%		

* Includes only Xerox AMERICAS and Rank Xerox Operations.
Key:
(a) — acquired by the company (complete or partial equity acquisitions are combined)
(b) — built by the company

Occidental Chemical and Xerox are much younger companies, and each
has grown rapidly. Xerox photocopier technology is a highly proprietary
process, and Xerox corporate growth has been due primarily to expansion.
Occidental Chemical has grown primarily by acquisitions.

All three companies manufacture chemicals with hazardous properties,
but the companies' main product lines differ. Oxychem produces only industrial chemicals, so consumer exposure is not a major issue. Both Du Pont
and Xerox produce chemicals to which consumers are exposed, so hazards
to both workers and consumers are important concerns.

Table 3.4 summarizes the ownership arrangements and the manner of acquisition for each of the foreign facilities studied. Occidental Chemical has
the highest proportion of jointly owned foreign facilities. This is probably

Figure 3.20
Total Occupational Injury Incidence Rates for Xerox, Du Pont, Oxychem

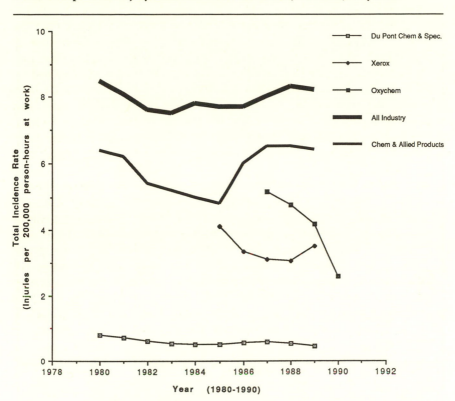

Year   (1980-1990)

related to the fact that its technologies, unlike those of Du Pont and Xerox, are not proprietary. The manner of acquiring facilities also differs among the three corporations: While Xerox and Du Pont tend to build their facilities, Occidental tends to acquire existing facilities from other companies.

All three corporations have well-developed management systems for EH&S, with clearly articulated philosophies and corporate involvement. The philosophies and management systems, however, have very different histories. Du Pont's concern with safety has its origins in the nineteenth century, when gun powder was its first and only product. Since then, the corporation has developed a highly sophisticated safety culture and is widely recognized as one of the world leaders in that area. Occidental Chemical (1981) and Xerox (1980) are more recent converts to the concept of high-level corporate involvement in EH&S management; both were awakened to the question by incidents that resulted in undesirable publicity.

The only numerical data providing direct cross-corporate comparisons for the three companies are the standard reported total occupational injury rates. As shown in Figure 3.20, all three companies show a general downward trend with time, although Xerox shows certain departures from the trend after 1987. Although Occidental Chemical and Xerox are among the leading corporations with regard to EH&S management, their occupational injury rates are still approximately an order of magnitude higher than Du Pont's. (This suggests that there is considerable room for improvement by even the best.) Notably, there is a definite convergence in the overall rate pattern, with a hypothetical baseline being asymptotically approached by Du Pont. By comparison to other industries, all three corporations have substantially lower average rates of occupational injury than the chemicals and specialties industrial sector or even the aggregated private sector. In sum, the available statistical data suggest that the three corporations under study are among the industry leaders in keeping occupational injury rates to a minimum.

The statistical data also suggest some counter-intuitive company-specific conclusions regarding facility performance differences between domestic and foreign facilities. In aggregate, the internal data provided by the corporations suggest that their foreign facilities have tended to outperform their domestic U.S. facilities and that this is particularly true of facilities in developing countries. (As has been noted, these differences must be interpreted with caution because cultural differences may influence the reporting of occupational injuries.) On the other hand, the data provided by the three corporations regarding compliance with occupational exposure standards show no systematic differences between domestic and foreign facilities.

THE HOST COUNTRIES

Development and Factory Licensing in India and Thailand

The current development policies of India and Thailand have evolved in very different ways and from very different historical roots. In India, the policies are the result of decades of intense national public debate, critical self-examination, and a continuing self-conscious search for pragmatic solutions to openly articulated social problems. Each of India's five-year development plans are drafted initially by the Planning Commission and then presented to Parliament, where each plan's "objectives, priorities and targets could be reviewed in detail with the widest public discussion" (Planning Commission 1961, p. 23). In contrast, Thailand's development debate has, until recently, been confined to a small circle of governmental officials whose views have been shielded from public debate (Christensen 1989, p. 181).

Following independence, India's first two decades of planned development were inward-oriented in the Soviet style and aimed at large-scale rapid industrialization and an increasingly self-reliant economy (Planning Commission 1961, p. 3). A severe balance of payments crisis in 1957 resulted in increased emphasis on the drive for self-reliance, and infused the planning process with a perceived need to conserve foreign exchange expenditures (Srinivasan 1990). In its quest for self-reliance, India's industrialization was to be guided by three prominent social aspirations:

1. the assurance of equal opportunities for all, regardless of class, caste, or region;
2. reduction of the extreme gap between social groups at opposite ends of the economic spectrum and prevention of new inequalities; and
3. prevention of monopolistic growth and concentration of economic power in the hands of a few (Planning Commission 1961, p. 31).

Current Indian policies related to industrial location, size, indigenization, and ownership, as well as the active involvement of government authorities in regulating investment activities, are all rooted in these post-independence goals and experiences. In the case of multinational facilities, these policies restrict location and ownership options, impose production quotas, enforce local procurement of parts and materials (up to 80 percent of value of the manufactured product), and require integration of the manufacturing process through the so-called Phased Manufacturing Program (PMP).

Thai development policies are not rooted in a rich history of highly visible public debate and overt development choices. While India's five-year development plans represent blueprints for coordinated national efforts toward both economic and social objectives, Thailand development plans serve primarily as a general guideline for government agencies. The Thai five-year development plans are not intended to mold national identity or produce social transformation. Indeed, a high-level official at Thailand's National Economic and Social Development Board (NESDB), who is a co-author of the recent plans, remarked, "The process of drafting a plan is more important than the final product, as it brings the best minds together and creates a lively and productive debate."

Thailand's strong commitment to a free market economy has resulted, without significant public debate, in the acceptance of economic growth (and limited governmental intervention) as the central development objective. The administrative structures and procedures currently employed to regulate MNCs still reflect the fundamental development philosophy adopted by post-war Thailand: openness to foreign investors, facilitation of economic growth, and minimal interference by the government. Not surprisingly, multinational corporations generally judge Thailand's business climate to be very good. As one high level official at the Board of Investment of Thailand stated, ". . . a foreign company can come freely to Thailand and when its technology is within the government's priority areas it can do whatever it likes."

A closer examination of the licensing process for foreign-owned manufacturing facilities reveals additional differences between the development phi-

Figure 3.21
Structure of India's Industrial Approval System*

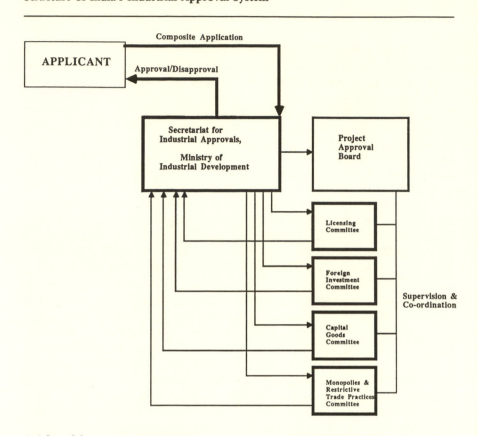

* Adapted from Martinussen (1988)

losophies of Thailand and India. Figure 3.21 outlines India's approval system for siting MNC facilities. The Secretariat for Industrial Approvals, located within the Ministry of Industrial Development, plays a key role in the process. Essential responsibilities of the secretariat include the receipt of all forms for industrial licenses and foreign collaboration agreements, appropriate channeling of these through the concerned approval committees, monitoring of delays, and the ultimate issuance of industrial licenses and letters of intent.

The Project Approval Board is a coordinating and supervisory body for the secretariat; it oversees the operation of the Licensing Committee, the Foreign Investment Board, the Capital Goods Committee, and the Monopolies and Restrictive Trade Practices Committee. The board and each of the committees are directly assisted by a Secretariat for Industrial Approvals (SIA), which operates within the Ministry of Industrial Development. The application process begins when a corporation submits to the minister of industrial development a letter of intent to apply for a factory license. The first response to the letter is the formation of a technical committee within the ministry, consisting of appropriate technical and development experts from the Ministry of Industrial Development and other branches of the government. The primary role of the committee is to determine whether the proposed technology is consistent with India's development objectives and hence desirable. Key factors considered in this initial review include domestic need for the product, prospects for indigenization of the manufacturing process, projected export value of the product, sophistication of the technology, projected magnitude of the employment, and (for highly polluting or resource-intensive industries such as paper manufacturing or mining) the potential environmental impact of the technology.

If the technology is approved by the Technical Committee, the applicant receives a letter of intent to consider an application for industrial license from the Secretariat of Industrial Approvals. This letter is equivalent to an invitation to enter the Industrial Approval System shown in Figure 3.21. That process is characterized by intense negotiations between the applicant and the host country's government and may take two to three years. Depending on the facility's size, proposed foreign equity percentage, and degree to which the proposed activity conforms to India's industrial sector priorities, the applicant will need to pass through powerful committees (Licensing, Foreign Investment, Capital Goods, and Monopolies and Restrictive Trade Practices), which are overseen by the Project Approval Board. For example, the Foreign Investment Board is chaired by an official from the Finance Ministry and includes the secretary of the Planning Commission, the director general of the Council for Scientific and Industrial Research, the director general of Technical Development, and various secretaries from other economic ministries as well.

The negotiations, which culminate with issuance of an operating license and a foreign collaboration license, typically settle the issues of location, ownership (including the value to be assigned for non-cash equity contributions), technical integration of the manufacturing process, production quotas, contribution to foreign trade, and contribution to indigenization of technology. Sites within large urban or industrial centers are effectively excluded from consideration. Potential industrial sites are categorized in four groups:

"A" sites, which have well-developed infrastructure and an established industrial presence but need more industry;

"B" sites, which have good infrastructure and some industries;

"C" sites, which have no infrastructure but some industry; and

"D" sites, which have neither infrastructure nor industry.

Industries that locate in "D" areas are classified as "pioneer industries" and receive a seven-year exemption from business taxes. Industries that locate in a C areas receive a six-year exemption from business taxes.

By comparison, the Thai licensing system is quite simple. Except for a number of very routine procedural approvals (such as commercial registration, business tax registration, and residence and work permits for non-Thai employees), a proposed investment that complies with the equity restrictions established by the Alien Business Law of 1972 will require no specific government approval other than an industrial license. (International Legal Counsellors 1980, p. 49; Business International Corporation 1989, p. 5). And in most cases, an application for an industrial license is processed within a few months through routine administrative channels. Ordinarily, there are no direct negotiations between the MNC and the government. The applicant has substantial flexibility in deciding the size and sophistication of the technology.

Thai authorities do exercise some influence over location of facilities, but the philosophy underlying their siting strategies is fundamentally different from that of India's authorities. India's policies are intended to promote long-term regional development, but the government assumes only the most minimal responsibility for providing infrastructure to support remote industrial locations. Thai policies are intended to relieve congestion in Bangkok while encouraging foreign investment; to serve these ends, the government assumes responsibility for providing superior infrastructure in government-managed industrial estates.

Given its efficient processing of industrial license applications and its generally unrestrictive business atmosphere, Thailand's principal means of influencing MNC conduct is a strategic incentives system. For example, Thailand uses a system of import duties to encourage local content in its production (Business International Corporation 1989, p. 7). The incentive system is managed by the Board of Investment (BOI), which has as its primary objective facilitating the conduct of business. This board is the central Thai government agency responsible for investment promotion. It provides a range of services designed to help investors at all stages of their projects, from identifying investment opportunities to solving specific operational problems. The BOI Investment Service Center provides a coordinating link with other government agencies, enables investors to obtain necessary approvals and permits, processes visas for foreigners investigating potential business opportunities, and actively seeks potential local business partners. BOI also manages a publicity campaign praising the investment climate of Thailand.

Established in 1960 as a relatively obscure entity, the BOI is perhaps best known now for its power to grant a wide range of attractive incentives (known as "privileges") to multinational corporations judged to deserve "promoted status." The Board of Investment is empowered by the 1977 Investment Promotion Act to "formulate an investment promotion programme" that furthers Thailand's development and to participate in preparation of the

National Economic and Social Development Plans. The incentives available to the board include:

1. guarantees against export restrictions, competition by new state enterprises, state monopolization of similar products, nationalization, price controls, and imports by tax-exempt state agencies or enterprises;
2. protective measures such as import surcharges or bans on competing foreign products;
3. exemption from the Alien Business Law restrictions on foreign-equity shares;
4. permission to employ foreign technicians and experts, to own land, and to take or remit foreign currency abroad; and
5. a wide range of tax incentives, such as exemptions from import duties and business taxes on raw materials components and re-exported items, exemptions from duties and business taxes on exports, and annual deductions from taxable incomes based on export performance (Business International Corporation 1989, p. 15).

In awarding privileges, BOI gives priority to projects that demonstrate clear importance for national development. The specific criteria by which the desirability of projects are judged reflects a broad range of social and economic objectives, including sophistication of technology, desirability of technology (vis-à-vis the government-promoted industrial and agricultural sectors), foreign exchange earnings, degree of domestic co-ownership, willingness to locate in government-designated industrial estates or in the provinces, magnitude of prospective employment, conservation of energy, and ability to develop a base for further industrial development (Board of Investment 1989, pp. 14–15). The relative weights assigned these several criteria are not equal. For example, the BOI application forms do not include questions regarding the environmental effects of the proposed projects. Similarly, a high-level BOI official interviewed by this research team assigned much less importance to implementing policies of regional development or natural resource management than to advancing economic growth and business development policies.

Despite its lack of direct authority to issue industrial licenses or to attach conditions to such licenses, the magnitude of the BOI's incentives and privileges make it a key regulatory body with respect to MNC activities. A majority of MNCs investing in Thailand do apply for promoted status and do choose to locate their facilities in a government industrial estate. These interactions with BOI, concerning the negotiation of incentives and privileges within the context of siting decisions, are the only times that most MNCs will directly confront the host country's development objectives. The agency's prominent role in the siting process is strengthened by the fact that its principal objective—to help investors in all business matters—is perfectly consistent with Thai policy regarding multinational corporations: to promote economic growth and exports by attracting foreign investors.

Regulatory Structures in India and Thailand

In Thailand, responsibility for developing national environmental policy is assigned to the National Environment Board (NEB) and to its executive arm, the Office of the National Environment Board (ONEB). The revised Conservation of National Quality Act of 1978 gives NEB and ONEB the responsibility to develop national environmental policies; recommend standards on environmental quality to other agencies having statutory power to implement and enforce them; coordinate efforts by government agencies to implement the environmental statutes; and report to the cabinet on the state of the nation's environment.

NEB and ONEB are primarily advisory, coordinating, and planning bodies, not enforcers or implementers. This limitation on NEB/ONEB authority is reinforced by its location in the central administrative structure of the country. In 1979 the NEB was transferred from the office of the prime minister to the newly created Ministry of Science, Technology and Energy (MSTE). Since the primary mission of MSTE is to promote certain industries, the regulatory objectives of NEB would appear to be structurally subordinate to the promotional objectives of its parent agency.

Friction occasionally arises between ONEB and BOI, usually over specific decision timetables. While ONEB may want one to two years to evaluate the environmental impact of a particularly complex project, the tight schedules of BOI may require much more rapid decision making. Although the prime minister has authority to resolve such matters, solutions to conflicts between economic and environmental objectives are usually negotiated among all the affected parties rather than imposed by one authority.

Authority to implement NEB environmental standards and to regulate the environmental activities of industrial facilities rests with the Ministry of Industry. The Ministry of Industry has promulgated standards for industrial effluents and air emissions since the early 1970s, as it was empowered to do by the Factories Act of 1969. By 1978 the regulatory authority of the Ministry of Industry was extended to include atmospheric chemical and mineral dust standards in the workplace and groundwater quality standards for drinking purposes.

In practice, enforcement of environmental standards is very weak in Thailand. In part, this is due to the limited authority and resources granted ONEB. In part, it can be attributed to the virtual absence of local enforcement authorities: All enforcement activities must be carried out by the ministries and departments of Thailand's highly centralized national regulatory structure. At government-managed industrial estates (which, thanks to superior infrastructure and BOI incentives, are increasingly selected by MNC affiliates), enforcement is largely delegated to the estate management, the Industrial Estate Authority of Thailand (IEAT). IEAT sets and enforces effluent standards, monitors discharges, and participates in the licensing process by specifying the conditions for environmental and occupational safety practices within the operating license. The advantages and disadvantages of delegating regulatory and enforcement authority to IEAT, an agency with multiple missions, are evident in the case studies presented in Chapter 4.

In contrast to Thailand's highly centralized system, India's legislative and administrative system for environmental regulation of industrial enterprises is characterized by the division of power between the central government and state governments. The main responsibility for environmental protection lies with the Ministry of Environment and Forests. The Central Board for Pollution Control acts as the central government's implementing and coordinating authority, while eighteen state pollution control boards have been established for more local supervision of statute implementation. The state boards are empowered to control pollution primarily through issuing discharge permits.

Functioning of India's administrative machinery is supported by the enactment of various environmental regulations. Prior to 1984, the primary environmental regulations were the Water Prevention and Control of Pollution Acts of 1974 and 1977, and the Air Prevention and Control of Pollution Act of 1981. Following the Bhopal accident in 1984, and in view of the shortcomings of earlier environmental regulations, the government of India enacted a comprehensive Environmental Protection Act in 1986 (Bowonder and Arvind 1989). As general legislation on environmental protection, the act coordinates the activities of various regulatory agencies; creates and empowers authorities for environmental protection, such as the plant closure authority given to the Ministry of Environment and Forests; regulates the discharge of environmental pollutants and handling of hazardous substances; enables speedy responses to accidents; and punishes those who endanger human environment, health and safety. Section 6 of the act explicitly empowers the central government by giving it rule-making authority for:

1. standards of quality of air, water, or soil for various areas and purposes;
2. maximum allowable limits of concentration of various environmental pollutants (including noise) for different areas;
3. procedures and safeguards for the handling of hazardous substance;
4. prohibition and restrictions on the handling of hazardous substance in different areas;
5. the prohibition and restriction of the location of industries and the carrying on of processes and operations in different areas; and
6. procedures and safeguards for the prevention of accidents that may cause environmental pollution and for providing for remedial measures for such accidents.

The 1986 rules contain industry-specific emission/discharge standards for a broad range of industrial activities. The 1986 rules also empower the central government with authority to prohibit or restrict the location of industries and the continued operation of existing operations.

Table 3.5
Characteristics of the Host Countries Relevant to the Siting of Manufacturing Facilities by Multinationals

CHARACTERISTICS \ COUNTRY	THAILAND	INDIA
1. Development Philosophy	Economic growth as the means to prosperity and social change	Simultaneous Social & Economic Change
2. Policies Towards Location of Facilities by MNCs --		
• Key expected benefits to the country	Economic growth; Export earnings	Technologic self-sufficiency, satisfying domestic demand
• Main purpose of government intervention	To facilitate	To regulate
• Extent of government intervention	Low initially, minimal after licensing	High initially, continuous throughout facility life
• Instruments of government intervention	Operating license, incentives	Operating license, permits, quotas
• Objectives of locational policy	Relieve urban congestion, provide infrastructure	Promotion of regional development
3. Issues in Negotiating MNC Facilities		
• Direct Negotiations	Minimal	Intense
• Duration of Licensing	Months	Approximately 2 years
• Location	Industrial Estates are encouraged	"Backward" areas are encouraged
• Infrastructure	Provided by government	Companies are on their own
• Joint Ventures	Required in some cases; otherwise encouraged	Required; exceptions exist
• Minimum Employment Quotas	Not an issue	Not an issue
• Sophistication of Technology	Encouraged through incentives	Required; Phased Manuf. Plan
• Domestic Production Quotas	Not an issue	Imposed if monopoly possible
4. Environmental/Occupational Protection		
• Laws	In place	In place
• Role of central authority	Prominent	Prominent
• Role of regional/local authority	Minimal	Prominent
• Agency with regulatory authority	Ministry of Industry; Industrial Estate Authority	State Pollution Control Boards
• Power of Environmental Agency	National Environmental Board • advisory • coordinating	Ministry of Environment & Forest: • advisors State Pollution Control Boards: • Regulators & enforcers
• Instruments of Environmental & Occupational Regulation of Facilities	Industrial license	Environmental emission & discharge permits

Using the British Factories Act of 1937 as a model, India's Factories Act of 1948 codified for the first time the international principle that workers employed in a hazardous manufacturing process should have their health protected, safety ensured, and welfare attended to. In accordance with the provisions of this act, facilities must pass state inspections and receive a license for safe operation from the state boards. The Factories (Amendment) Act of 1987 provides better safeguards in the use and handling of hazardous substances in factories, mandates the creation of emergency response procedures, and allows for more stringent punishment for noncompliance with the provisions of the Act. For hazardous industries, the 1987 act specifies provisions controlling the facility siting for the protection of neighboring communities, creates compulsory disclosure of information by corporations, and ensures that the person ("occupier") who has ultimate control over the affairs of the factory is responsible for implementing safety and hazard management. Concerning hazardous facility siting, a mandatory siting procedure involving the creation of a site appraisal committee has been instituted. This committee is to consist of the chief inspector of factories of the state (as chair), an expert in the field of occupational health, and representatives from the State Pollution Control Board's meteorological department. This committee has the power to call for any information from the industry prior to siting a factory (Bowonder and Arvind 1989).

Despite the existence of an extensive regulatory structure for environmental protection, enforcement in India is weak. Administrative and technological constraints, coupled with the reluctance of governments to take firm actions when the interests of strong and influential private groups are put into jeopardy, provide common hindrances to the enforcement capabilities of India as well as other developing countries (Eskeland and Jimenez 1991).

SUMMARY

Against this background of two fundamentally different national development philosophies, rooted in different economic and political systems and conditioned by different institutional and national histories, in the early and mid 1980s Du Pont and Occidental Chemical initiated business ventures in Thailand, and Xerox initiated a venture in India. Table 3.5 summarizes the philosophical differences between the two countries, which are reflected in a wide spectrum of contrasting policies and administrative systems, including, for example, the extent of government intervention; the instruments of that intervention (e.g., incentives versus strict and short-lived licenses and permits); the degree of control imposed on the foreign corporations; and the support provided by the host country to the corporations.

Not unexpectedly, the contrasts in business environment between Thailand and India create different expectations of how the siting process for foreign facilities would proceed in each country. *From the company perspective,* the expectation in Thailand would be for a relatively efficient siting process, with minimal negotiations between the host country and the company and with a large degree of autonomy maintained by the company in making key design choices: design and complexity of technology, location, and environmental and occupational control systems. In India, the company might expect a slower siting process, one that would involve multiple government agencies at both the state and central levels. It would likely require extensive negotiations and might leave the company little flexibility in making key design choices. India's process would be more likely than the Thai process to create a perception (independent of the actual outcome) by both participants that the solution was less than optimal.

But one might also expect certain similarities between the two national situations. Since both countries have fairly weak enforcement systems, the companies all might expect to have relative autonomy in achieving compliance with EH&S regulations and in choosing their own combinations of engineered and management controls for implementing their EH&S policies.

REFERENCES

Board of Investment. *Answers to Your Questions*. Bangkok: Board of Investment, Office of the Prime Minister, 1989.

Bowonder, B., and S. Arvind. "Environmental Regulations and Litigation in India." *Project Appraisal*. 4:4 (1989): 182–196.

Business International Corporation. *ILT Thailand*. New York: Business International Corporation, July 1989.

Christensen, Scott R. "Thailand in 1989: Consensus at Bay." *Asian Survey*. 30:2 (1989): 178–180.

Du Pont Thailand. *Policy Manual for the Bangpoo Plant*. Bangpoo, Thailand, 1981: p. 1.

Du Pont Thailand. *Operating and Procedures Manual for the Bangpoo Plant*, 1982: Bangpoo, Thailand.

The Economist Intelligence Unit. *Thailand, Burma: Country Profile 1989–1990*. London: The Economist Intelligence Unit, 1990.

Eskeland, Gunnar S., and Emmanuel Jimenez. "Curbing Pollution in Developing Countries." *Finance and Development*. 28:1 (1991): 15–17.

Friedman, Frank. *A Practical Guide to Environmental Management*. Washington, DC: Environmental Law Institute, 1991. Second edition.

International Legal Counsellors, Ltd. *Thailand Business Legal Handbook*. Bangkok: Board of Investment, 1980.

Kohli, Atul. "Politics of Liberalization in India." *World Development*. 17:3 (1989): 305–328.

Martinussen, John. *Transnational Corporations in a Developing Country: The Indian Experience*. New Delhi: Sage Publications, 1988.

Overseas Business Reports. *Doing Business with India*. Washington, DC: U.S. Department of Commerce, 1985.

Planning Commission. *Towards a Self-Reliant Economy*. New Delhi: Government of India, 1961.

Snidvongs, Kasem, and Kosit Panpiemras. "Environment and Development Planning in Thailand." Pages 347–360 in UNEP (ed.), *Environment and Development in Asia and the Pacific: Experiences and Prospects*. Nairobi: UNEP Reports and Proceedings Series 6, 1982.

Srinivasan, T. N. "External Sector in Development: China and India, 1950–1989." *American Economic Review*. 80:2 (1990): 113–121.

Tambunlertchai, Somsak. "Economic Prospects and External Economic Relations of Thailand." *Asian Development Review* 7:2 (1989): pp. 88–112.

Wyatt, David K. *Thailand: A Short History*. New Haven, CN: Yale University Press, 1984.

Xerox. *Environmental Health and Safety Manual: Safety and Environmental Control Standard* (1982): p. 2.

CHAPTER 4

Tales of Three Facilities

This chapter assembles the main body of raw data collected through the case studies; it consists of a detailed description of the events that took place in the course of establishing the three facilities. Although occasionally peppered with interpretive commentaries, these are fundamentally narrative descriptions of the three chronologies. The chapter concludes by identifying the variables that may explain the nature of the interactions among the principal participants observed in the three facility transfer processes.

The vital statistics of the three facilities studied are summarized in Table 4.1. All were constructed and brought on line during the 1980s. The two Thai facilities generate products for domestic consumption and employ a relatively small work force, while the Indian facility is significantly larger and significantly committed to exports. All three handle materials with potential occupational and environmental hazards. The stories of the facilities have been reconstructed from different types of elements: interviews with company managers and executives in the United States and in the host countries who had personally participated in the events; analysis of documents such as industrial licenses, technical agreements, joint venture agreements, internal letters, and memoranda; site visits at the foreign facilities; and associated interviews with employees at the foreign facilities. Additional insights were gained from the collaborating research teams in India and Thailand, who independently met with the executives and managers of the facilities and conducted site visits.

In comparison, interactions with host country officials possessing either first-hand or indirect knowledge of the three cases were much more modest. Only the Modi Xerox case included an interview with a high level official who had participated in considering the company's application for a license.

Table 4.1
Case Studies

	Thailand **Du Pont Agrichemicals** Bangpoo Facility	Thailand **Occidental Chemical** Bangpoo Facility	India **Modi Xerox** Rampur Facility
Year of Establishment	1982	1984*	1986
Principal Products	Herbicides, Fungicides, & Insecticides	Chrome Compounds for Leather Tanning	Photocopiers Electronic Boards Photoreceptors Developers & Toners
Marketing	Domestic • Thai Farmers	Domestic • Thai Leather Industry	Domestic & International (>30%)
Number of Employees	25	42	272**
Operating Schedule	1 Shift 7 Hours/day 6 Days/week	3 Shifts 24 Hours/day 7 Days/Week	1 Shift 9 Hours/day 5 Days/Week
Ownership	Wholly Owned	Joint Venture	Joint Venture

* Originally Established by Thai-Pakistani Interests;
  Re-Started in 1986 by Diamond Shamrock and then continued by Oxychem following 1986 acquisition.
** 96 of these are former land owners who are employed primarily as grounds-keepers.

This can be attributed to the several-year interval since the events under study. Furthermore, in Thailand both facility transfers were accomplished through routine administrative procedures, without extensive involvement by any one individual government employee.

It was not possible to interview the Modi Xerox or Oxychem joint venture partners.

MODI XEROX FACILITY IN RAMPUR

Negotiations

The joint venture between Rank Xerox and Modi Rubber was primarily initiated by Modi Rubber in the late 1970s. The prospects for photo-reproduction technology in India, which at that time had no domestic manufacturers of photocopiers, were bright. After considerable activity prior to 1982, the two companies formed the India Export Company and inaugurated a 100 percent export assembly facility located in Bombay. Following governmental relaxation in 1982 of severe restrictions on that technology, Modi Rubber established Indian Xerographic Systems Limited, and the venture partners (Rank Xerox and Indian Xerographic Systems) submitted a letter of intent to the Ministry of Industrial Development (MID) to form a collaboration and to set up a factory. The letter provided a general description of the proposed technology. In accordance with the standard administrative procedures for licensing foreign enterprises in India, the first response to the letter of intent was the formulation of a technical committee representing the Ministry of Industry and other governmental agencies. The following issues were considered during that initial review: domestic need for the product; prospects for indigenization of the manufacturing process; projected export value of the product; and sophistication of the technology. Also considered, but to a lesser degree, were the projected magnitude of the employment and the potential environmental impact of the technology. Consideration of environmental factors, though included, was limited at this stage to ascertaining whether the proposed project was resource intensive or highly polluting (neither of which was the case with the proposed facility).

Upon the initial approval, issued in mid-1982 by the technical committee, the venture partners were encouraged to apply for the industrial license and foreign collaboration license. The submission of the applications for these licenses was followed by a period of negotiations between the government and the newly formed company regarding the location, size, equity arrangement, technological sophistication, and export requirements for the proposed facility. The participants in the negotiations included the minister of industry for the central government of India, the managing director of Rank Xerox, the president of Indian Xerographic Systems Limited, and, later on, a representative of the government for the state of Uttar Pradesh.

From the company's perspective, an ideal site for the proposed facility would have the following attributes: access to the means of transportations (good roads, railroad, airport); access to skilled labor; other essential infrastructure (electricity, telephones, sewage, drinking water, etc.); dust-free air (important in the manufacturing of electronics); cultural and educational amenities that would make it sufficiently attractive to Indian and expatriate employees. These criteria (with the exception of dust-free air) led them to propose potential sites in highly industrialized areas of the country.

In contrast, the government's criteria for selecting a suitable site were primarily concerned with promoting regional development. Its first proposal focused on Kashipur, a town in the state of Uttar Pradesh (the home state of the minister), classified as a "D" area. The site had no industry, and its lack of infrastructure included the absence of paved roads and railroads.

Both sides flatly rejected each other's proposals, and the negotiated compromise solution emerged as the town of Rampur, approximately 120 miles east of Delhi and also in Uttar Pradesh. The area was at that time classified as "C". The principal disadvantages to the company of locating in Rampur were the lack of reliable power supply, lack of skilled labor, unattractiveness to the potential employees because of unavailability of good primary education and cultural and social life, and high level of airborne dust. As shown later, the company has since made significant progress in compensating for these deficiencies or in reducing them. The advantage of the site was its location on Delhi-Lucknow-Calcutta National Highway 24 and the proximity to Amritsar-Lucknow-Calcutta Railroad line. The nearest airport was approximately 40 miles away in Pantnagar.

It appears that the compromise made by the venture partners, from an "A" to a "C" area, was greater than that made by the host country authorities from a "D" to a "C" area. This skewed outcome was, according to the company, a reflection of the government's smaller concern that the deal might fall through; in this case the locational benefits of the facility were perceived as outweighing its other potential economic and social benefits.

The conditions specified in the letters of intent to grant the industrial and foreign collaboration licenses, issued in July 1983 by the Ministry of Industry, indicate that approximately a year after initiation of the formal approval process, the key decisions had been made. These included equity participation by Rank Xerox of 40 percent; export obligation of 30 percent for five years; annual production ceiling of 9,500 machines destined for domestic sales (no ceiling on exports); compliance with phased manufacturing program, and indigenization plan; location in a backward district category "C". This was also the year that Rank Xerox and Indian Xerographic Systems Limited established Modi Xerox Limited.

The limit on the level of production was dictated by the country's attempt to prevent monopolistic market domination by Modi Xerox, which in the early 1980s was the only manufacturer of photocopiers in India (this is no longer an issue). Indigenization policy, as applied to the proposed Rank Xerox facility, required that within five years approximately 80 percent of the value of the product manufactured at the facility be contributed by the local industry—either made at the facility or purchased from the local vendors. The company is free to choose which parts of the final product it will import and which it will obtain locally, as long as the overall financial value of the imports is reduced annually at a predetermined rate. Since the policy is enforced through semiannual renewal of import licenses, the intense negotiations between the corporation and the government are practically continual.

In accordance with the provisions of the national phased manufacturing policy, Rank Xerox was required to transfer to Rampur increasingly complete stages of the complete array of the xerographic technology: machine and electronic boards manufacturing, as well as the chemistry of the photocopying process (toner, photoreceptor, and developer). That such integration required a major departure from the company's usual investment practices is apparent from Table 3.1; the Rampur facility is the only one among Xerox and Rank Xerox manufacturing facilities worldwide that has all photocopier technologies concentrated under one roof. The departure is even more striking if one considers that the Rampur facility is among the smallest in capacity.

From the business perspective, manufacturing of toner in India would not be cost effective until the toner facility could operate on three shifts, a goal not expected to be achieved for several years after start-up. Nonetheless, the operating license specifies the construction of toner, developer, and photoreceptor plants a year after completion of the hardware facility.

Notably, environmental issues were not part of the negotiations between the company and the central government. Similarly, at no point did the government express any expectations of Rank Xerox regarding the size of the proposed work force.

The operating license and the license for foreign collaboration for the Modi Xerox facility were issued in June 1984. The industrial license reiterated the conditions articulated a year earlier in the letters of intent and specified Rampur as the site of the facility. In addition, several general conditions of compliance with the state environmental regulations were included.

The rigid restrictions imposed on the Rampur facility are in contrast to the flexibility afforded by the authorities to the first Xerox facility (jointly owned by Rank Xerox and Modi Rubber as part of the Indian Export Company) established approximately two years earlier in Bombay and producing exclusively for export. Starting with a location significantly more attractive than Rampur's, the facility is exempt from the indigenization and PMP requirement, import duty and customs duty, and has no production ceiling. The only requirement is that the final product has value added through local labor and materials. Accordingly, the production entails only assembly of machines and parts that are, by and large, imported. The difference between the two facilities vividly illustrates the trade-offs made between different dimensions of achieving technological self-reliance in India. In this case, the trade-off is made between two mutually desirable goals, promoting technology transfer and balancing foreign trade.

The negotiations between the joint venture partners, respectively representing Rank Xerox and Indian Reprographic Systems (IRS), proceeded in parallel with the negotiations with the government. As early as 1981 the partners agreed, in a memorandum of understanding, on the form of management for the new enterprise. According to the agreement, during the first five years IRS would nominate the president and vice president, with an option of Rank Xerox also nominating a co-president. In the case of such joint presidency, the Rank Xerox president would be responsible for technical matters. After five years the company would have only one president, nominated by IRS, and one vice president, nominated by Rank Xerox. In addition, the agreement assigned to Rank Xerox the sole authority for product quality control over the life of the facility, which included stopping production if necessary. The financial management was assigned to Rank Xerox for the first five years and to Indian Reprographic Systems thereafter. The emphasis on product quality was consistent with the general corporate objectives in considering foreign investments, as described in Chapter 3. The agreement did not address management of environment, health, and safety.

The formal joint venture agreement and the accompanying technical agreements were signed by the partners in 1983. It specified ownership to be 40 percent by Rank Xerox, 40 percent by Indian Reprographic Systems, and 20 percent by public share holders. The 40 percent ownership by Rank Xerox was the ceiling on foreign ownership of Indian companies as defined by law (the original breakdown has since been changed to 35 percent Rank Xerox, 35 percent Modi, 20 percent public, and 10 percent institutional).

With regard to the management of the facility, the documents were concerned primarily with the transfer of know-how—such as design and engineering of the plant, and specifications of equipment and its maintenance, manufacturing process, and quality control—by the multinational to the domestic partner. The joint venture agreement is brief on other aspects of joint venture management as well. Furthermore, what functions were specified in the joint venture agreement were altered in response to the needs. For example, the initial assignment of technical management to Rank Xerox (engineering, design, construction, installation, product quality) and business management to Modi changed when it was clear that certain elements of the Rank Xerox business management were more appropriate than those of Modi. In the course of the case study, the executives of the company repeatedly stressed that there was one culture and one management system, that of Modi Xerox. "There is no Modi partner and Rank Xerox partner, there is simply Modi Xerox" were the words used by one.

However, each partner clearly brought its own strengths to the enterprise, and these strengths were displayed at different times. During the negotiations, Modi was helpful in arranging the purchase of 96 acres, a difficult task considering India's limitations on land ownership (a ceiling of 12.5 acres). The partner's knowledge of the country's prevailing business practices also would prove helpful in dealing with local suppliers, officials, and customers. As in the 1981 document, the issues of EH&S are not included.

The design and management of environment, health, and safety were not explicitly assigned to either partner in the joint venture agreement, but it has been implicitly understood by both parties to be the purview of Xerox through its subsidiary Rank Xerox. The elements of that system in the Modi Xerox facility are described later.

Construction

The construction of the facility started in November 1983, a few months before the official issuance of the operating license. The production ceiling imposed on the facility created a challenge for the company. It could build a large facility, similar to its other worldwide plants, and simply run it well below the capacity for an unknown period of time. Alternately, it could build a smaller plant. The main advantage of choosing the first option was that the company would approach the task with extensive and well-tested experience in designing the plant and procuring the necessary equipment; the main disadvantage was that it was not a cost-effective solution. The choice made by Xerox, to build a scaled-down plant, presented a different challenge. The Rampur facility would be but one-third the size of the smallest similar facility in the world of Xerox. Such a drastic reduction in size implied that there could be significant changes in the basic design and in the choice of equipment. The adjustment that these changes might require in order to achieve product quality and facility safety equivalent to other worldwide Xerox operations were not completely known at the outset of construction.

The plant was designed by an Indian architectural firm whereas the technology specifications for the manufacturing process, equipment, and engineered pollution and safety controls were designed by Rank Xerox engineers at the Dutch facility (toner), the U.K. facility (photoreceptor), and the Dutch and the French facilities (assembly of machines and electronic boards). Corporate EH&S personnel were included in the process. The Indian venture partner had little involvement in the designs for the facility or in the oversight of its construction. This was clearly the domain of the owner of the technology.

The technology design required modifications in the standard blueprints to meet the small scale of the plant and the integration of the diverse technologies (for example, in the design of a water treatment plant, waste disposal, and emergency response system). The construction was performed by local contractors. Errors were made and corrected. In one instance the local contractors, anxious to meet deadlines, finished the toner building without providing a sufficient explosion-relief system. Upon the insistence of Rank Xerox management, the buildings had to be partially demolished.

The design of the toner plant reflects the adjustments the company made in scaling down the facility while retaining all features associated with maintaining product quality. The process generates fine dust in the respirable range and beyond. The workers most exposed to the inhalable dust are cleaning staff, control operators, and materials handlers. The primary hazards of airborne toner dust consist of adverse health effects from inhalation, explosions, and fires. Since air concentrations sufficient to protect workers from adverse effects provide a wide safety margin for explosions, for both types of hazards, dust control is the most effective preventive measure. The major sources of dust emissions are at transfer points between the steps. Automation and infrequent changes in the product lines (generally requiring reassembling of equipment) are therefore the most effective methods for reducing dust generation. In addition, maintaining cleanliness in the plant prevents the already settled particles from becoming airborne again, thus reducing the risk of secondary explosions.

In the large Xerox toner facilities, most transfer steps are automated.

However, the relatively small size of the Rampur facility and the modest initial scale of production did not justify extensive automation. The manual operations at the facility included hoisting of the bags of starting materials to the Banbury mixer located on the upper level (since automated by an elevator), most transfers between steps, and bottling. At the outset, management was concerned that the manual operations would generate more airborne dust than the automated operation, but the lack of prior experience with a small operation such as this did not allow them to make accurate predictions on the magnitude of such increase. An alternative solution, chosen by the company as an interim measure, was to use individual personal respiratory protection (disposable dust masks) once the facility went into operation. The measure was accompanied by the installation of an extensive personal monitoring system. This and other health and safety systems installed at the facility are discussed later.

The employment of personal protective devices instead of engineered controls was clearly a temporary solution that would be effective only for a modest production scale at the plant. The system would not, according to the initial predictions, meet the demands of a two- or three-shift production schedule. (These predictions were later confirmed during a brief acceleration of production). As the system was being put in place, the plans for further modifications of the key sources of emissions also were being developed by the EH&S personnel for future implementation.

During the construction, the partners occasionally differed on capital spending for engineered safety. In one instance, at issue was installation of a fire protection system: Whereas the Indian partner aimed for a system that would assure the lowest possible fire insurance and no more, the Western partner aimed for a system capable of meeting certain performance standards. The disagreement was resolved in Xerox's favor when it became clear that protecting the factory from destruction in fire was more cost effective than other alternatives.

Startup and Operations

The construction of the first part of the machine assembly plant was completed early in 1985 and the toner, developer, and photoreceptor plant approximately a year later. The 42 acres on which the facility is located can be accessed directly from National Highway 24. It is a single-lane, two-way paved road that serves the needs of long-distance travelers and delivery trucks, as well as the local population. The trucks, automobiles, buffalo-drawn carts, and pedestrians, including children, all coexist on that road. The average car speed is probably below 30 mph, and the 120-mile trip from the company's headquarters in New Delhi takes four to five hours. The shoulders of the road are lined with vehicles damaged in collisions, not surprising considering the crowds, the total absence of lighting at night, and the failure on the part of many drivers to use headlights after dark. Sometimes the road is closed altogether because of religious festivals or political rallies.

The facility manufactures half a dozen different models of photocopiers and electronic boards, as well as photoreceptor, toner, and developer. Its products are identical to those manufactured at other worldwide plants. At the time of this study, the facility operated 9 hours per day, 5 days per week. As the demand for machines grows, the facility may expand to two and three shifts. There are 272 employees, 96 of whom are the former occupants of the land (primarily employed as groundskeepers). In 1988–89 the factory produced at a rate of 1,000 machines per month. Five thousand machines were exported that year to Bulgaria, Czechoslovakia, Poland, Soviet Union, the United Kingdom, Holland, Spain, and Zimbabwe.

In 1988–89 Modi Xerox commanded 40 percent of the domestic market share in India, up from 36 percent in 1986–87. The number two competitor had 15 percent of the market that year.

In addition to the manufacturing areas, the facility has laboratories for routine chemical analyses and a modest R&D unit. The R&D efforts are primarily directed at improving the existing processes and materials and responding to the unique needs of the customers. One of its recent accomplishments was a modification of the photoreceptor manufacturing process to meet the needs of Japanese customers.

Despite the remote location of Rampur and a shortage of cultural amenities, Modi Xerox had no difficulty in attracting and keeping a highly skilled work force. Company executives attribute the success to the management style at Modi Xerox and the attraction of high technology represented by a well-known multinational corporation. Another reason for the company's success in attracting a professional work force is its significant efforts to improve the quality of life of the workers. More than half of the 96 acres owned by Modi Xerox in Rampur has been used for housing, recreation, and educational purposes. The Modi Academy, established in 1987, offers fine elementary schooling for approximately three hundred children of the employees and other Rampur residents. There are company housing, recreational areas for employees, and medical services. Following the well-established tradition of Indian companies, Modi Xerox "adopted" two very poor local villages. The company's improvements in the villagers' lives have included building a modest schoolhouse, erecting solar panels, dust and mosquito control, hygiene education, job training, and medical services.

Changes in the business climate of the area have been disappointing, however. Although the workers contribute to the local economy, spin-off industries associated with the Modi Xerox technology have not been established in the area, most likely because of the small size of the production. Since the establishment of the Modi Xerox facility, the area has been re-classified from "C" to "B." Clearly, the location policies of the Indian government that pressured Rank Xerox into siting its facility in the poorly developed area of Rampur only partially accomplished their objectives: The enterprise brought jobs and infrastructure to the area and, for some people, improved living conditions, but it did not attract satellite industries.

The manufacturing activities at the Rampur facility are associated with multiple occupational hazards. Chronic health impairment may occur from prolonged inhalation of particulates in the toner plant, from inhalation of selenium and arsenic in the photoreceptor plant, and from exposure to vapors in the paint shop. Several materials generate toxic fumes when ignited. As stated earlier, there is a substantial risk of fire and explosion in the toner plant because toner is a combustible dust. In addition, there are the usual hazards associated with operating a variety of mechanical equipment in the toner plant, the photoreceptor plant, and the machine assembly plant: accidental damage to the limbs, eyes, the body.

The company selectively practices all forms of occupational protections at the facility: engineered controls, if feasible, personal protective devices, training workers in safe occupational practices, monitoring potential and actual exposure levels of workers, and an emergency response system. The engineered controls in the toner factory, where the risk of fires is the greatest, includes a dust exhaust system, fire doors, and pressure relief panels built into one of the walls of the building. The paint shop is extensively automated. Other engineering controls include safety switches on equipment, local exhaust ventilation, remote control operations, and machine guarding.

The workers in the toner and photoreceptor plants wear respiratory equipment known to permit occupational exposures that are lower than Indian national or Xerox standards. Respiratory protection in the toner plant consists of selected approved disposable masks. The personal monitoring of airborne dust, conducted since 1987, has shown compliance with company standards in most areas, and the mandatory wearing of masks has been confined to the operators of the Banbury mixer where emissions are the highest. The masks are light but become quite uncomfortable with prolonged wear, especially in hot and humid weather. Gloves, glasses, and other protective clothing are required where necessary.

Compliance with Xerox occupational dust standards in the Rampur toner facility, as in all other Xerox facilities, is ascertained by way of personal monitoring in the breathing zone. Dust particles down to 0.3 um in diameter are collected by personal dosimeters attached to the collars of workers. As shown earlier (Figure 3.3), the Rampur facility has been in compliance with the standard since opening and on par with other Xerox toner facilities. Similarly, Figures 3.4 and 3.5 show that the photoreceptor plant is in compliance with Xerox's arsenic and selenium standards, although the safety margins are wider than for dust. Relative to other Xerox facilities, the Rampur plant has also performed well in occupational injuries, as shown in Figure 3.6, although the small sample size (based on two incidents annually) and uncertainty with regard to reporting practices, suggest caution in data interpretation.

Official corporate audits are conducted at the Rampur facility biannually. In addition, Rank Xerox's EH&S manufacturing manager travels to the plant on an average of two to three times per year. Local audits are conducted at the facility each month, and the results are reported to the corporate headquarters of Rank Xerox and Xerox.

When the facility first opened, safety training was conducted by a consultant engaged for that purpose. In addition, the safety manager, who had a post-graduate diploma and five years of relevant safety experience in India, went for one month of training in England. Twenty-five percent of the two-day training of new employees in manufacturing jobs is dedicated to safety. The annual evaluation of performance includes a section on safety practices of each worker.

Discussions with the management of the Rampur facility revealed a group of professionals deeply committed to the Xerox safety philosophy. Achieving and maintaining safety behavior among workers that is consistent with the company's standards requires, however, continual monitoring and feedback. The obviously dangerous violations, such as smoking or using spark-prone instruments in the toner plant, are rare. Other, less obviously hazardous activities, take time to eliminate. The workers' acceptance of the uncomfortable face masks took time. During our brief tour of the facility we saw some workers without protective glasses, and we observed pneumatically operated fire doors that were left open. As explained during the site visit by one of the managers, the fire doors had been installed only recently, and the workers are only slowly becoming accustomed to the new practice.

Like all systems that rely on modification of human behavior, that one is vulnerable to unusual circumstances. The Rampur facility may be uniquely vulnerable on this count because:

1. The average worker in India is entitled to approximately 30 percent of workdays off each year because of numerous holidays, which requires frequent shifts of workers between jobs.
2. The toner facility is more dependent on worker compliance than other, similar Xerox facilities because of less automation.
3. A rapid increase in demand might increase the production level several-fold (the plant currently operates at approximately 60–70 percent of single-shift capacity) with the result that the manual step would become the bottleneck.

The Rampur facility produces liquid and solid hazardous waste: The solid waste consists primarily of difficult-to-handle fine carbonaceous powder. Liquid waste contains arsenic and selenium. From the outset, the corporation was given to understand by the state authorities that a license to transport any waste from the site was unlikely to be granted. This constraint has required Rank Xerox to devise and provide suitable waste treatment technology. Programs were initiated in-house and with the U.K. Harwell Envi-

Figure 4.1
Chronology of Events for Occidental Chemical, Du Pont, and Xerox Facility Sitings*

XEROX		DU PONT		OXYCHEM	
CEO of Modi Rubber Initiates Business Relationship with Rank Xerox	Late 1970s	Du Pont Agricultural Products Are Marketed by Individual Distributors	1960		1983
				Facility is Built by Thai-Pakistani group	
Rank Xerox & Indian Reprographic Systems Agree on important Management Issues of the Potential New Enterprise	1981				1984
Rank Xerox Submits a Letter of Intent to the Ministry of Ind. Dev. to form a Collaboration & a build facility.	1982				
Initial Approval Granted by The Technical Committee	Mid 1982	Du Pont Far East is Established; Repackaging & Labelling by local contractor	1971	Diamond Shamrock Purchases Facility	1985
Rank Xerox Applies for Foreign Collaboration License & an Industrial License	1982				
Negotiations With Indian Gov. -- • Location • Equity Participation • Export Obligation • Facility Scale • Indigenization				Industrial License Granted by BOI & IEAT Bangpoo Re-Start	Jan. 1986
		Deteriorating Relationship With Local Contractor	1978		
Letters of Intent to Grant the Industrial and Foreign Collaboration Licenses are Issued by Ministry of Industry	Mid 1983	• Decision to Build Facility • Meetings with BOI & IEAT Bangpoo • Securing Thai permits • Start-up Planning • Construction Specifications		Facility visit by Occidental Pertroleum V.P.	Oct. 1986
Joint Venture Agreement & Technical Agreements are signed by collaborating partners	Mid 1983			Acquired by Oxychem	Nov. 1986
				Industrial License is renewed with few changes	
• Facility Design by Rank Xerox • Further negotiations with Indian Gov.		Appropriation Request for the Facility is Approved	July 1981	Safety & Env. Assessment by Oxychem	Mid. 1987
Construction of Facility is Begun	Nov. 1983	Ground-breaking for facility	Late 1981	Education of workers is commenced	Late 1987
Operating and Foreign Collaboration Licenses are Issued by Ministry of Industry	June 1984	• Construction • Operating Procedures Manual • Hiring & Training of Workers			
Construction of Machine Assembly Plant Completed	Early 1985				
Construction of Photoreceptor, Toner and Developer Plants is Completed.	Early 1986			Start of construction for plant expansion	Aug. 1988
Two-Day New Employee Training For Manufacturing Jobs Stresses Safety	Feb 1986	Facility Begins Production	Oct. 1982		
Assembly Production Begins	Fall 1986			End of construction for plant expansion	Mid 1989
Photoreceptor & Toner-Developer Production Begins					
Modi Academy is Established	1987				

* Note: Different time scales apply to each chronology

ronmental Centre in 1988 to devise processes that would ensure solid and liquid discharges from the site met permissible levels for toxic constituents. These levels are more stringent than in the United States. The solid discharge was required to be a stable waste, meeting the U.S. Environmental Protection Agency criteria for landfill disposal. The solid waste program was managed by Dames & Moore International Ltd., environmental engineering consultants to the corporation. The liquid waste program was managed by Modi Xerox using Rank Xerox Welwyn Garden City (British) expertise for process development and scale up.

The interim period of awaiting the development of these technologies has required on-site storage and management of wastes in volumes greater than planned. Two innovative solutions were developed by Modi Xerox engineers to reduce waste volumes and handling problems:

1. The design, fabrication and implementation of a solar evaporator to reduce bulk liquid effluent volumes and give a residual slurry for later processing or sale. The company is considering potential buyers of the enriched selenium-containing waste. It is carefully evaluating potential buyers to assure that the buyer will handle the material in an environmentally responsible manner.
2. The design, fabrication, and implementation of a solar cooker in which the powder waste from the toner plant is fused into blocks by the use of the sun's heat.

Summary

The story of the Du Pont facility in Thailand, outlined in Figure 4.1, is ically in Figure 4.1, is that of a series of adjustments made by a multinational corporation in response to the sharply focused agenda of a host country, which restricted the corporate choices in location, ownership, size and sophistication of the technology, and links with local industries.

The government policies were successful in several respects:

- The backward area of Rampur has benefited from upgraded infrastructure—a new school, housing and recreational areas, a hotel, and contribution to the local economy.
- The quality of life in two Modi Xerox adopted villages has been transformed.
- The process of indigenization, as measured by the rate of decrease in imports, is on target.
- The toner facility—the outcome of the PMP process—has provided stimulus for the on-site research and development unit to generate a toner with qualities requested by a client.
- The 30 percent export quota has been exceeded.

Although the facility did not stimulate growth of other industries in the area, the company's initial concern—that the unattractive location would interfere with attracting a skilled work force—proved to be unfounded.

The adjustments made by Modi Xerox were extensive, including the design of the manufacturing process as well as the management system. They led to a facility functionally equivalent to the U.S.-based facilities in EH&S performance but relatively more vulnerable to human error, sudden increases in production volumes, and planned-for future shifts in the management arrangements.

DU PONT AGRICULTURAL FACILITY IN BANGPOO

Negotiations

Du Pont's presence in Thailand dates back to the 1960s when several of its products were marketed by individual distributors. Crop protection chemicals were in great demand among Thai farmers, and by the end of the decade these chemicals accounted for half of Du Pont's business in Thailand. In 1971 Du Pont made a modest official start of its branch in Thailand by opening an office of Du Pont Far East in Bangkok. The company started by marketing agricultural chemicals, plastic products, and synthetic rubber. At that time the formulated agrichemicals were shipped in bulk containers from the United States to Thailand, where the fully formulated products were re-packaged and labeled by a local contractor.

Business was good during the 1970s, especially for agrichemicals, and the local contractor was soon given the additional task of formulating the agri-chemicals. By 1980 the sales of agrichemicals in Thailand totaled $5 million, which accounted for some 70 percent of total sales of Du Pont in Thailand. Du Pont had 7 percent of the $74 million pesticide market in Thailand. All through the 1970s, the market in Thailand was—and remains—very competitive. All major international agrichemical suppliers participated. Several of those, including Bayer, Shell, Union Carbide, and Hoechst, had their own local formulation/repackaging facilities while Du Pont relied on contractors for that service. The rate at which the Du Pont agrichemical products could be introduced into the Thailand market was determined by the rate at which the local contractor formulated, packaged, and labeled the materials. Especially important in the local market were small packets (as small as three grams) to serve the small farms typical of developing countries.

During the 1970s the sales of the chemicals continued to grow. By 1978 Du Pont's business relationship with the local contractor deteriorated. First, the packaging step became a bottleneck in Du Pont's ability to meet the needs of the Thai market. Second, the company was dissatisfied with the contractor's low safety and product quality standards. (For example, the contractor's baby food repackaging operations shared a warehouse with their pesticide operations). After considering various options (contracting with other local business interests, contracting with other multinationals, building a formu-lating/repackaging facility) the decision to construct a facility was a logical next step because other options did not guarantee long-term improvement in the situation, were not considered cost effective, and evoked concerns about proprietary information. The option of building a new facility thus emerged as the most attractive and profitable alternative. This solution would also most likely increase Du Pont's chances of expanding its share of the local market.

The series of events that, over time, led to the decision to build a facility in Thailand, from the initiation of marketing in the 1960s to the actual siting of a manufacturing facility two decades later, is characteristic of the company's entrance into a foreign market, as discussed in Chapter 3. Gradual entry allowed Du Pont to become familiar with the Thai market and with the country's cultural, economic, and political environment. Also during that time Du Pont was able to build important working relationships with a net-work of local contractors, suppliers, customers, and government officials. In short, the company has, over time, gained the advantages that would be otherwise brought by a local business partner in a joint venture partnership arrangement.

In considering the location of the proposed facility, the corporation sought an area with sufficient infrastructure to support manufacturing (roads, water, sewage, telephone, electricity), proximate to a major port, and accessible to prospective workers. Other factors, such as good schools and cultural and recreational resources, were minor considerations in this case because the management of the facility was to be all Thai, but would have been important if expatriate U.S. employees were to be assigned to these positions. The po-tential sites were all in the Bangkok area. One was an industrial estate located in Bangpoo, 20 miles southeast of Bangkok. Established in 1977, Bangpoo was one of the first such estates in the country. It currently hosts approxi-mately 100 plants, with a capacity for 300, and is one of the few estates that accept chemical industry (approximately 74 percent of all facilities in the estate process or manufacture chemcials).

In return for agreeing to locate in Bangpoo, Du Pont received exemption from import duties as well as guarantees against nationalization, direct gov-ernment competition, and product price controls. Du Pont was also permitted to own the land. The company benefited from choosing this site in other ways. First, the estate provided an important infrastructure, such as perim-eter and interconnecting roads, electrical power, drinking quality water, and a central waste treatment facility. Secondly, the management of the estate facilitated the permitting process by contacting, on behalf of the company, all the necessary government agencies.

From the company's perspective, there were also disadvantages to that location. Heavy concentration of chemical industry in that area increased the potential for accidental releases, events outside the company's control.

Table 4.2
Permits Required to Construct Du Pont Thailand Facility in Bangpoo

Permit	Agency	Time (months)
Approval for setting up factory	Minister of Industry	2
approval for construction	Minister of Industry	2
approval for operating industry	Minister of Industry	1
approval for bringing in foreign technicians	Board of Investment	2
approval to own land	Board of Investment	2
approval for production/storage of toxic substances	Ministry of Agriculture	2

That possibility was particularly disturbing because the estate also did not control the growth of residential housing around it, a likely consequence given the rapid growth of the Bangpoo Industrial estate. To the contrary, the original development plan designated 20 percent of the land within the estate for residential housing. (This was abandoned on economic grounds; the land is too expensive for blue-collar workers and not sufficiently attractive for those who can afford it.)

The six permits required for the Du Pont facility, the permitting agencies, and the time it took to receive them are listed in Table 4.2.

Du Pont's application for a factory operating permit, signed by the Thai Industrial Estate Department, was issued in 1981. It stipulated thirteen EH&S conditions, ranging from keeping the factory clean, to worker medical check-ups at three-month intervals, to personal safety equipment. The total permitting process, which did not include the Office of the National Environmental Board, took three to five months to complete and was so uneventful that the Du Pont executives and managers interviewed for the study had practically no "story" to tell.

Several factors account for the ease of siting of the Du Pont facility. First, it was a small operation with uncomplicated technology that was simple to review. Second, since the enterprise was expected to have a small impact on the environment and on the economy, it did not trigger high-level involvement by the authorities. Third, Du Pont did not seek major privileges such as tax exemption, which would have been available from the Board of Investment had the facility produced primarily for export, installed sophisticated technology, entered into joint ownership with local business interests, or created many new jobs. The facility simply did not meet these criteria. The involvement of BOI, which might otherwise have led to serious negotiations, was instead only a routine matter. Fourth, the efficacy was consistent with the investor-friendly business climate of Thailand.

Construction

While the permits to set up and operate a factory were being sought by Du Pont in Thailand, the blueprints for the facility were prepared in the United States. They consisted of extremely detailed construction specifications for the local contractor and covered all aspects of the construction: the appropriate fill grade, the construction of structures, tie-ins with the electric, water, and sewage companies, all manufacturing equipment, the screws and bolts, and so on. The specifications left nothing to chance or imagination. This was to be another Du Pont facility that happened to be in Thailand. The contractor performed the work with minimal profit for the experience of building the Du Pont facility. Construction started late in 1981 and was completed a year later.

The formulating and repackaging operations in the plant are very simple. The herbicide and fungicide/insecticide operations are in two separate buildings. The starting materials (paper bags for solids and barrels for liquids) are manually emptied from bulk containers into charging stations (areas where the ingredients are loaded into the mixing vessel). After mixing, the filling machine deposits premeasured quantities into containers that move on the belt underneath. The rest of the operation—the addition of an aluminum tamper-proof seal, a screw cap and a label—are manual.

All transfer points in the process—the charging and container-filling areas— are ventilated under hoods to prevent any dust from escaping into the indoor air so the operators do not have to wear respirators or face-masks, even when working with the acutely toxic Lannate. This is important in the Thai climate where face-masks would be uncomfortable and difficult to enforce. The central exhaust system and several other related engineered safety systems are consistent with Du Pont's preference for engineered controls over personal protective equipment.

Startup and Operations

The Bangpoo facility opened in October 1982. The simplicity of the manufacturing process requires simple skills of the operators. Currently, the plant employs 25 people, 7 hours per day, 6 days per week. It consists of three operations: herbicide repackaging (Karmex and Hyvar X); fungicide and insecticide repackaging (Lannate 90, Benlate, Manzate D, Delsene MX 200, and Curzate M8); and liquid insecticide formulation and packaging (Lannate and Vydate L).

The hazardous properties of the materials processed in the Bangpoo plant are summarized in Table 4.3. The insecticides are members of the carbamate family. The fungicides are dithiocarbamates and carbamidazoles. The her-

Table 4.3
Hazardous Properties of Materials Processes in Du Pont Facility

	LD 50 mg/kg		LC 50 mg/l	Chronic NOEL	TLV (AEL)
	Acute Oral Dosage	Acute Dermal Dosage	Inhala-tion		
Methomyl Technical	17 - 24	>5,000	0.30	100 ppm in food	2.5 mg/m^3
Lannate L (24%)	130	5880	0.68	--	
Lannate 90 Insecticide	--	--	--	--	--
Benalate (50% Benomyl fungicide)	>10,000		>2	500 ppm in food	10 (5) (Benomyl is a Teratogen)
Manzate B (80% Manet fungicide)	6,400	2,000	--	250 ppm in food	-- (2 for Maneb)
Hyvar X Herbicide (80% Bromacil)	5,000	>5,000	>4.8	250 ppm in food	10 (10) for Bromacil
Krovar Herbicide (40% Bromacil 40% Diuron)	5,980	>7,500			10 (10) for Diuron

MeNCO: methyl isocyanide; HCN: hydrogen cyanide; n-BuNCO: butyl isocyanide

ADI	Irritant Allergen (route)	Decomposition	Flammability	Explosive	Non-human Toxicity
0.025 mg/kg-day	eye irritant, damages cornea.	All formulations slowly decompose. Accelerated by impurities, temperature & some solvents	Combustible, highly toxic fumes: MeNCO, HCN.	airborne dust (5% to 75% vapor in air) is explosive; badly decomposed formulations will explode	Bees, aquatic organisms, and birds.
	eye irritant, damages cornea.	All formulations slowly decompose. Accelerated by impurities, temperature & some solvents	Same as Methomyl Technical	Same as Methomyl Technical	Bees, aquatic organisms, and birds.
--	eye irritant, damages cornea.	All formulations slowly decompose. Accelerated by impurities, temperature & some solvents	Same as Methomyl Technical	Same as Methomyl Technical	Bees, aquatic organisms, and birds.
--	allergen	Slowly decomposes in the presence of impurities, temperature, & water.	Toxic fumes n-BuNCO (tear gas)	Same as Methomyl Technical	Aquatic Organisms
	Irritating to the eyes, nose, throat & skin.	Slowly decomposes in the presence of impurities, temperature, & water.		Same as Methomyl Technical	Aquatic Organisms
	Irritating to the eyes, nose, throat & skin.	Slowly decomposes in the presence of impurities, temperature, & water.		Same as Methomyl Technical	Aquatic Organisms
	Irritating to the eyes, nose, throat & skin.	Slowly decomposes in the presence of impurities, temperature, & water.		Same as Methomyl Technical	Aquatic Organisms

bicides are of urea and uracil families. Methomyl and its two formulations Lannate 90 and Lannate L are acutely toxic, while its chemical relatives, benomyl (formulated as Benlate) and maneb (formulated as Manzate), are much less so. The herbicides have very low toxicity to humans but their environmental release may be destructive to vegetation and some desirable crops. These agents can produce irritation of skin, nose, eyes, and mouth and can produce allergic reactions.

Explosions and toxic fire are serious hazards associated with the processes at the Bangpoo plant. The airborne dust and vapors (as low as 5 percent in the air) are explosive if exposed to high temperature or sources of ignition. Fires and explosions of some products can occur under storage conditions that lead to decomposition in sealed containers. Decomposition produces heat and gases that can ignite spontaneously. The chemical decomposition of these products during combustion also sometimes generates highly toxic fumes. For example, Benlate generates a highly effective teargas, n-butyliso-cyanate, and methomyl and Lannate formulations emit the deadly poisons cyanide and methylisocyanate.

The facility bears the unmistakeable marks of a safety-conscious management: Safety glasses and hard hats are mandatory, the doors have outlines on the floor to indicate in which direction they open, there is emergency equipment for chlorine in case of an accidental release in the chlorine facility adjacent to the Du Pont plant, and there is a large-capacity water pump to augment the fire fighting capabilities of the industrial estate. The building is constructed to withstand a major earthquake. A manager of another U.S. company with a subsidiary in Thailand, who had visited the plant, remarked to us: "If our facilities are Jeeps, the Du Pont facilities are Cadillacs."

Hazardous wastes produced by the facility are all solids, consisting primarily of empty shipping containers. Du Pont's original plan was to dispose of these containers at an appropriate local sanitary landfill. When none was identified, the company in 1982 installed an incinerator with a capacity of 150 pounds per hour. The Du Pont solution to waste disposal is not unique among the residents of the Bangpoo Estate, which does not offer waste disposal services; many resident facilities own on-site incinerators.

The responsibility for selecting and training new workers rested with the new facility management. The plant manager had been a long-time Thai employee of the company, whereas the production supervisor was new. Both were trained for six weeks in the United States. They were also members of the task force that designed and started up the plant. By the time the first group of workers was hired, management of the facility was clearly ready to indoctrinate them in the safety philosophy of the company.

The workers were hired into the facility only after careful selection, with preference given to recent technical school and high school graduates, and were meticulously observed during the probationary first six months of employment, including soliciting their personal views on risks and safety. The turnover during the first six months was significant.

In addition to training the plant workers, the company trained local institutions in hazard management when it was considered mutually beneficial. These included the local fire department's response to emergencies at chemical plants; the local hospital in treating victims of accidents at chemical facilities; and neighboring hazardous facilities at the Bangpoo Industrial Park in emergency response at their own plants, one of which manufactured chlorine and the other matches.

How does a company control the safety of its product beyond the boundary of the facility? Underlying this question are several vexing problems unique to crop protection chemicals. Three scenarios of human exposure are of primary concern: in the field during application and immediately after, through misuse of empty containers, and through accidental releases such as floods, fires, or transportation accidents. The chemicals can also contaminate ground water if improperly applied.

Du Pont has been active in controlling these downstream hazards. One way is in packaging, which presents unique local challenges. First, there is the possibility of product adulteration through removal of material from unopened containers and replacement with another ingredient using hypodermic syringes. Second, because of the widely practiced reuse of containers in Thailand, there is a possibility of mistaking the liquid pesticide for a beverage and accidentally drinking it. To address the first problem, the containers are made of thick polyethylene, difficult to puncture with a needle, and aluminum seals that show puncture marks are put on all bottles. To address the second problem, the liquid products are dyed bright blue, and hazard information is included on the label.

Since the plant opened in 1982 a single dealer has been the major distributor for Du Pont's agricultural products in Thailand. The dealer warehouses the materials and sells them directly to farmers. The warehouse is located directly on a canal, water being the main route of transportation in the area. The man and his family live in the warehouse, and the cartons of packaged agrichemicals are stored in their living room. The major hazard of this unorthodox arrangement is that in a fire the people could be exposed to toxic fumes and chemicals might be carried into water. The company provided safety training to the distributor and offered to install a sprinkler system in his house, but the man declined the latter. The problem was solved by Du Pont by building a warehouse on the Bangpoo property, which is scheduled for completion at the end of 1992.

Protection of the rural population from acute poisoning by the chemicals presents perhaps the greatest challenge for Du Pont. Seventy percent of Thailand's population lives on farms, mostly small, family-owned one- to two-acre properties. Education is low among the rural population. To reach, educate, and train these 40 to 50 million people is a monumental task (in comparison, there are approximately 10 million farmers in the United States). The company has an extensive outreach program. It conducts workshops in villages and distributes protective clothing specially designed for the local climate and farming practices. The clothing is sold to farmers at cost. Significant research has been dedicated to developing new materials for protective uniforms.

The company has also expressed concern for potential ground water contamination through misapplication of pesticides. While no direct sampling-and-analysis program is in place, the primary emphasis is on prevention through farmers' education.

Summary

The story of the Du Pont facility in Thailand, outlined in Figure 4.1, is that of gradual and carefully planned entrance of a seasoned U.S. corporation into a new host country market. In that process the company meticulously controlled all aspects of building and starting up the plant and was able to essentially recreate its U.S. technology and culture. The local adaptations in the design of the facility and in management style were primarily to adapt to the unique conditions of the country and the site, such as lack of suitable land disposal of chemical waste, hot climate, or proximity of other hazardous facilities. The Bangpoo facility is first and foremost a Du Pont facility that happens to be located in Thailand.

THAI OCCIDENTAL CHEMICAL FACILITY IN BANGPOO

Acquisition and Negotiations

Thai Occidental Chemical, Ltd. is a joint venture of Occidental Chemical Corporation and certain Thai business interests. Occidental owns 49 percent, one venture partner owns 36 percent, and another 15 percent. The facility manufactures chrome compounds for the local leather-tanning industry.

The operation, dating back to 1983, was originally built, owned, and operated by certain Thai and Pakistani interests. The facility never worked to full capacity because of the poor quality of the product. After lengthy disputes with the local tanneries, the owner of the facility decided in 1985 to sell the facility to the partnership consisting of U.S.-based Diamond Shamrock Corporation (49 percent) and a local industrialist (36 percent). The previous owner retained a minor partnership in the enterprise (15 percent) that he continues to hold.

According to the contract, the company would have two managing directors, each nominated by one venture partner, and a board of directors represented by both companies. With respect to EH&S, the following excerpt from the contract specifically required that the environmental standards observed at the facility would be those specified by Diamond Shamrock and that both partners would contribute the funds necessary for their achievement, according to their respective shareholdings:

The parties agree to cause the Company to bring the Project up to environmental health and safety standards prescribed by Diamond Shamrock Chemical Corporation (DSCC) and thereafter to maintain the Project in accordance with said standards and all applicable Thai environmental health and safety laws and regulations. If the Company has insufficient funds or cannot borrow the funds needed to achieve the standards prescribed by DSCC, then the parties will contribute such funds to the working capital of the Company in proportion to their respective shareholdings.

The industrial operating license, signed by the Industrial Estates Authority, was approved by the Ministry of Industry in a routine administrative move, with no direct negotiations between the company and the central authorities. The license was accompanied by a set of EH&S compliance conditions, as follows:

- The quality of the waste water must comply with IEAT standards;
- The company must provide safety equipment such as masks and gloves to employees;
- Workers who work with acid must wear "long rubber shoes" and "rubber gloves";
- The company must install a ventilator system to remove gas that might cause harm to workers;
- The company is to be "very careful" so that there are no acid leaks that cause danger to workers;
- The company "must use water or inorganic material" to clean up spilled acid;
- The company must have voice and light alarms in case of emergency;
- The company must have a first-aid room and first aid equipment; and
- The company must provide annual physical check-ups to staff.

Clearly, these are simple criteria. The most notable among them is the combined role of the Industrial Estate Authority in facilitating plant licensing and its EH&S regulation.

Diamond Shamrock upgraded the facility and restarted it in January 1986. Shortly after that, in November 1986, Occidental Chemical Corporation acquired a majority of the worldwide chemical operations of Diamond Shamrock. This included the Diamond Shamrock portion of the Thai joint venture, along with forty-four other chemical plants throughout the world. The negotiated agreement included sharing the potential costs of environmental remediation at these facilities. Sixteen of the 45 facilities acquired by Oxychem from Diamond Shamrock were subsequently sold. The Bangpoo facility was kept by Oxychem under the same venture partnership agreement as before, including the written agreement that Oxychem EH&S standards would prevail at the facility. In fact, the transition from Diamond Shamrock to Oxychem was so smooth at the facility level, with no changes of employees, that the workers were aware of it only through the change of the company's name and the gradual introduction of more stringent safety and environmental procedures and rules.

After the decision to acquire the Diamond Shamrock chemical facilities, the Oxychem staff had two weeks to assess the environmental and safety conditions at these plants and to estimate the future costs of environmental remediations. The environmental audit records of all Diamond Shamrock international facilities were reviewed and visits to most of the facilities were made. The international facilities that were visited were those that used dangerous chemicals and/or were large in scale; the overriding concern was the possibility of explosions or acute releases on the plant premises or on-site burial of solid waste. The Thai facility was relatively small and did not produce explosive or acutely toxic substances and therefore was not among those facilities most in need of an immediate inspection. Another reason for not visiting the plant was that the management of Oxychem was avoiding potentially sensitive situations with business partners and therefore did not perform on-site inspections of joint venture operations.

The Oxychem's decision to keep the Thai facility was consistent with the company's general objectives in seeking foreign investments, as outlined in Chapter 3. The operation was the only manufacturer of leather-tanning chemicals in the country, with only limited competition from other Asian countries (Japan and China), and was potentially profitable. The combined local (40 percent) and export (60 percent) market for the product was large enough to justify the economy of scale and, with foreign leather manufacturers investing in Thailand, was likely to expand in the future. Oxychem was a manufacturer of one of the raw materials for the Thai facility in its domestic operations and was therefore quite familiar with the product. The company was also able to negotiate maintaining influence over the operation of the facility through the majority ownership and through the written stipulations regarding EH&S management. Finally, the business and political climates in Thailand were favorable, with bright prospects for the future. In summary, all major criteria usually applied by the company in considering foreign investment pointed to keeping the Bangpoo facility.

The particulars of the business arrangement between Occidental and its business partner had several long- and short-term consequences. First, making few changes in the original contract between Diamond Shamrock and the Thai group meant that obtaining government approvals and licenses would be a relatively straightforward task. Occidental applied for, and received, the BOI privileges accorded to foreign investors who own less than 50 percent of their Thai subsidiaries and who locate in the government-promoted industrial estates. The three-year renewable factory operating license was obtained from the Ministry of Industry with no delays. The license specified an identical set of conditions as the 1986 license issued to Diamond Shamrock. No separate environmental permits were needed. It is noteworthy that the conditions specified in the 1989 Factory License were also signed not by a representative of the Office of the National Environmental Board (NEB) or by the license granting agency, the Ministry of Industry, but by the management of the Bangpoo Industrial Estate. This illustrates the distant role of the central government in overseeing the safety and environmental activities of the companies. The government has *de facto* delegated this function to the semiautonomous Industrial Estate Authority of Thailand.

Office of the National Environmental Board became involved in the process only briefly, upon the request by the Ministry of Industry, to inquire about on-site chemical storage procedures. In particular, adequate protection against spillage into the Gulf of Siam was reviewed. The question was particularly appropriate for the Bangpoo industrial park, which is located in a large, filled wetland in the coastal area. During the on-site inspection that preceded the issuance of the license, the government inspectors identified the need to install a scrubber but did not make the license contingent upon its immediate installation (no such condition appeared within the Factory License); rather, the government set the expectation that the scrubber would be installed before the license was renewed in three years' time (a scrubber has been installed since). In summary, the main purpose of the government inspection was to confirm that the technology specified by the company in the license application, both for manufacturing and safety, was indeed in place. No particular attention was given to the issues of safety or pollution control.

Preserving the essential features of the Diamond Shamrock partnership had various consequences at the facility level as well. On the one hand, no significant changes in personnel were needed so continuity of the operations was maintained. On the other hand, the company was confronted with imposition of its own EH&S philosophy and system on the team of people who were trained within a different culture. Since Diamond Shamrock had a more relaxed attitude toward management of safety and environment than did Occidental Chemical, substantial changes clearly were required.

Perhaps the greatest unknown in the transition process, at least from the environmental and safety perspective, was the new relationship with the major Thai venture partner. As leader of a major manufacturing group of over 22,000 employees, the partner—in the words of an executive of Oxychem, "a vanishing breed of entrepreneurs in Thailand"—was in complete control of financial decisions of his enterprise, savvy in identifying new business opportunities, but had only limited interests in day-to-day management of facilities. The major benefit such entrepreneurs bring to the partnerships is to "provide the foreign company with a license to operate in that country" through fulfilling the government-favored ownership arrangements and the ability to deal with local authorities, local legislation, and local markets. The technology and the systems for marketing, accounting, and management are, in such partnerships, left to the foreign company.

Oxychem was therefore in a strong position to achieve one of the important aspects of its policy regarding international subsidiaries: to maintain major influence over the operation of the facility. Although the provisions of the written joint venture contract were not specific beyond the ownership arrangements, less formal agreements assigned specific functions to each partner: Oxychem was responsible for technology, general management of the facility (including EH&S), and for export markets; the Thai group was responsible for dealing with the Thai government (permits, licenses, inspections, reports) and for interactions with local customers and suppliers.

Entering into a partnership also meant that the management styles of the two partners, which were very different, would require mutual adjustments. With regard to environment, health, and safety, for example, the Oxychem slogan of "pay now or pay later" would have to be accommodated by the partner. Because the history of the facility indicated that it would almost certainly require significant initial investments for pollution control, a decision that would require approval by both partners, the slogan would be put to the test almost immediately.

The adjustment in the management styles of two partners would be particularly important because the managing directorship of the joint enterprise would be shared by two individuals, each representing one of the venture partners. Thus, there would be an Oxychem managing director and a Thai managing director. Furthermore, because the contract also provided for shifting management into the Thai hands after several years, institutionalization of Oxychem's safety and environmental culture at the new subsidiary during the initial years of the partnership was essential.

In short, there were several EH&S-related uncertainties with regard to the blending of the joint management at Thai Occidental Chemical Company, including the Thai partner's philosophy, his willingness to accept immediate costs of upgrading the pollution control technology, and his acceptance of the Oxychem's structured style of managing environment, health, and safety.

Shortly before the acquisition of Diamond Shamrock was completed in October 1986, Occidental Petroleum Corporation's vice president for health, environment, and safety visited the facility in Thailand to explore these questions. The direct involvement of the parent company, Occidental Petroleum, in the EH&S affairs of its subsidiary, Occidental Chemical, speaks to the importance of this matter to the parent corporation. He was accompanied by a consultant specializing in environmental management. The visit had three purposes:

1. to evaluate the potential managerial changes that would be required in order to install the Occidental system of environment, health, and safety;

2. to identify improvements needed immediately at the facility; and

3. to introduce the venture partner to the Occidental environment and safety philosophy and to establish a working relationship with him in that area.

The outcome of that visit would weigh heavily in the company's decision of whether to enter into the partnership or to sell the Thai facility. Occidental was prepared to invest significantly in upgrading the safety-and-control technology, by up to 15 percent of the purchase price. With respect to the venture partner, Occidental was prepared to negotiate the timetable for introducing the changes in the technology and management of EH&S but not the nature of these changes; the option to pull out of the partnership was definitely open.

To the satisfaction of the U.S. corporate representative, the potential partner was open to the Oxychem ideas on environment, health, and safety. The two basic principles of Oxychem environmental and safety philosophy, that safety and environmental awareness pays and that safety/environment requires long-term investments, also appealed to his business instincts. According to company officials, the slogan "pay now or pay later" was particularly persuasive. During the visit several environmental and safety measures were requested by the U.S. team for immediate implementation on the premises, with the venture partner's consent. These included installation of a scrubber, construction of dikes, and installation of safety gates. In the middle of the next year, a systematic implementation of the Oxychem safety system was initiated at the facility.

Transition and Additional Construction

In mid-1987 a full safety and environmental assessment was conducted at the facility by the Oxychem Manager of Safety and Environment International. One of the major conclusions reached during the assessment was that the plant manager was too busy to effectively manage health and safety issues and that an individual was needed at the plant level with health and safety responsibilities as part of the formal job description. The individual eventually employed in the newly created position was sent to the United States for two weeks of training, one in safety and one in environmental management. Currently, he spends approximately 75 percent of his time on health, safety, and environmental management. In addition he is assisted by the laboratory manager for environmental matters and by the production manager for safety matters. He reports to the plant manager and, indirectly, to the Thai Occidental managing director responsible for environment, health, and safety matters. The second key outcome of the assessment was development of a specific long-term EH&S program, including specific actions and target dates. Again, the responsibility for the implementation was given to the Oxychem managing director.

The systematic education of the workers in the Occidental safety practices started approximately a year after the acquisition and included all employees. According to the company, the transition was easy. As the managing director, also a former employee of Diamond Shamrock, recalls, Occidental filled a vacuum left by the previous owner: "These people (vice president for EH&S at Occidental Petroleum and the international manager of environmental safety at Occidental Chemical) came in and brought a structure to it." The most important aspect of that education was not the series of improvements in the engineered safety systems or the new procedures, but the awareness of the issues. Once the philosophy of safety was accepted and the awareness of safety and environment was built into the management style, according to the managing director, changes simply followed as the most logical operating procedures.

The changes that took place at the facility since the acquisition went beyond management systems and upgrading the safety technology. By mid-1989 the manufacturing capacity of the plant had doubled through major expansion. One of the key changes in the technology was a shift from using dry chromate to wet chromate as feedstock. There are several advantages to the new process: Workers are not exposed to hexavalent chrome dust, which is potentially carcinogenic; using liquids allows for making all the transfers in a closed system (a liquid chromate is pumped directly from a truck into a process storage tank and then to a reaction vessel); the process is more automated because manual opening of bags is eliminated; efficiency is greater; there is no need to dispose of empty bags.

The design and construction of the expanded facility was a joint project of the Thai engineers and plant managers and the U.S.-based experts, with the Thai team playing a significant part in all decisions. This effective transfer of technology was undoubtedly facilitated by two factors: First, this was a simple technology, with no proprietary elements beyond what one may describe as the "art of getting a high quality product" by finding just the right combination of the ingredients, the temperature, and the duration of the chemical reaction; second, there was no equivalent Occidental facility in the United States that would provide the blueprints for the Thai facility.

The construction also afforded the opportunity to introduce a number of safety and environmental systems that would be expected at an equivalent U.S. facility. In particular, spill control was stressed, including paving and trenching of critical areas, thus enabling recycling of spilled materials. Like the technology for manufacturing, the safety and environmental technology was "transferred" into the Bangpoo facility. The engineering and management team in Thailand closely interacted with the U.S. experts in that area and jointly produced the most appropriate design.

Another consequence of changing the feedstock from powder to liquid was the requirement of obtaining a permit to import. Although such a permit does not routinely involve environmental considerations, Thai government (National Environmental Board) insisted on receiving assurances from the company that the transfers and transport of the chromate liquid would be conducted in a safe manner. This was accomplished by Occidental Chemical through purchase of the transport vehicle.

Operation

Currently, there are 42 employees in the plant, which operates on 3 shifts, 24 hours a day, 7 days a week. The operation consists of a plant manager, a production manager, a quality control manager, and an administrative manager. The main functions of the administrative manager are safety, industrial hygiene, and environmental management.

The assessment scores for safety management at the facility have been steadily improving since the acquisition, as shown earlier in Figure 3.17, and although they continue to lag behind other international and U.S. facilities, the gap appears to be narrowing.

There are two hazardous raw materials used in the process: sulfuric acid and sodium bichromate. The final product is trivalent chrome, which is considerably less hazardous than hexavalent chrome. The toxic properties of the chemicals used at the plant are quite well established. Sulfuric acid is highly corrosive to biological tissues and will destroy skin, the respiratory tract, and the digestive tract upon contact. Tri- and hexavalent chromium compounds are also irritating to the skin and may cause allergic reactions upon long- or short-term exposure. Chronic exposure to airborne hexavalent chromium is also destructive to the respiratory tract and can lead to ulceration of nasal passages, perforation of nasal septum, and lung cancer.

The facility produces no process effluent, although there are two air emission point sources, a scrubber and a reactor vent, none of which are routinely monitored. The facility does not generate waste classifiable in the United States as hazardous. Empty raw material bags that contained potentially hazardous chemicals under the old "dry" manufacturing system are incinerated. The incinerator ash is being stored in the plant pending the construction of a planned secure landfill in Thailand. There are several hundred kilograms of that ash. Recently, the facility chemist has initiated experimental procedures for extracting chromium from the ash, thus rendering it nonhazardous. All other wastes are sent to the local landfill.

All the changes that took place at the facility since the acquisition were primarily motivated by the company, with some involvement of the Thai licensing authorities. The management of the industrial estate was notably absent. At times, there have been concerns at the Occidental plant about the air emissions from one of its neighbors, a matter that would be quite appropriate for the estate to handle, but the latter did not take the initiative. The participation of the estate management in the environmental and safety matters of individual facilities primarily focuses on setting and monitoring the pretreatment waste water standards.

The tanning industry served by the Thai Occidental products has a less conscientious attitude toward materials for leather tanning, and environmental and occupational safety. In Thailand leather tanning is a trade passed through generations within families and has been traditionally confined to certain social groups. The tanneries are small, family owned and operated, and mostly concentrated in one geographical area not far from Bangkok. In the past, that area was quite remote but recent spread of industry and housing into a wider and wider area outside the capital has changed that. Recently, the discharges from the tanneries into surface waters became a nuisance to local housing developments, shrimp farms, and other local enterprises. In response to the increasing dissatisfaction among those adversely affected by the pollution, the government authorities became involved. In the course of a few years the tanning industry found itself under growing social and institutional pressure to change its operating practices and to clean up. The pressure was sufficiently intense to open to question the very survival of that industry.

The potential decline of the leather-tanning industry in Thailand became a serious business concern of Thai Occidental Chemical (its major supplier), and the company became actively involved in seeking solutions. Oxychem, in cooperation with Thai government, facilitated implementation of a study of sound environmental management options among the tanneries. The World Environment Center, a U.S.-based nonprofit organization providing technical assistance to government and industry in developing countries, was selected to undertake the study. Occidental is also considering switching to manufacturing a new leather-tanning product, appropriately named ENV, which was originally developed in Taiwan because of the environmental concerns there. The agent is absorbed by leather more effectively than are the currently manufactured products and thus produces less waste.

Perhaps the most difficult aspect of the relationship between the business partners has surfaced recently as the two corporations are getting ready to consolidate the shared managing directorship of the Thai enterprise in the hands of one individual. According to the contract, that person should represent the Thai side of the joint venture. Clearly, the U.S. corporation has a stake in the decision because of its desire to maintain a major role in the management of the facility and because of a need to ensure that the safety culture of the company does not change. This is where the differences in the management styles of the two partners play a role. The preference of Oxychem would be to hire from the outside a highly professional individual who would share the management style and safety philosophy with Oxychem. In short, the individual would represent the rapidly growing class of Thai business school graduates. In contrast, the Thai partner would prefer to choose a loyal associate from among the employees of the Thai group. Personal loyalty to the group and a long-standing association with that enterprise would be among the key criteria applied in making the selection. From the

Oxychem perspective these selection criteria would produce an uncertain outcome and would therefore be less desirable.

Summary

The chronology of Thai Occidental Chemical tells a story of a relatively smooth transition of co-ownership, in three years, of a joint venture manufacturing enterprise in Thailand. During that period the facility's safety and pollution control system was significantly upgraded and the manufacturing system was expanded to double capacity. The safety record at the plant saw steady improvement and is approaching the safety performance of older Oxychem facilities. Similarly, the management of the Thai subsidiary appears to have adopted the Oxychem safety philosophy and practices. The story also highlights the challenge to a multinational corporation with a commitment to environment, health, and safety created by acquisition of a foreign facility and by entering into a joint venture partnership.

EMERGING RELATIONSHIPS

The three case studies of facility transfer illustrate the complex interactions among principal participants in facility siting who are guided by their respective policies relative to development, business, and health, safety, and environment, and by the necessity for mutual adaptations.

At the same time, each case highlights a different dimension of the transfer process. Modi Xerox's is a tale of a corporation making adjustments to a set of direct controls imposed by a host country while simultaneously accounting for the objectives of a joint venture partner and pursuing its own business and environment, health, and safety objectives. The case follows in detail the making of these adjustments and the complexity of implementing corporate EH&S policies in the presence of two other active participants: host country and joint venture partner. It also reveals how one corporation resolved what it perceived as an aggregate set of mutually desirable but at times competing objectives.

In contrast, the Du Pont case describes a facility transfer in an environment characterized by a relatively low level of direct controls by the host country in the absence of a joint venture partner. This case reveals how one corporation with a strong sense of commitment to environmental and occupational safety chose to transfer that commitment to its foreign affiliate in the absence of significant external constraints. It also illustrates the site-specific adaptations the company made in pursuing its self-defined standards of safety and the effects that the host country's attempts to facilitate business may have on corporate EH&S.

The Occidental Chemical case represents a middle-of-the-road set of external constraints on a multinational corporation. Like Du Pont, the company in this case had few direct controls imposed by the host country. Unlike Du Pont, however, the corporation was confronted with two other constraints: acquisition of an existing facility, with environmental and occupational performance below its own standards of acceptability, and acquisition of a joint venture partner whose presence on the scene preceded its own. Arguably the most illuminating aspect of the Occidental Chemical case is the study of how the company managed a transition among an existing work force (including the management) to conform another company's safety philosophy and policies to its own and how it managed to extend its own principles of environmental and occupational safety to the venture partner.

Clearly, the three cases are substantially idiosyncratic in nature, precluding any possibility of making meaningful comparisons among them. This is due to the large number of variables involved, and the researchers' inability to change these variables one at a time while keeping the others constant. Furthermore, the research depended upon self-selected multinationals and their volunteering for study of their individual facilities and corresponding data related to environment, health, and safety. As a group, however, the cases highlight three types of factors that appear to play crucial roles in the management and performance of overseas facilities of multinational corporations: corporate safety culture, host country development policies, and business arrangements at foreign affiliates. The cases also show that in the dynamic and highly interactive facility transfer process, the three types of variables play different roles at different stages. The management system for EH&S at the facility level and its performance are the product of both: the nature of the three variables in each case and their mutual interactions over time.

In the three chapters that follow, each of these variables is explored in depth, both from a theoretical perspective and in reference to the case studies.

CHAPTER 5

Host Country Development Policies and EH&S

Industrialization is among several dimensions of development actively promoted by governments of developing countries through the mobilization of domestic and external resources. Multinational corporations contribute to that process when they engage in any one of several forms of foreign investment, such as non-equity participation (subcontracting, licensing, technical assistance, consulting, and turnkey projects) and direct investments in wholly or jointly owned manufacturing facilities. Figure 5.1 summarizes this broad context, with multinational facilities representing one of the dimensions of development.

Multinational corporations contribute to industrialization of developing countries by increasing domestic production capacity, importing sophisticated technology and management skills, conducting business efficiently, producing consumer goods and exports, developing backward areas, developing infrastructure, and creating employment. There may also be adverse effects, such as excessive costs of technology transfer, social and economic disruption, concentration of capital, interference with political and economic policies of host countries, erosion of environmental quality, and adverse effects on human health and safety. The challenge to the host country government is to maximize net benefits associated with multinationals' manufacturing facilities through incentives and controls consistent with its broader development philosophy.

Host countries, multinational corporations, and joint venture partners (if any) enter the facility-siting process with established policies regarding technology transfer, environmental protection, and occupational health and

Figure 5.1
MNC Facilities in the Context of Industrialization and National Development

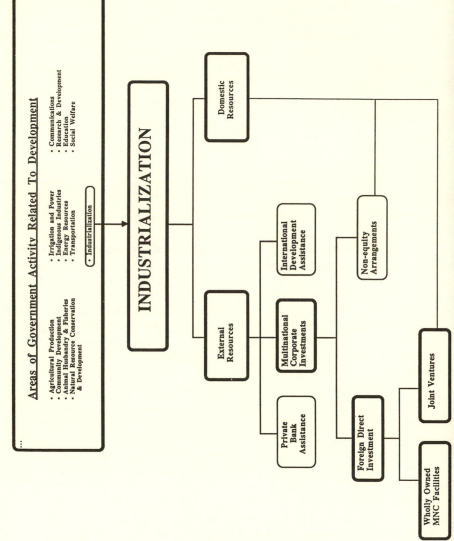

safety. The facility-siting process is initiated when an application for facility approval by the multinational corporation induces the principal participants to proceed with implementation of their respective policies. It entails a complex chain of interactions among the principal participants in the course of negotiations, facility design, permitting, and start-up, which may involve many time-dependent decisions by each party as well as mutual adjustments to those decisions by all participants. A student of such a process has many independent variables to study (and most are not truly independent of each other) and many ways to define *dependent variables.*

This chapter examines, through the prism of the three case studies, the effect of host country policies that are related to the DE&I values on environmental and occupational hazard management at the facility level. The specific objectives of this chapter are:

1. to explore the mechanisms of interactions among the principal participants in the facility transfer process;
2. to identify the points in the process at which the actions that bear most significantly on the facility-level outcomes take place;
3. to illuminate the roles of the principal participants in the outcomes; and
4. to identify any trade-offs between development objectives of the host countries and EH&S at the facilities that can be attributed to the host country's pursuit of its DE&I values.

Although the analysis takes into account the chronology and multiple dimensions of the interactions in the facility transfer process, the scope of the main line of inquiry is narrow. The host country's policies toward multinational corporations are the key independent variable, the initiators that set all other variables into motion. The extent to which the DE&I and EH&S values are served by each MNC facility—with special emphasis on environment, health, and safety management and performance—is the key dependent variable, the outcome.

There have been numerous efforts to analyze India's and, to a lesser extent, Thailand's progress in pursuing their respective policies regarding technology transfer by multinational corporations, generally by means of a variety of quantitative indicators of national trends (see, for example, Ahluwalia 1985; Brahmananda and Panchamukhi 1985; Kumar 1985; Mahajan 1985; Nair 1988; Sekhar 1983; Subrahmanian 1985; Patrasuk 1991; and Komin 1991). Given the nature of data generated by case studies, we do not intend to significantly contribute to that large-scale mode of analysis. However, by allowing a close-up look at the anatomy of decisions involving host countries, U.S. multinationals, and joint venture partners, the case studies uncover specific interactions among the participants and their policies, and allow us to elicit the hows and whys of the relationship between the independent and dependent variables.

Figure 5.2
Forms of Intervention by Developing Countries in the Activities of MNCS

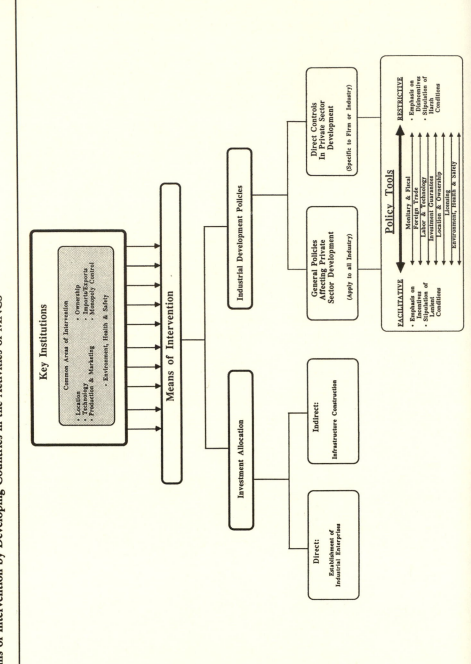

DEVELOPING COUNTRIES
AND MULTINATIONAL CORPORATIONS

Developing countries use many different methods to shape the role of the industrial sector and of MNC participation in that sector. As noted by Donges (1976), in many developing countries "virtually every important aspect of manufacturing activity appears to be potentially influenced by some form of government intervention: the level, composition, and location of production; the methods of production; the prices of products and factor in puts; the type and concentration of ownership of production, facilities; the nature and degree of market competition." Cody, Hughes, and Wall (1980, pp. 5–6) identify two general forms of government influence: investment allocations and industrial development policies (Figure 5.2). Investment allocations may directly target industrial enterprises or infrastructure such as roads, ports, or public utilities. Investment allocations for infrastructure development are more common and more resource-intensive, yet less visible in most developing countries than allocations for public or private industrial enterprises. This is to be expected, as infrastructure development has become an unquestioned responsibility of all governments, even those with the most extreme free market economies. Additionally, unlike most infrastructure investments, allocations for the establishment and ownership of industrial enterprises are prone to negative publicity from national and international private and public interests.

While investment allocations by the government can exert significant influence on the behavior of international and national corporations, most developing countries have also resorted to direct intervention through industrial development policies. Among those, general industrial development policies of finance, taxation, labor, location, and foreign trade are designed to fulfill multiple functions in the management of a nation's economy and play a prominent role in defining a country's overall business environment for investment by multinational corporations. Restrictions, or location requirements, are crafted to ensure that individual enterprises fulfill specific industrialization strategies and are intended to have lesser effects on other aspects of the national economy (Cody, Hughes, and Wall 1980, p. 6).

Industrial development policies, both general and direct, are considered facilitative to multinational direct investments when the policy tools for furthering national industrialization emphasize incentives and lenient conditions. Policies are considered restrictive when the policy tools emphasize disincentives and stipulate restrictive conditions.

Underlying these policies is a set of broad development, equity, and independence values. These and related values may be grouped into general conceptual domains (see Hughes 1980; Killick 1981; Kirkpatrick, Lee, and Nixson 1984). For example, Kirkpatrick, Lee and Nixson (1984, pp. 193–194) suggest a fundamental division of industrial development goals into two "higher order" categories: "efficiency-related" goals of industrial development, concerned with maximizing the total welfare accruing to the economy from the efficient use of scarce resources; and "distribution-related" goals, concerned with achieving the most satisfactory distribution of total welfare among people. Killick (1981, p. 33) identifies three categories: "efficiency," "social justice," and "national cohesion." In a similar manner, Hughes (1980) suggests that the principal issues of industrial development are those of "growth and efficiency," "equity and welfare," and "national independence" (p. 11). All three classifications share the common notions of equity and national sovereignty, in addition to those of growth and efficiency.

Because broad aspirations such as growth, equity, and self-determination, or self-reliance, are too general to guide a host country's government in the conduct of its development-related functions (in the case of facility transfer, influencing in the activities of multinationals), they may be disaggregated into "subsidiary" objectives, capable of providing precise enough guidance to formulate specific development policies and investment allocations. Such subsidiary objectives may include dispersion of industries into underdeveloped areas, facilitation of industrial development through the provision of infrastructure, and maintenance of local control. Various institutions further articulate these objectives through specific laws, regulations, and policies and are empowered to implement them through a variety of policy tools (Figure 5.2).

Officials of most developing countries will quickly agree on the importance of the limited set of broad values (listed previously) in guiding their long-term development process. However, the relative priorities given to each will vary widely. For example, "equity now, growth later," "growth now, equity later," and "growth with equity" each represent fundamentally different development approaches. The two countries included in this study represent the extremes of the national development spectrum, with India representing the growth-with-equity model and Thailand favoring the growth now, equity later model.

Differences among countries become even more visible in the area of subsidiary development objectives and policies. Whereas some countries do much to help the industrial sector (e.g., Hong Kong), other countries (e.g., Tanzania) extensively regulate the industrial sector's structure, conduct, and performance. For example, the facilitative noninterventionist countries let institutions allocate funds for infrastructure and enact industrial policies with incentives and lenient conditions of entry and operation. Reliance on direct investment allocations, disincentives, and restrictive industrial controls would be less prominent, or at least less visible. Restrictive interventionist countries, on the other hand, would be more inclined to put direct restrictions on production, employment, foreign investment, technology choice, imports, and exports. The most facilitative countries allow unlimited entry by multinational corporations whereas the most restrictive countries have consciously refused foreign investment as a matter of policy (Laya 1988, p. 31).

Thailand's recent facilitative industrial policies are representative of several small African, Caribbean, and Pacific countries that have consistently maintained relatively "open door" stances toward foreign investors. (U.N. 1983, discussed in Kirkpatrick, Lee, and Nixson 1984). India's policies, on the other hand, have been representative of the handful of relatively large and industrialized developing countries, such as Argentina, Brazil, Chile, Mexico, Indonesia, Republic of Korea, and Venezuela. Recently, most of these countries, including India in 1991, have been recently engaged in a liberalization of some of their most stringent policies, with Mexico becoming a leader among them.

Multiple development objectives, and the institutions pursuing them by a variety of measures, collectively make up a complex web. In that web, the means used to attain one type of objective do not necessarily promote the attainment of another. For example, measures used to achieve greater equality of income may impede the efficient mobilization of resources. Similarly, measures used to achieve dispersion of industry may interfere with, or thwart altogether, the efficient conduct of business. In such cases, trade-offs would be expected, either through explicit recognition of the incompatibility and clever use of multiple policy options, or implicitly and incrementally through defaults or multiple small adjustments. Furthermore, the means of pursuing development objectives may either promote or compete with other objectives of the host country, such as worker safety or environmental protection, or with the objectives of the corporation, such as profit, safety, or product quality.

DE&I VALUES AND RELATED POLICIES IN INDIA

Among the political leaders and scholars in India, the search for goals and paths in the country's economic and social development dates to many years before liberation from colonial rule. Mahatma Gandhi had a profound influence on the articulation of such thought. For Gandhi, the main objective of India's development was to eliminate as fast as possible the poverty among the masses of rural and urban population. He advocated decentralized administrative structure down to the village level, austere consumption, and an inward-looking economy, with small, craft-oriented industries and self-sufficient rural communities as fundamental social units. Gandhi's vision of India underwent fundamental changes during the Nehru era. Nehru shared Gandhi's deep concern for the overwhelming poverty that afflicted much of India's population and was deeply committed to its elimination. He also shared his mentor's deep belief in social justice, peaceful coexistence, and cultivation of national heritage. His major difference with Gandhi was, however, over industrial development strategy. Whereas Gandhi vehemently opposed the "soul-less" machine, which he equated with "soul-less" society, Nehru's vision of India was that of a strong and self-reliant economic power built through carefully planned industrialization. In that process, the large-scale industrialization would emphasize capital and heavy industry — the big machine — and mastery over modern technology (Bhatt 1980). Nehru also believed that the state should actively promote industrial development through economic planning and through ownership of certain key industrial sectors.

A decade before independence, Nehru influenced India's Congress to establish the National Planning Committee, which he chaired until his death in 1964. After independence the committee became responsible for producing five-year development plans and other major policy documents related to national development. One such key document was the First Industrial Policy Resolution of 1948. The resolution set the foundation for the socialist pattern of society in India by allowing the state to assume complete monopoly in several industries and by articulating the future growth of state ownership as a long-term trend. At the same time, the 1948 model provided for a mixed economy in India, with a thriving private sector (Lok Sabha Secretariat 1989).

India's government continues to actively regulate the economy. The country's economic and social development is guided through a series of planned programs (Nair 1988). The five-year plans outline the priorities with respect to the investment and use of India's resources. The objective of the First Five-Year Plan (1951–1955) was, in the words of the planning commission, "to initiate a process of development which will raise living standards and open out to the people new opportunities for a richer and more varied life" (Planning Commission 1952, p. 7). By the Third Five-Year Plan, India's key industrial development values had become sharply focused (Planning Commission 1962, pp. 4–5):

These values or basic objectives have recently been summed up in the phrase "socialist pattern of society." Essentially, this means that the basic criterion for determining lines of advance must not be private profit, but social gain, and that the pattern of development and the structure of socio-economic relations should be so planned that they result not only in appreciable increases in national income and wealth. . . .

The accent of the socialist pattern of society is on the attainment of positive goals, the raising of living standards, the enlargement of opportunities for all, the promotion of enterprise among the disadvantaged classes, and the creation of a sense of partnership among all sections of the community. These positive goals provide the criteria for basic decisions.

All of India's five-year plans have played an important role in defining its pace and direction of development and continue to provide an important forum for articulating the key DE&I values of the country. Self-reliance, growth and prosperity, prevention of concentration of economic power, and attainment of social justice and equity are the fundamental themes of the development documents in India during the past four decades. Furthermore, these broad aspirations do not appear to have been given any clear priority over one another. The reluctance to assign priorities to these highly desirable but obviously not always mutually compatible goals, or at least to realistically assess their economic and social costs, has, in fact, at times retarded the pace of India's development (Nair 1988).

Industrialization as the means for pursuing the key development objectives has been the cornerstone of India's strategy from its very conception. In the Industrial Policy Resolutions of 1948, 1956, and 1973, and in the Industrial Policy Statement of 1980, industrialization has been linked to economic growth and prosperity, political and technological self-reliance, and to the broader social agenda. The Industrial Policy Statement of 1980 lists, for instance, the following socioeconomic objectives: rapid industrialization, increased availability of goods at fair prices, larger employment, higher per capita income, increased productivity, correction of regional and sectoral imbalances, promotion of exports, promotion of economic federalism, consumer protection, and prevention of concentration of economic power.

To India, self-reliance has meant technological independence, promotion of indigenous industries, and, where necessary, import, absorption, and adaptation of foreign technology. The emphasis on domestic technology, in preference to imports, as a means to technological self-reliance and independence from foreign products is clearly the objective of the Technology Policy Statement of 1983 (Planning Commission 1983):

Fullest support will be given to the development of indigenous technology to achieve technological self-reliance and reduce dependence on foreign inputs, particularly in critical and vulnerable areas and in high value added items in which the domestic base is strong. Strengthening and diversifying the domestic technology base are necessary to reduce imports and to expand exports for which international competitiveness must be ensured.

As suggested by Subrahmanian (1985, p. 423), technological self-reliance is consistent in India with the use of a mix of imported and indigenous technologies, a mix that seeks to reduce imported technologies over time. It is sought by an "import-adapt" strategy, which seeks selective import of foreign technology and its subsequent absorption, adaption, and upgrading to suit the domestic resources and conditions by increasing domestic R&D activities.

At the conceptual level, technological self-reliance may be defined as a process of increasing through domestic R&D efforts the nation's capacity to acquire, absorb, and adapt imported technologies to facilitate further innovation, thereby increasing technological capacity while reducing external technological dependence. Thus, in the pursuit of technological self-reliance on a national scale, the government recognizes the necessity for inflow of foreign technology. At the same time, however, four decades of national development betray an ambiguity toward foreign enterprises. While recognizing the necessity of foreign direct investment, the government's basic philosophy has been to develop its resources through the efforts of its own people. It has repeatedly stated its intention to rely on indigenous workers, capital, technology, skills, and other resources even where it means slower growth, poorer quality, domestic undersupply, and higher prices (Stoever 1989, p. 485). Thus, the import of foreign technology has been generally viewed as the last resort, primarily as a vehicle for the transfer of technology required by the country, and has been restricted to technology in sophisticated and high priority areas where India's skills and technology are not adequately developed, in export-oriented or import substitution manufacturing, or for support of indigenous industries (Lok Sabha Secretariat 1989).

Phased manufacturing programs and indigenization plans for individual enterprises, described in Chapters 3 and 4, reflect India's import-adapt strategies. The essential strategy of India is to induce the multinational corporations to establish fully integrated manufacturing processes there and to stimulate local satellite industries by requiring procurement of indigenously produced parts and materials.

In addition to self-reliance and growth through industrialization, the Indian government has, over the years, emphasized the need for balanced regional development through the dispersion of industries. Since its inception in 1951, the industrial licensing process has served as the major instrument for achieving this objective. Enforcement through the licensing process increased, and by 1977 the government prohibited the establishment of licensable industries within certain geographic limits of large metropolitan cities and urban agglomerations with a population greater than 500,000 people (Sekhar 1983). In addition to direct controls through industrial licensing, industrial dispersal has been promoted through policies of input rationing, the use of interregional price controls of certain basic materials such as cement, and increasing reliance on market mechanisms. The 1980 Statement on Industrial Policy suggests the growing importance of incentive mechanisms to achieve industrial dispersal into so-called backward areas:

Industrialization will play an important role in correcting the regional imbalances and reviving the industrial growth to lead the economy once again to the take-off stage. For the achievement of this goal, Government have decided to encourage dispersal of industry and setting of units in industrially backward areas. Special concessions and facilities will be offered for this purpose and these incentives will be growth and performance oriented (Lok Sabha Secretariat 1989, p. 43).

Despite such efforts, marked regional differences color industrial development in India. From the viewpoint of efficiency, these differences are not surprising, as various theories of location have articulated, because natural resources are not evenly distributed and there are economies of scale, agglomeration in production processes, labor costs, and costs of transportation and infrastructure (Sekhar 1983). The regional differences in industrialization in India have taken the form of increasing the concentration of population, economic activities, congestion, and pollution at selected locations such as Bombay and Calcutta, and severe disparity in welfare among different regions within the country—in short, the pattern of urban polarization typical of Third World regional development.

In the late 1970s, partly in response to the ineffectiveness of these policies, the planning commission set up a National Committee on the Development of Backward Areas (NCDBA) to "formulate appropriate strategies for effectively tackling the problem of backward areas" and "to recommend programs and policy measures for influencing and controlling the locational pattern of industrial activity" (NCDBA 1980, pp. 197–198). For medium and large facilities, the NCDBA has been advocating the "growth center" concept, defined as the areas having no less than 50,000 people in the 1971 census and having less than 10,000 workers in non-household manufacturing. The growth center concept recognized the need for governmental provision of infrastructure and the viability of business investment in terms of critical mass of labor and market demand. This concept was reiterated again in the 1980 Industrial Policy Statement, which called for "economic federalism" through setting up so-called nucleus industries intended to generate ancillary industries in backward areas (Lok Sabha Secretariat 1989).

The government's involvement in the location of industries traditionally has been justified on both economic and social grounds, namely: (1) the disparities are a result and cause of inefficiencies and will therefore hinder further economic growth; (2) the disparities are inequitable and therefore not socially just. Measured by the achievement of their stated objectives, these policies have drawn severe criticism from the World Bank (Sekhar 1983). First, the World Bank found that the government's location policy had been implemented without adequate, simultaneous development of infrastructure by the government. Second, whereas controls effectively prevented industries from being set up in certain regions, they could not induce industrialists to invest in the most underdeveloped areas. This has been demonstrated in a failure to thrive by many industrial estates set up by the government in rural areas. Furthermore, the incentives offered by the government in a form of subsidies usually failed to compensate for the other disadvantages of the location. The result has been decreased investment in restricted areas without a compensating increased investment in other areas (Sekhar 1983).

The economic inefficiencies that have been associated with the industrial location policies in India have not been, according to the 1983 World Bank report, justified on the social equity grounds either, particularly as a tool for correcting intrastate disparities. This is because the mobility of the population and labor force assures that people will move toward jobs much more efficiently than if industry is brought to where the people are.

Despite the criticism, regional development through, among other means, government influence on dispersion of industrialization, remains a significant national policy objective in India. For example, the Seventh Five-Year Plan (1985–1990) describes the

. . . dispersal of industries and balanced regional growth [as an] important objective of planned development. This is necessary not only from the point of view of balancing development regionally, but also for relief from transport in the industrialized urban centers (Planning Commission 1985, p. 173).

The fundamental development philosophy in India entails the simultaneous pursuit of multiple economic, social, and technological objectives. The philosophy is conducive to active and far-reaching governmental involvement, and has given rise to proliferation of policies and public institutions empowered to implement these policies. The Industrial (Development and Regulation) Act of 1951 gives the central government broad authority to implement several key policies related to planned and carefully controlled industrialization, such as the promotion of certain industries, location, public ownership, or export promotion. In relation to MNC facilities, this authority translates to close scrutiny and extensive restrictions on the business and technical decisions of the prospective investors.

India's extensive development agenda translates into a careful review of proposals from potential direct international investors. All proposals for foreign facilities are carefully screened to determine their necessity to the economy and potential contribution to indigenous technological development. The government expresses a clear preference for "technical collaborations" (sale or licensing of technology) over equity collaborations (joint ventures) and is least receptive to equity arrangements for packaged technology imports involving substantial foreign ownership. The strict limitation on equity participation under the Foreign Exchange Regulation Act of 1973 (FERA) reflects the overall policy of retaining control over foreign investors and treating them as vehicles for achieving specific development objectives such as technology transfer and foreign currency earnings through exports. Despite the negative effects of FERA limitations on the volume of foreign investments (Nair 1988), India has preserved that requirement over the years. The Monopolies and Restrictive Trade Practices Act of 1969, aimed at preventing capital concentration, represents another form of control through selective imposition of production ceilings on foreign investors (as was indeed the case with Modi Xerox).

From the perspective of foreign investors, two principal instruments of implementing industrial policy in India have been: a system of industrial licensing under the Industries Development and Regulation Act (1951) and a system of import licensing and other trade policy measures under the Import and Export Control Act (Nair 1988). The Ministry of Industry is the key regulatory agency for both. Given the breath of development objectives India is pursuing through its industrial policy, facility licensing is the principal instrument of government's participation in that process (incentives, the second major instrument, plays a significantly lesser role). As explicitly stated by the government (Lok Sabha Secretariat 1989, pp. 8–9), India's licensing system is an "essential part" of the government's industrial policy, which is aimed at attaining wide economic, political, and social objectives: by optimal use of investable resources; and allocation of investable resources. This is done with a view to:

1. meeting need-based requirements of industries in accordance with national priorities;
2. preventing the concentration of economic power;
3. securing balanced development of various parts of the country;
4. securing the widest possible dispersal of entrepreneurship and distribution of income;
5. stimulating employment with particular accent on absorption of agricultural surplus as well as discouragement of rural-to-urban migration;
6. locating the nucleus of economic activity in a dispersed manner so as to widen the industries' base; and
7. achieving optimal balance of the public sector, organized private sector, and small private enterprise sector.

The licensing process for a joint venture, described in Chapter 3, commences with a receipt of a letter of intent from the Department of Industrial Development. The letter is equivalent to a "provisional industrial license" and is issued upon conformance with the development policies of India. The licensing process does not end with issuance of an industrial license because import licenses must be renewed every six months. Thus, as long as the manufacturing process uses imported materials, the central authorities are active participants in the operations of the enterprise.

The first two decades of planned development in India witnessed large-scale industrialization. By the 1970s, however, India's inward-looking policies were increasingly criticized for having contributed to India's alienation from the global modernization process and having resulted in relatively low overall economic growth rates (3.5 percent per year) in comparison with the growth performances of some outward-looking Asian nations. Attributing many of India's developmental problems to inefficiencies within the public sector, India embarked upon a liberalization process, which was initiated under the Janata government (1977–1980), carried forward under Indira Gandhi (1980–1984), and then accelerated under Rajiv Gandhi (1984–

1989). In addition, the central government began devoting serious attention to the adverse environmental effects of technology. The Industrial Policy Statement of 1980 explicitly recognized the need for preserving ecological balance and improving living conditions in the urban centers of the country. However, not until the issuance of the Environmental Guidelines for Industry by the Ministry of Environment and Forests in 1985 was an active role of the central government established in controlling industrial locations for environmental reasons. The Environmental Protection Act of 1986 provided further support for the central government's involvement by including environmental considerations in the licensing process.

For multinational corporations, the liberalization process signified a more favorable climate in India for direct foreign investments, characterized by relaxed and streamlined licensing procedures and the opening up of a wider segment of the economy to foreign investment initiatives. These changes notwithstanding, today India's government remains deeply committed to the social policies of regional and sectoral equity in development, to the goal of technological self-reliance, and to the concept of active participation of the authorities in achieving these social objectives through, among other means, regulation of foreign investors in India. Rigid locational requirements, indigenization requirements, and phased manufacturing programs are among the key manifestations of this development philosophy.

DE&I VALUES AND RELATED POLICIES IN THAILAND

In contrast to India, which chose to create its own unique national model of development, the evolution of development strategies in Thailand has proceeded along a path parallel to that of many other developing nations. The search for, and debate on, the national identity in development has been also relatively modest among Thailand's leaders and intellectuals. Consequently, fewer government documents and scholarly analyses have been written on that subject in Thailand.

Thailand's First National Economic Development Plan in (1962–1967) marks the beginning of the government's formal role in pursuing its vision of the country through a planned and systematic process of economic development. That vision identified economic growth as the key instrument for achieving national self-reliance, improved living conditions, international recognition, and social equity. The government's role in pursuing growth would be to provide the necessary infrastructure and to reorganize the country's administrative system in order to facilitate rapid and unrestrained growth of the private sector. The provision of infrastructure and selective encouragement for private initiative provided the foundation for the First Development Plan (1962–1966) as well as for subsequent plans. For example, the "Objectives and Policies" section of the Second Development Plan (1967–1971) explicitly states that the mobilization of human and natural resources for optimum utilization in expanding the productive capacity and national income of the country, so that the benefits of development can be shared equitably by all classes of people (discussed in Snidvongs, Kasem, and Panpiemras 1982, p. 349).

This development philosophy also provided the essential conceptual framework for the subsequent structuring of policies and institutions with the responsibility for interacting with multinational corporations. The Board of Investment (BOI), the Ministry of Industry (MOI), and the Industrial Estate Authority of Thailand (IEAT) are among Thailand's most visible such institutions. The missions and policy instruments of these institutions, and their relative status, are a direct reflection of that philosophy.

Established in 1960 as the first such institution in Southeast Asia, BOI's mission is:

1. to guide the country's development through participation in formulating the five-year development plans;
2. to formulate an investment promotion program, including selective encouragement of certain economic sectors;
3. to promote actively, though selectively, foreign investment by helping investors identify opportunities, overcome operational problems, and obtain governmental clearances.

Despite the lack of authority to issue licenses or attach conditions to such licenses, BOI enjoys high status, partly because of its direct link with the cabinet (along with National Economic and Social Development Board, it is one of the two offices within the Office of the Prime Minister), and partly because of its key role as the ultimate allocator of substantial investment incentives (see Chapter 3 for details). The combination of attractive incentives (so-called privileges), high status, and broad functions gives BOI the unprecedented role as one of the architects of the national development strategy as well as its main interpreter and implementer.

Key point of interaction between a foreign corporation and the central authorities is the process of applying for, and negotiating the terms of, the BOI privileges. At this stage the host country exerts strong influence on a company to act in conformance with the country's development agenda. This stage is conceptually equivalent to the process of considering an application for industrial license in India. There are, however, differences in the respective agendas of the two countries, the participating institutions, and the extent of government control over the applicant. First, in India the process includes multiple agencies and involves a broad agenda, including social and economic considerations. In Thailand, on the other hand, the context is significantly narrower, with a single agency—the BOI—taking the leadership and dominating the agenda, with economic growth having precedence over other development objectives. Furthermore, since adoption of the BOI incentives is voluntary, the host country's influence on the key choices of a corporation—location, sophistication of technology, scale of technology, environmental controls, and others—is essentially indirect, leaving significant flexibility in the corporate decision making. The key mandatory step—securing an industrial license from the Ministry of Industry—is relatively simple in Thailand and made simpler yet through the help of BOI and the Industrial Estate Authority, as described later. This freedom is in contrast to the negotiations and directly imposed controls experienced by corporations entering India.

The primary mission of the Industrial Estate Authority of Thailand (IEAT), the third primary participant in the interaction between foreign corporations and the government, is to develop and maintain infrastructure for manufacturing facilities, both domestic and foreign, through establishment of well-serviced industrial estates. The agency was created in the early 1970s and until the 1980s operated two industrial estates outside Bangkok: Bangpoo Estate, established in 1977, and the home of two case-study facilities, and Bangchan, established in 1972. By 1991, there were 19 such estates, operating or under construction throughout the country (12 of these were within 45 miles of Bangkok, and only one was located in the less-developed northern part of the country).

Although some industrial estates are owned and operated by the government, most are joint ventures between the government and the private sector. A typical ownership agreement calls for the government to provide the initial infrastructure—roads, electricity, water, sewerage, waste treatment, and basic communications—and to maintain it over time. The private developer, who owns the land, is responsible for building additional infrastructure as the estate grows. The developer also chooses the buyers of the land and decides on the location of the new facilities. The IEAT's functions include the regulation and enforcement of environmental and occupational safety standards. The IEAT's influence on the location of facilities within the estate is restricted to a veto power: It may refuse to accept a new applicant at the estate. In exercising that power, however, the agency would risk creating a conflict with its venture partner.

Although maintaining safety at the estate is among the responsibilities of IEAT, insufficient influence on land allocation severely limits its options. IEAT's ability to enforce sound environmental management among the industries at the estate is also restricted. In principle, it has the authority to close the factories that violate pretreatment waste water standards, mismanage their waste, or otherwise pollute. In reality, however, such action is unlikely. First, it would reflect poorly on the image of the estate and thus be viewed with suspicion by the venture partner. Second, the primary role of IEAT is not that of a regulator but rather that of a facilitator, through provision of infrastructure and help with permits. If faced with a necessity to become involved in environmental management issues, the agency would choose a negotiated rather than an imposed solution.

The direct, though admittedly limited, authority of IEAT in regulating and enforcing environmental and occupational health and safety is in contrast to the indirect and diffuse authority of the National Environmental Board, described in Chapter 3. The contrast is more striking because it is the board, not IEAT, that is legislatively empowered to implement the National Environmental Act of 1975 (and its 1978 revisions).

The heavy investment in the industrial estates speaks to the commitment of the Thai government to influencing location choices of the foreign investors. Although India and Thailand are similar in that both influence location of MNC facilities, the similarities end there. In India, the location policies are aimed both at reducing regional inequities and at relieving urban congestion. Accordingly, this objective is usually pursued with no particular concern for its effect on business: Industrial facilities are located in remote areas but companies must develop their own essential infrastructure. The objectives of the Thai location policies are primarily to facilitate foreign investment by providing infrastructure for industries, with a second goal of relieving urban congestion of Bangkok. The government-industry estates accomplish both objectives: Ninety percent of existing and planned estates are located south of Bangkok proper in areas relatively attractive to prospective businesses.

This development strategy has brought remarkable success to Thailand as measured by standard economic indicators. Between 1960 and 1970, the annual growth rate of gross domestic product (GDP) averaged 7.9 percent, compared to 2 to 3 percent prior to 1960. Industrial production grew even faster during that period, at 10.9 percent annually, and economic transformation from agriculture accelerated its pace; the relative share of agriculture in total GDP dropped from 39.8 percent in 1960 to 28.3 percent in 1970 (and to 17.5 percent in 1985). After a slowdown in the early 1980s, the economic growth rate again accelerated to 10 percent for three consecutive years, 1986–1988 (Krongkaew 1988).

International Monetary Fund data published by the United Nations for Thailand reveals that Japan and the United States are Thailand's leading foreign investors, accounting for 26.7 percent and 14 percent, respectively, of total investment. Recent trends show that the foreign component of Thailand's capital stock continues to increase as average annual inflows of foreign investment have risen from $82.5 million during 1975–1980 to $280.3 million during 1981–1985. Data for 1988 alone reveal that the foreign investment component of governmental approvals exceeded 50 percent. The remarkable inflow of foreign technologies into Thailand has without doubt contributed to the nation's rapid industrial growth and transition from a mostly agricultural economy to that characterized by a mix of agriculture, service, and manufacturing.

Until the late 1960s, development policies in Thailand focused primarily on economic growth. However, toward the end of the decade the nation's leaders and intellectuals were recognizing the need to include in the concept of development such factors as income distribution, public health, and other aspirations of the Thai society (Snidvongs 1982). These changing perceptions were not unique to Thailand and reflected the fundamental shifts within the global community in the vision of development, as progressively articulated in the 1971 *Founex Report,* the 1972 Stockholm Declaration, the 1974 Cocoyoc Declaration and, more recently, in *Our Common Future* (World Commission on Environment and Development 1987). During the 1970s and 1980s, the development agenda in Thailand gradually widened to include EH&S values and a larger menu of DE&I values.

Attention to environmental issues in development planning started with the establishment of the first environmental committee in 1971 and in 1974 establishment of an environmental division in the National Economic and Social Development Board (NESDB). After the creation of the National Environmental Board (NEB) in 1975, NESDB continued to maintain an environmental division, primarily for liaison with NEB, so that the views of the environmental agency would be taken into account in NESDB evaluations of proposed environmental projects and in the five-year plans. Environmental issues were first introduced into the Fourth National Economic and Development Plan (1977–1981), but it was the fifth plan (1982–1987) that contained a separate section dedicated to environmental issues. The Sixth National Economic and Development Plan (1987–1991) emphasized the need to prevent the deterioration of the country's natural resources and environmental quality and sectoral/regional equality. According to a high level NESDB official, the key issues for the seventh plan, which were being debated at the time of this study, were environmental management and inclusion of public participation in that process, social adaptation to the increasingly industrial character of the economy, and regional equity in development.

Despite these changes, the primary development philosophy in Thailand has remained faithful to its initial precepts, which held development and independence values supreme to others. Outward-looking economic growth and limited governmental constraints on private enterprises, including MNCs, thus are the key paths to other desirable goods: social transformation, equity, and health and environmental protection. BOI continues to be the leading interpreter of the national development agenda with regard to multinational corporations; the partnership of BOI and IEAT continues to provide the key instruments for facilitating business and for exerting control—mostly by indirect approach and while internally balancing its own competing agendas over the behavior of the manufacturing affiliates of multinational corporations. The role of NEB in regulating corporate behavior, significantly strengthened over the years by increased staffing and participation in long-term planning, remains relatively weak.

Emerging in the Thai context then, is a multinational corporation which, once permitted to enter the country, commands a significant freedom in most, if not all, key business and safety decisions: location, sophistication of technology, size and design of technology, safety systems, and environmental management.

THE OUTCOMES

India and Thailand have erected elaborate structures in order to influence the activities of multinational corporations. These structures consist of multiple policies, institutions, and instruments of policy implementation. Some institutions have narrowly defined missions and unambiguous agendas, such as Thailand's BOI; others have complex missions, such as the Ministry of Industry in India, which implements several developmental objectives through licensing. Others still have poorly defined or ambiguous missions, such as IEAT in Thailand. Similarly, for some policies—such as location policy in India—the measures of implementation are straightforward, whereas others—such as the Indian policy of indigenization—require multiple tools for implementation (phased manufacturing program, import policies, local procurement requirements, etc.).

The three case studies have demonstrated that host countries' policies toward MNCs that site manufacturing facilities within their territories have been effective in attaining several specific objectives. Thailand's aggressive pursuit of foreign investment, through liberal policies of facilitation and minimal governmental interference with the business activities of MNCs, was originally conceived as a means of import substitution; increasingly, it has been sought as a means for rapid, export-oriented industrial growth, and has proven very successful.

Du Pont and Occidental Chemical located their facilities within industrial estates, according to the Thai government's preferences, and one of them entered into a joint venture arrangement. While meeting these objectives, the government kept the entire approval process to a brief two- to three-month period in each case. Thailand's expediency stands in contrast to the two-year process of approval for Modi Xerox in India. Administrative expediency has continued in Thailand since the completion of the two facilities because of the minimal participation of the administrative bodies in their daily activities.

The Modi Xerox case exemplifies the effectiveness of India's pursuit of technology transfer and absorption through policies of phased manufacturing process (PMP). In exchange for the opportunity to enter the large xerography market in India, Rank Xerox was required to import the full manufacturing process, and is continually required to ensure that necessary materials and parts are acquired locally rather than imported. Despite certain difficulties, such as delays, inconsistent quality of materials, and perhaps additional costs of doing business, Modi Xerox is well on its way to achieving the main objective of the national indigenization policy: to have 80 percent of the value of the product contributed by local manufacturers. Currently, the facility is also fully integrated and capable of conducting product innovation on a modest scale on the premises.

The Modi Xerox case also demonstrates the advantages of the host country's active participation in regulating the EH&S aspects of MNC facilities. The restrictions placed by the state pollution control boards on the waste management practices at the facility proved no obstacle to business development, and they stimulated innovation in on-site hazardous waste treatment.

As noted, both countries emphasize industrial dispersal through industrial location policies. Although India has historically placed greater emphasis on directly controlling the location of industries in "backward" areas via industrial licensing requirements, Thailand's use of incentives to encourage the location of MNC facilities within industrial estates represents the government's relatively recent objective to relieve infrastructure overloads within and around the Bangkok area. The two cases indicate that both approaches have proven successful, suggesting that India and Thailand have in place effective policies for influencing the siting of MNC facilities in accordance with industrialization objectives. The case studies also show that Thailand has supplemented its location policies with heavy investment allocations in infrastructure development whereas India provides less infrastructure. Largely through the provision of infrastructure, Thailand has been able to offer investors alternative locations that are economically viable and thus congruent with corporate business objectives.

The three case studies also highlight the undesirable effects that implementation of each country's development policies can have on EH&S practices at the MNC facilities level.

Thailand's policy of minimal governmental interference with business activities, in conjunction with a weak regulatory infrastructure for environmental and occupational health and safety, does not assure the best EH&S performance of industrial enterprises in general. The licensing process—efficient and primarily in the hands of the Ministry of Industry—limits the participation of the occupational and environmental agencies. The corporations operating in Thailand are in effect free to implement the EH&S systems of their choice, without significant input from the host country's authorities. The corporate commitment is therefore the fundamental determinant of safety and health within these factories. The two Thai case studies exemplify strong corporate EH&S systems, well-articulated policies, strong oversight by the parent corporation, tight lines of communication, and clear recognition by the corporation of the need to adapt to local conditions and to develop a strong safety awareness among the local employees. Although the facilitative approach of the Thai authorities has worked well for the two corporations, it may not be so in all cases. It is reasonable to assume that multinationals with less corporate commitment to EH&S might, in that climate, choose a less responsible behavior, leading to environmental degradation and compromised occupational safety and health.

The India case study brings to light a different dimension of suboptimal EH&S outcome precipitated by well-intentioned host country development policies. The primary issues during negotiations between the central government and Xerox were sophistication and size of the technology, ownership arrangement, location, prospects for indigenization, and exports. The matters of health, safety, and environment, perceived as not inherently prominent in the photocopying technology, which is neither resource intensive nor highly polluting, clearly took the back seat to the other items on the agenda, presumably to be addressed by the state regulatory system. In that early stage, the combination of the antimonopoly and technology transfer policies of India imposed two contradictory requirements on the company: to backward integrate according to the phased manufacturing plan and to keep domestic production volume low. These requirements led the corporation to choose a scaled down and highly integrated facility and, in the pursuit of cost-effective solutions, to opt for a manual rather than an engineered safety system in the toner production portion of the facility. Although the adjustment was clearly adequate to meet the stringent internal corporate occupational standards, it nevertheless put to the test the overall safety philosophy of the parent corporation: to use engineered health and safety systems whenever possible. It also made the facility more vulnerable to the unanticipated changes in the work environment: sudden increases in workload, labor disruption, and change in management. To ensure maintenance of EH&S standards under these conditions would require a persistent and focused corporate commitment to safety, both by the developing country subsidiary and the parent company.

Notably, the cause of the vulnerability of health and safety structure in the India case is opposite to that in the Thai case; whereas the former resulted from the low level of control by the host country authorities over multinational enterprises, the latter was caused by the multiplicity and inflexibility of such controls. The instruments used by India to implement policies of indigenization, monopoly prevention, and regional development led to trade-offs among five desirable objectives: indigenization, prevention of monopoly, regional development, economic efficiency, and preferred safety system. Furthermore, the regulatory environment of India relative to multinational corporations assured that the trade-off would be made by the corporation—either on the cost effectiveness or on the safety side—and not by the host country. This is for two reasons. First, with the exception of highly polluting or resource-intensive technologies, EH&S is not explicitly incorporated in the negotiation phase of the facility-siting process, and it is precisely during that stage that the issues of backward integration and down-scaling of production were negotiated. Second, the regulatory philosophy of the host country in relation to multinational corporations, and the multi-agency administrative structure driven by inertia and tradition, favors a scenario in which the authorities impose requirements and the corporation adapts, which is precisely what happened in the Modi Xerox case.

From a corporation's perspective, the highly controlled business environment of a host country, as the India example illustrates, may delay business conduct. Recurrent renewal of import licences, travel between the facility and the corporate headquarters in New Delhi, and delays in procuring locally made equipment, parts, and materials, all serve as examples. While promoting other desirable objectives of the host country, these restrictions are costly to the corporation and, as disincentives to potential new investments, may be costly to the host country.

It is partly to shield foreign investors from these and other delays that the Thai government created industrial estates and the Industrial Estate Authority of Thailand (IEAT). The industrial estates serve as a magnet for foreign investors through incentives because of their superior infrastructure. Their investor-friendly administrative structure is an additional attraction. However, the geographic benefits of the estates for Thailand are partly offset by their suboptimal, if unintentional, management of EH&S. First, the estates concentrate large number of hazardous facilities in close proximity to each other. In the case of the Bangpoo Estate—the home of the two Thai case study facilities—three-quarters of the resident facilities manufacture chemicals, plastics, or pharmaceuticals. Furthermore, the lack of effective zoning restrictions in Thailand, which is common among developing countries, eliminates the possibility of maintaining a distance between the industrial and residential areas.

The multiple functions of IEAT illustrate even more strikingly the effect of the pursuit of efficiency on the management of EH&S at the facility level. Initially created primarily to manage the industrial estates, IEAT has also been given other key functions: to facilitate business by helping foreign corporations in obtaining necessary permits and to set and enforce environmental discharge standards among the resident facilities. Although the concentration of multiple functions within one government agency is not unique to IEAT or to Thailand (it is true for the Ministry of Industrial Development in India, which, through industrial licensing, implements several policies simultaneously) IEAT stands out in two ways. First, it serves three distinct interests, namely the central authorities, the multinational enterprises, and its own business partners in jointly owned estates. Second, its multiple functions as a facilitator, regulator, and manager may at times be in conflict with each other, and thus internally weaken the agency. When confronted with such conflicts, IEAT would most likely favor trade-offs of business interests of the joint venture partner, growth and efficiency desired by the government, and its own environmental and occupational safety objectives. Under those circumstances, the freedom of corporations in choosing their EH&S systems, good and bad, is considerable.

The chronological four-stage model outlined in Figure 2.1 provides a different perspective on the effect of host country development policies on EH&S outcomes. Those development policies were manifested during the negotiation stage of the siting process: the location policy in Thailand (which catalyzed the selection of Bangpoo estate); the EH&S conditions imposed by IEAT during facility licensing; and government controls on the size and technological integration of the facility in India.

Notably, although the decisions made during the first stage had significant consequences for the EH&S management later on, the issues related to environment, health, and safety were not explicitly included in the negotiations between the host countries and the corporations at that stage. From the country's perspective, this was partly because the three technologies were viewed as neither highly polluting nor resource intensive. Furthermore, it appears that the environmental and safety issues were perceived by the host countries as the domain of the permitting process, to be addressed adequately during the subsequent stage.

The undesirable effects of various well-intentioned industrial policies of developing countries, often in a form of interference with the host country's pursuit of other desirable development objectives, have been previously explored by Kirkpatrick, Lee, and Nixson (1984). These authors point to several such inherent conflicts:

- industrial licensing systems may be used to promote industrial growth in remote regions (to meet distributional objectives) but cause new establishments to be sited in high-cost locations (contrary to efficiency objectives);
- minimum wage legislation may promote a more equitable distribution of income but over-encourages capital-intensive methods of production;
- restrictions on transnational corporations may encourage the use of more "appropriate" technologies and stimulate self-reliance and nation-building but deprive less-developed countries of entrepreneurial skills and capital resources;
- high import duties may stimulate the growth of output and employment in the indigenous manufacturing sector, but the protection it receives may also lead to a fall in technical and productive efficiency.

They also note that apparent consistencies between subsidiary objectives and higher order development values may, upon scrutiny, turn out to be in conflict with each other or with other development values. In one specific case, a policy of industrialization of backward areas, while leading to an increase in the average income of the inhabitants of the region (and thus promoting spatial equity) also increased the disparities in the individual incomes among the population (and thus reducing per capita equity). Furthermore, pursuit of such spatial balance objectives by means of locating industries in remote areas is unlikely, according to the authors, to be consistent with efficiency objectives.

The case studies provide support for Kirkpatrick's observations of inconsistencies in development policies. They also bring to light an additional type of inconsistency, not emphasized by other authors, namely between policies related to DE&I values and those related to EH&S values. Furthermore, when such strain materialized in our cases, its origins could be traced to aggressive pursuit of mutual development objectives by the host country in the course of facility licensing. We also note that the relationship between the implementation stages of these host country development policies and the EH&S outcomes can be indirect and delayed, consisting of incremental adaptations by MNC to the host country's policies. The adaptations were made implicitly by the key actors rather than through direct negotiations.

REFERENCES

Ahluwalia, Isher J. "The Role of Policy in Industrial Development." Pages 388–411 in P. R. Brahmananda and V. R. Panchamukhi (eds.), *The Development Process on the Indian Economy.* Bombay: Himalaya Publishing House, 1985.

Bhatt, V. V. 1980. "The Development Problem, Strategy, and Technology Choice: Sarvodaya and Socialist Approaches in India." Pages 151–175 in Franklin Long and Alexandra Oleson (eds.), *Appropriate Technology and Social Values.* Cambridge MA: Ballinger Publishing Company, 1985.

Brahmananda, P., and V. Panchamukhi. "The Development Process: An Appraisal." Pages xxvii–xxxxxxviii in P. R. Brahmananda and V. R. Panchamukhi (eds.), *The Development Process on the Indian Economy.* Bombay: Himalaya Publishing House, 1985.

Cody, John, Helen Hughes, and David Wall. "Introduction." Pages 3–9 in John Cody, Helen Hughes, and David Wall (eds.), *Policies for Industrial Progress in Developing Countries.* Oxford: Oxford University Press for the World Bank, 1980.

Donges, J. B. "A Comparative Survey of Industrialization Policies in Fifteen Semi-industrial Countries." *Weltwirtschafitlches.* Archiv. 112:4(1976): 626–659.

Hughes, H. "Achievements and Objectives of Industrialization." Pages 11–37 in John Cody, Helen Hughes, and David Wall (eds.), *Policies for Industrial Progress in Developing Countries.* Oxford: Oxford University Press for the World Bank, 1980.

Government of India. Technology Policy Statement. 1983.

Guisinger, S. "Direct Controls in the Private Sector." Pages 189–209 in John Cody, Helen Hughes, and David Wall (eds.), *Policies for Industrial Progress in Developing Countries.* Oxford: Oxford University Press for the World Bank, 1980.

Killick, T. *Policy Economics: A Textbook of Applied Economics for Developing Countries.* London: Heinemann, 1981.

Kirkpatrick, C. H., N. Lee, and F. I. Nixson. *Industrial Structure and Policy in Less Developed Countries.* London: George Allen and Unwin, 1984.

Komin, Suntaree. Social Dimensions of Industrialization in Thailand. *Regional Development Dialogue* 12:115–134 (1991).

Krongkaew, Medhi. "The Development of Small and Medium-Scale Industries in Thailand." *Asian Development Review* 6:2 (1988): 70–95.

Kumar, N. "Technology Policy in India: An Overview of its Evolution and Assessment." Pages 461–492 in P. R. Brahmananda and V. R. Panchamukhi (eds.), *The Development Process on the Indian Economy.* Bombay: Himalaya Publishing House, 1985.

Lall, Sanjaya. "India." Pages 309–336 in John Dunning (ed.), *Multinational Enterprises, Economic Structure and International Competitiveness.* Chichester, England: John Wiley & Sons, 1985.

Laya, Jamie. "Economic Development Issues." Pages 31–40 in Lee Travis (ed.), *Multinational Managers and Host Government Interactions.* Notre Dame: University of Notre Dame Press, 1988.

Levy, F. S., A. J. Meltsner, and A. B. Wildavsky. *Urban Outcomes.* Berkeley, CA: University of California Press, 1974.

Lok Sabha Secretariat. *National Industrial Policy.* Government of India, 1989, pages 38–49.

Mahajan, O. "Indian Economic Planning in Retrospect and Prospect." Pages 734–740 in P. R. Brahmananda and V. R. Panchamukhi (eds.), *The Development Process on the Indian Economy.* Bombay: Himalaya Publishing House, 1985.

National Committee on the Development of Backward Areas. *Report on Industrial Dispersal.* Government of India Press, 1980.

Nair, Ronald A. "The Role of India's Foreign Investment Laws in Controlling Activities of Multinational Corporations." *Syracuse Journal of International Law and Commerce* 14 (1988): 519–553.

Patarasuk, Waranya. The Role of Transnational Corporations in Thailand's Manufacturing Industries. *Regional Development Dialogue* 12:92–112 (1991).

Planning Commission. *First Five-Year Plan.* New Delhi: Government of India, 1952.

———. *Third Five-Year Plan.* New Delhi: Government of India, 1962.

———. *Technology Policy Statement.* New Delhi: Government of India, 1983.

———. *Seventh Five-Year Plan.* New Delhi: Government of India, 1985.

Pressman, J. L., and A. B. Wildavsky. *Implementation.* Berkeley, CA: University of California Press, 1973.

Sekhar, Uday A. *Industrial Location Policy: The Indian Experience.* Washington, DC: World Bank Staff Working Paper Number 620, 1983.

Snidvongs, Kasem, and Kosit Panpiemras. "Environment and Development Planning in Thailand." Pages 347–360 in United Nations Environmental Programme, *Environment and Development in Asia and the Pacific: Experiences and Prospects.* Nairobi: UNEP Reports and Proceedings Series 6, 1982.

Stoever, William A. "Foreign Collaborations Policy in India: A Review." *The Journal of Developing Areas* 23 (1989): 485–504.

Stubbs, Roy C. *Environmental Administration in Thailand.* Honolulu: East-West Environment and Policy Institute. Research Report No. 5, 1981.

Subrahmanian, K. K. "Towards Technological Self-Reliance: An Assessment of Indian

Strategy and Achievement in Industry." Pages 420–446 in P. R. Brahmananda and V. R. Panchamukhi (eds.), *The Development Process on the Indian Economy.* Bombay: Himalaya Publishing House, 1985.

United Nations. *Transnational Corporations in World Development: Third Survey.* New York: United Nations ST/CTC/46, 1983.

World Commission on Environment and Development. *Our Common Future.* Oxford: Oxford University Press, 1987.

CHAPTER 6

Corporate Culture and Technology Transfer

Jeanne X. Kasperson and Roger E. Kasperson

Locating industrial facilities in developing countries, as the preceding chapters make clear, confronts corporations with a stream of choices and potential conflicts among corporate objectives. How these choices and competing objectives are interpreted and reconciled depends heavily upon the meanings that are attached to them and the values that are brought to bear in corporate decision making. Accordingly, much depends on what has come to be called *corporate culture* and the extent to which this culture actually guides the behavior of its managers through the various stages of developments that result in the acquisition, construction, or operation of a facility in a developing country. This chapter inquires into this issue in the case of E.I. du Pont de Nemours and Company, or Du Pont, widely cited as having a particularly well-developed corporate culture.

Corporate culture is, of course, not a new concept; it has, in fact, several diverse roots of origin. Members of the "Carnegie School" of organizational theory (Simon 1951, March and Simon 1958, Homans 1958, and Blau 1964) conceived organizations as entities that make contributions in exchange for inducements and incentives. Social anthropologists, such as Kluckhohn (1951) and Levi-Strauss (1963), have included organizations in their more general writings on culture. As early as 1951, for example, Elliot Jaques (1951, p. 251) observed:

The culture of a factory is its customary and traditional way of thinking and of doing things, which is shared to a greater or lesser degree by all its members, and which new members must learn, and at least partially accept, in order to be accepted into service in the firm. Culture in this sense covers a wide range of behavior: the methods of production; job skills and technical knowledge; attitudes toward discipline and punishment; the customs and habits of managerial behavior; the objectives of the concern; its way of doing business; the methods of payment; the values placed on different kinds of work; beliefs in democratic living and joint consultation; and the less conscious conventions and taboos.

Attention to corporate culture as a way of understanding the behavior of corporations has ebbed and flowed since these early writers first proposed this approach. The focus of scholarly writings on corporations has shifted from scientific management, organizational structure, and rational or strategic planning during the 1970s and early 1980s. The "surprise" of the two OPEC oil crises in the 1970s, the growing competition for American industry from foreign competitors, and particularly the stunning competitive success of Japanese firms in both smokestack and high-technology industries have rekindled interest in corporate culture as a framework for analyzing corporate performance and behavior.

This chapter examines the ways in which corporate culture enters into, and affects, the process by which a multinational corporation locates facilities in developing countries. In particular, it seeks to clarify the concept of corporate culture, assess the extent to which such a culture exists at Du Pont, and the role that this culture played in the location of a Du Pont facility in Thailand. The discussion begins by examining the concept of corporate culture and its relevance to the issues of the technology transfer treated in this book. Recent research into high-reliability organizations and their management of hazards and safety adds another dimension to the analysis. Using these conceptual approaches, the chapter then examines in detail one of the three case studies treated in this volume, the location of Du Pont's Bangpoo factory in Thailand (Chapters 3 and 4). Du Pont has achieved global recognition as having a distinctive and well-developed corporate culture, and Thailand itself is a culture very different from settings in the United States; thus, the case provides a particularly rich context in which to explore these issues.

CORPORATE CULTURE: FUNCTIONS AND PROCESSES

Given the several theoretical origins of research on corporate culture and the flourishing interest in it during the 1980s, it is not surprising that a variety of frameworks and theoretical perspectives has emerged. It is useful to characterize these major approaches before examining how corporate culture entered into technology transfer in the case of Du Pont's Bangpoo facility.

Distinguishing major approaches to the analysis of corporate culture is

unavoidably somewhat arbitrary given the great diversity of available perspectives. Particularly relevant for this study are four approaches: culture as
social functions, systems of common beliefs, systems of shared knowledge,
or *patterns of symbolic discourse.*

The *functionalist approach,* in search of patterns that may have implications for organizational effectiveness, examines variations in managerial
and worker perceptions, attitudes, and behavior across organizations and
countries (e.g., Ronen and Shenkar 1985). In this view, corporate culture is
an internal attribute of the corporation that can enhance the effectiveness of
the firm and provide a potential competitive advantage over other corporations. Research, therefore, is a quest to understand how such cultures differ
and the means by which they might enhance corporate performance. This
approach led sometimes to what might be termed *corporate-culture engineering,* in which managers emphasize the manipulation of corporate culture
as a powerful lever to achieve some other end, such as safety performance or
some specific corporate goal. Managers, proponents argue, must find ways
to use stories, legends, and symbols to achieve these corporate goals (Peters
1978).

This culture-engineering approach is apparent in the nuclear industry's
calls for a safety culture. In the U.S. Nuclear Regulatory Commission's
view, a *nuclear safety culture* is

a prevailing condition in which each employee is always focused on improving safety,
is aware of what can go wrong, feels personally accountable for safe operation, and
takes pride and ownership in the plant. Safety culture is a disciplined, crisp approach
to operations by a highly trained staff who are confident but not complacent, follow
good procedures, and practice good team work and effective communications. Safety
culture is an insistence on a sound technical basis for actions and a rigorous self-
assessment of problems (GAO 1990, p. 28).

In analyzing safety problems at the Savannah River nuclear plant, the
General Accounting Office found that this safety culture had not kept pace
with changes in the commercial nuclear power industry and that the old culture (whatever that was) continued. Accordingly, Westinghouse, the operator
of the plant, was required to produce a comprehensive implementation plan
involving specific changes needed in the safety culture, milestones for their
accomplishment, and measurement indicators of cultural change (GAO
1990, pp. 31–32).

A second view of corporate culture, one that overlaps with the functionalist approach, sees corporate culture as *a fabric of shared beliefs and
values.* For many analysts (e.g., Deal and Kennedy 1982, Liedtka 1988)
values form the heart of corporate culture. Such values define in concrete
terms success and standards of achievement for employees. In corporations

with highly developed, or strong, corporate cultures, which will be discussed later in this chapter, members share a rich and complex system of values and talk about them openly and without embarrassment.

A third approach conceives corporate culture as *shared knowledge,* the conceptual and ideational systems and the language and metaphors that are enlisted to make sense out of the corporate world. The semantics reflect the world view of corporate members, whereas language and communication offer a rich means for interpreting the thought patterns that sustain particular forms of behavior. Social interaction occurs through the exchange of symbols that have a shared meaning for members of the set or organization. The methodology for this approach is akin to that of ethnomethodologists or the postmodernists in their embrace of qualitative interpretation of specialized meanings attached to various aspects of routine life, the rules and scripts that guide action, and a generally subjectivist view of social reality (Smircich and Calás 1982). Gregory's (1983) study of how Silicon Valley technical professionals understand their own careers exemplifies this approach.

Finally, some see corporate culture primarily as *patterns of symbolic discourse* (Pondy et al. 1983). These patterns, or themes, require deciphering and interpretation, following the work of the anthropologist Clifford Geertz (1973). Ingersoll and Adams (1983), for example, seek to identify the meta-myths that lie behind organizational behavior and managerial practices. Analyzing business literature and executive biographies, they find rationality celebrated continuously as a managerial metamyth. Others (e.g., Rosen 1985) use a social-drama metaphor to examine how the symbolic rites and ceremonies of corporations contribute to social order and patterns of political control. Stories also may provide clues to culturally based values and assumptions (Martin 1982).

It is important to appreciate that these approaches proceed from different and sometimes incompatible assumptions and concepts. They do each offer important insights into or illuminate faces of corporate culture. Rather than debate the relative merits or correctness of each, we draw upon these several approaches to define the concept of corporate culture that prevails in this chapter.

Corporate culture, in the authors' views, refers to the basic values, beliefs, norms, and fundamental assumptions that members have about the corporation, its environment, and human nature; the organizational structures and rules of behavior that emerge from these values and shared meanings; the discourse, relationships, and symbols that provide coherence to the organization; and the policies, programs, and procedures that implement the goals and norms.

Following Mitroff and colleagues (1989), the authors envision corporate culture as having an onion-like quality (Figure 6.1). At the core of the culture is the root mission and identity of the corporation and its members' most basic beliefs about the world, the corporation's place in that world,

Figure 6.1
An Onion Model of Corporate Culture

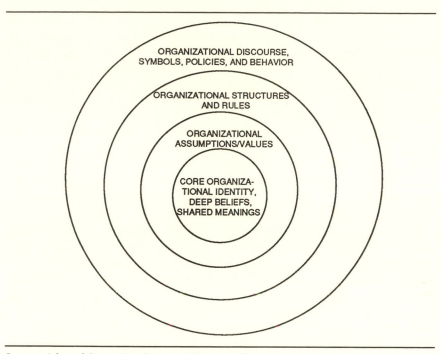

ORGANIZATIONAL DISCOURSE,
SYMBOLS, POLICIES, AND BEHAVIOR

ORGANIZATIONAL STRUCTURES
AND RULES

ORGANIZATIONAL
ASSUMPTIONS/VALUES

CORE ORGANIZA-
TIONAL IDENTITY,
DEEP BELIEFS,
SHARED MEANINGS

Source: Adapted from Mitroff et al. (1989, p. 272).

and the individual's place in the corporation. Although the factors that compose the core are usually the most decisive for shaping the behavior of the corporation, they are often the most difficult to articulate or discern. The next layer involves key organizational assumptions and values that give particular direction to organizational functioning and actions. These assumptions and values are typically expressed in particular organizational structures and systems of rules. The interactions, however, are two-way throughout the onion layers, so changes in the outer layers may also alter inner layers. As Giddens (1979) has noted, social structures cannot be said to exist without reference to the meaning that such structures have for the affected individuals. Thus, core identity/beliefs and concrete behavior/policies are mutually expressive. And the outermost layer of the onion composes the policies, behaviors, discourse, and symbols that express and maintain the structures and rules of the inner layers (Schein 1980, 1985).

Corporate culture, then, provides the core beliefs and assumptions that set the base for the rules and operating principles in which members of the corporation root their behavior. It also establishes the frames of reference and perspectives from which to interpret events and respond to surprises or

Figure 6.2
Mission and Consistency in Corporate Culture

MISSION

	A	B
CONSISTENCY	Clear Mission, High Consistency	Unclear or Divided Mission, High Consistency
	C	D
	Clear Mission, Low Consistency	Unclear or Divided Mission, Low Consistency

crises. In essence, it is a shorthand code that pervasively and subtly renders reality understandable and provides order and security to its members.

Not all corporate cultures are the same, of course; they differ in key attributes. Here we note, in the form of a matrix (Figure 6.2), several variables that are central to shaping the effectiveness and capacity of the culture to respond to surprises in its external environment.

Some corporations have a clear sense of mission; others do not. *Mission,* in the authors' usage, refers to *the shared definition of corporate goals and functions vis-à-vis the larger world.* A strong sense of mission provides clarity and direction to the behavior of managers and workers and a capacity to take action in novel, or ambiguous, or even emergency situations. It also provides an intrinsic sense of meaning and worth to the contributions of the corporation. A highly internalized sense of mission allows members to shape their behavior to distant ends that transcend short-term planning horizons or corporate targets. Denison (1990) cites the example of Medtronic, a corporation best known as a producer of cardiac pacemakers. A very distinctive part of Medtronic's unique culture was a powerful sense of mission ". . . to contribute to human welfare by application of biomedical engineering in the research, design, manufacture and sale of instruments that alleviate pain, restore health and life of man" (Denison 1990, p. 98). This strong mission of caring and commitment served as a magnet for building the corporation's work force, for developing an explicit ideology and behavioral norms, and for managing the corporation effectively with little internal control or accountability.

Consistency refers to *the extent to which managers and workers agree on corporate mission, values, and rules.* Highly consistent corporate cultures provide a strong basis for effective communication since values and meanings are widely shared. Agreed-upon expectations and norms shape behavior in ways that formal rules and organizational structures cannot. Two types of consistency may be envisioned. *Horizontal consistency* occurs when members in very different parts of the corporation can easily communicate and coordinate efforts. Such congruence and common knowledge contributes to effective working relationships, tacit agreements, and conflict resolution. *Vertical consistency,* by contrast, refers to a high understanding among workers regarding the expectations of their superiors and, conversely, to the understanding, on the part of management, of workers' assumptions and norms. High vertical consistency typically involves a sense that a member will be rewarded over the long term for short-term contributions and sacrifices (Camerer and Vepsalainen 1988, p. 121). Both types of consistency breed significant economic efficiencies as well as a capacity to respond to challenges and surprises.

Corporations possessing clear missions and high degrees of consistency are often described as having *strong cultures*. In such corporations, employees have a well-developed sense of purpose and an attachment to the organization. Clear mission and informal norms provide strong guidance for behavior—little time is wasted in seeking direction or interpreting events. Moreover, corporations with strong cultures are resilient to surprise and adversity. When Delta Airlines Flight 191 crashed in August 1985, for example, volunteers from Delta's management ranks immediately came forward to assist the families of victims and survivors. Although the corporation did not solicit or recruit them, many of its executives flew to Dallas where they gave their time and emotional energy, sometimes at great personal cost, to help in victim identification and burial arrangements. This response appeared to emerge largely from their identification with the "Delta family" and their sense that Delta was in a time of need (Isabella 1986, p. 175). Procter & Gamble is frequently cited as another corporation with a strong and highly consistent corporate culture, with a powerful tradition of listening and responding to its customers and a socialization process that builds values in key aspects of the corporation's operations (Deal and Kennedy 1982; Denison 1990, pp. 147–160). In their qualitative analysis of differential performance of some eighty companies, Deal and Kennedy (1982, p. 7) found that the only common denominator among the highly successful companies was that all were consistently "strong culture" companies.

To the extent that a culture's consistency is undeveloped or that other strong cultural identities exist and compete for loyalty among its members, however, a corporation is apt to harbor various *subcultures*. Such subcultures may be quite well developed and the systems of common beliefs and assumptions may depart substantially from those in the dominant corporate culture. This observation is akin to the argument of Thompson, Ellis, and Wildavsky (1990) that cultures are plural and not singular. Members of the health and safety departments of a corporation, for example, may embrace rather different beliefs and expectations about the corporation than do members of the accounting or marketing divisions. Blue-collar workers recruited from a particular ethnic group may differ substantially from white-collar managers. And, of course, in cases of corporations locating plants in developing countries, locally recruited employees may bring cultures profoundly different from those existing in the parent corporation.

Although much discussion and writing have centered on how strong cultures arise and are maintained, in fact these processes are not well understood. The notion that corporate cultures, like an administrative flow chart, can be easily engineered is particularly naive. It may well be, as Camerer and Vepsalainen (1988) argue, that strong corporate cultures simply arise without benefit of purposeful design. Some of the factors that other studies have found to be important in such emergence include:

Early history. The early history of a company can provide a strong stamp for mission, values, and assumptions. And since precedents, myths, and stories can be powerful forces, such cultures may change slowly.

Heroes. Charismatic leaders can be pivotal figures in establishing and embodying corporate values. They are symbolic figures who are both motivators and role models for members of the corporation.

Recruitment and socialization. Some companies consciously recruit particular types of individuals they feel personify or will fit and reinforce the corporation's culture. A variety of training and socialization processes may be used to create and maintain cultural identity, norms, and learning (Hayes and Allinson 1988).

Incentives and sanctions. Reward and penalty systems are often employed to reinforce corporate objectives, norms, and rules. Members who integrate well with the culture are rewarded and promoted; others languish or are let go.

Rites and rituals. How things are done in the company, even when highly routine, can develop and express corporate culture. Ceremonies place the corporate culture on display and provide memorable experiences; rituals express myths that sustain values and scripts that create meaning.

Later in this chapter, each of these factors is discussed in the context of Du Pont's establishment of the Bangpoo plant.

Some see a hierarchical structure for management in the dynamics of corporate values. In this view, top managers function as the cultural *value formulators,* those who by their actions and priorities signal key values and mission to the members of the corporation. The president and chief operating officer, in particular, ". . . provide the map that ultimately directs the behavior of employees" (Isabella 1986, p. 188). The middle managers are the *value translators,* who convey key values and assumptions into the structures, policies, and everyday procedures of the corporation. As translators, these managers reinterpret events and situations in a manner that communicates actual norms and rules to subordinates. Finally, the *value maintainers* are the lower managers who implement corporate values by making decisions and engaging in behavior that is consistent with the corporate culture. Although it is doubtful that any corporate culture functions in quite this idealized, top-down way, the distinctions among roles do relate to the onion conception of corporate culture and the cultural processes discussed here.

This brief overview of corporate culture provides a backdrop for a second stream of research. Work on high-reliability organizations is particularly relevant to the issues involved in the location of potentially hazardous facilities in developing countries.

HIGH-RELIABILITY ORGANIZATIONS AND RISK

Most studies of corporate culture give short shrift to the ability of high-technology firms to prevent catastrophic accidents, but this issue has emerged as a major societal concern. The Bhopal, Mexico City, Three Mile Island, and Chernobyl accidents all focused attention on questions of safety and reliability. Although still very exploratory, research during the 1980s addressed hazard-management issues that warrant integration with the more established, traditional approaches to studying corporate culture.

In 1984, Perrow published *Normal Accidents,* a book concerned with the increasingly complex technologies needed by society and the inherent problems in assuring safety, especially what is needed to prevent catastrophic accidents. Perrow devotes particular attention to two problem areas—*systems complexity* and *tight coupling*—that confront high-risk organizations. *Complexity* refers to such issues as potential for unexpected sequences in accident development, technological complexity, potential for interactions among apparently separate or incompatible functions, and the indirectness of needed information sources. *Tight coupling* refers to the lack of slack in systems, the time-dependent nature of many processes, invariant sequences of operations, and single means for reaching particular goals. In Perrow's view, serious accidents are normal in high-risk organizations because they are destined to fail. Because these organizations deal with highly sophisticated technologies that involve unanticipated interdependencies and interactions, they face a constant struggle to ensure high reliability. Indeed, reliability and safe operations, rather than productivity, become the chief goal (or, in the authors' usage, "mission"). In such systems, problems propagate in unexpected ways, and even high reliability in each and every part fails to ensure high system reliability. The coincidence of tight coupling and technological complexity, in short, creates conditions of interactive complexity that in turn poses unique problems and generates a new family of system-level failures that end up as catastrophic accidents.

Although Perrow sketched this argument in vivid hypothetical terms, the empirical basis and confirming evidence that he offered were still rather meager and debatable. Over the past seven years, a group of scholars at the University of California at Berkeley has further developed and modified the

Figure 6.3
The Relationship between Reliability and Technological Risk

TECHNOLOGICAL RISK

		HIGH	LOW
RELIABILITY	HIGH	**1** Air Traffic Control	**2** Urban Water Supply
	LOW	**3** Bhopal, Three Mile Island	**4** Handicrafts

initial hypotheses. High-reliability organizations, in their view, are those in which managers pay extraordinary attention to operational reliability because of the inherent dangers of a situation and because achieving desired outcomes (e.g., safety) related to reliability is otherwise impossible. Highly reliable organizations are considered to be those that repeatedly avoid catastrophic events even though the potential for such accidents is high (Roberts 1989, pp. 112–113). Put another way, the research centers on those cases that fall in Quadrant 1 of Figure 6.3.

LaPorte (1987), arguing that organizational research has generally shed few insights into the nature of high-reliability organizations, has called for detailed studies of the structures and behavior of such systems. He defines five pairs of knowledge/behavior patterns that make for high reliability:

- Nearly complete causal knowledge of the functioning of the technical and organizational system helps to assure expected outcomes. Based on this knowledge, both personnel and machines exhibit nearly error-free performance.

- Error regimes specify the small deviations from routines for both machines and operations and signal potential onset of failures in critical components. Associated with this are well-developed alerting systems and personnel with strong error-identification capabilities.

- Improved knowledge permits characterization of the consequences of given failures, particularly their potential for spawning damage throughout the system. Associated with this are strong error-absorbing capabilities in people responsible for appraising organization of technological malfunctions or lapses in human performance.

- Credible, exact knowledge of the environmental and social effects of technical operations provides the basis for comprehensive cost/benefit analyses. Associated with this knowledge is a continuous monitoring capability to detect external effects as the technology spreads and ages.

- System error specification regimes are sensitive to public concerns and interests. Alerting strategies address system errors and mitigate their consequences.

The Berkeley team has over the past several years examined four high-reliability organizations. The first is the Federal Aviation Administration's Air Traffic Control System in which controllers handle aircraft some 7.5 million times a year. Approximately 100 "near misses" (or, more accurately, "near collisions") annually require quick action by controllers and pilots, but mid-air collisions are rare (Rousseau 1989). The second is Pacific Gas & Electric Company, which provides 10,000 hours of electrical service to its 4 million customers, achieving 99.965 percent reliability in terms of avoiding outages. The third is nuclear aircraft carriers, incredibly complex technological systems that have achieved remarkable safety records in their flight operations and handle up to 300 cycles of aircraft preparation, positioning, launchings, and arrested landings (often at about 55-second intervals per day) (Rousseau 1989, p. 291). Finally, Roberts, Rousseau, and La Porte (1993) report on the culture of PAVEPAWS, an early-warning-system unit staffed by U.S. Air Force personnel.

These studies yield important insights to supplement, extend, or sometimes contradict research on corporate culture. Several are particularly germane to corporate culture and technology transfer as considered in this chapter. First, Rochlin (1989) argues that a key strength of high-reliability systems is their ability to be self-designing and to be able to translate organizational learning into standard operating procedures that members can be trained to follow. It is the organization that learns, Rochlin argues, and not its individual operators. System or organizational learning, in turn, depends strongly upon high accuracy in communication and quality of information. Hence the need for corporate cultures that make heavy investments in training and in developing detailed rules for making decisions. At the same time these cultures need to be *elastic,* in order, on the one hand, to promote conventional, routine behavior under normal operating conditions, while on the other providing high discretion and information-scanning proficiency under crisis conditions.

Second, researchers have found that high-risk organizations face unusually uncertain external environments of hazard and yet have high interdependence associated with high technological complexity. The environmental uncertainty gives particular value to organizational decentralization but the interdependence produces problems of coordination and control that managers often resolve through the use of extreme hierarchy (e.g., the ranking system used aboard aircraft carriers). Organizations appear to solve this conflict in different ways, such as through highly flexible hierarchy or special units to manage interdependence. Others fail to solve the problem and suffer severe failures.

An interesting finding from the aircraft carrier studies is that external forces continuously pressure for new technologies and technological fixes, whereas

Table 6.1
Motivations to Invest in Thailand: The First Three Choices of Importance

Motivation Factors	Number of Firms by Rank of Importance		
	First	Second	Third
Diversification of business	-	-	-
Access to local materials	1	6	4
Low wage costs	13	3	1
Disciplined labor force	-	-	-
Fewer language problems	-	-	-
Investment incentives	2	5	8
Good and efficient government	-	-	-
Political stability of host country	-	-	-
Risk-free environment	-	-	-
Strategic location	-	-	1
Adequacy of infrastructure	-	1	1
Adequacy of communication facilities	-	-	-
Availability of land	-	-	.-
Existence of industrial estates/IPZs	-	-	-
Other factors	-	-	-

Source: Patarasuk (1991, p. 97).

the operators of the carriers strongly resist their imposition. These operators view the new technologies as inherently less reliable than the old ones and as creating much more interdependent systems in which problems propagate. Accordingly, carriers turn out to be a fascinating mix of old and new technologies. Ship personnel manage state-of-the-art weapons systems, relying on 20-year-old computers and grease pencils. Carrier operators repeatedly told Berkeley researchers that the old technologies did the job when crises occurred or the electricity went off (Roberts 1989, p. 122).

The findings also point to a distinctive role for corporate culture in contributing to high reliability. A basic challenge posed by new technologies is that more and more of the work and operations have disappeared into the machines (Weick 1989). Trial and error are less available as a learning strategy because errors may produce catastrophes. As a result, managers and operators must increasingly rely on inference, imagination, intuition, mental models, symbolic representation of technology, and problem solving to understanding what is happening and to avoid accidents. Thus, a corporate culture that values and makes use of stories, storytelling, and storytellers may develop greater reliability because members know more about their system and the potential errors that might occur and have greater confidence in their ability to handle errors (Weick 1987, p. 113).

Finally, the research pinpoints a series of problems that all organizations with needs for high reliability (such as Du Pont's facilities worldwide) must confront:

- High reliability requires both hierarchy and decentralization. Technological complexity makes centralization and integration absolutely indispensable, yet many decisions are optimal when pushed to the lowest level commensurate with the skill.
- Asymmetrical reciprocal interdependence leads to very tight coupling, whereas flexible reciprocal interdependence requires loose coupling.
- Demands on high-risk organizations typically stimulate more introduction of technology, whereas budgetary constraints reduce the work force. What results is more tightly coupled systems and reduced slack.
- Training tends to be narrow and specialized, whereas uncertain events pose complex and interactive contingencies.
- High-reliability organizations are very expensive to operate, yet pressures almost always exist for efficiency and cost cutting (Roberts and Gargano 1990).

Thus, when corporations locate facilities in developing countries, they not only confront issues of culture transfer but must also find solutions to these problems. Several of the problems were, in fact, important issues in the Bangpoo case.

TRANSFERRING CORPORATE CULTURES AND ENSURING HIGH RELIABILITY

A multinational corporation contemplating the location of a production unit in a foreign country, particularly if it is a developing country, faces issues that have the potential to affect substantially the corporate culture that emerges in the unit and the eventual reliability, and profitability, of operations achieved. Chapter 2 takes up some specific considerations that emerged in the three cases examined in this volume. Generally, these issues include the technological environment and capabilities prevailing in the host country, the market advantages to be gained, labor costs, incentives offered by the host country, the stability of the political environment, the business arrangement, and, of course, cultural factors. Indeed, a recent study (Patarasuk 1991) of sixteen firms investing in Thailand suggests the importance of low wage costs, investment incentives, and access to local materials as motivations for corporations to open facilities in Thailand (see Table 6.1).

Although the issues associated with cross-cultural transfer did not play a prominent role in these survey results, they do represent pervasive issues that corporations must address. For example, the host-country culture may differ substantially from the corporate culture in attitudes toward authority and equality. Hofstede (1980), in a survey of some 88,000 employees of one multinational firm in 67 countries, found that respondents in developing countries were generally more receptive to hierarchical, authoritarian, and paternalistic relationships and that collectivism, rather than individualism, was a common norm. In many developing countries, kinship networks and family ties are powerful forces in the organization of the business environment and often serve as channels of communication among businesses and between business and government. If corporations adapt to these networks, significant advantages can accrue to the corporation through employee loyalty or superior access to information; conversely, failure to take account of such differences can leave corporations at a serious disadvantage (Austin 1990).

Cultural attitudes and values carry far-reaching implications for organizational decision making and, thus, corporate culture. Scandinavian workers expect superiors to encourage their participation, whereas Latin American and Asian workers expect managers to be paternalistic. Japanese firms encourage decision making in groups with input from all organizational levels. French firms generally have hierarchical structures in which decisions are made at the top and passed down through the organization (Ronen 1986, p. 349). Italian managers see a need to provide crisp, precise answers to workers' questions, whereas many U.S., Swedish, Dutch, and British managers emphasize helping subordinates to find their own solutions (Laurent 1983).

Even basic assumptions about and conceptions of incentives vary widely among cultures. In group-oriented cultures, singling out individuals for praise of their high performance—a practice of individually oriented cultures—sometimes produces a loss of face and threatens group harmony. Economic incentives work in some cultures but not others. Adler (1986, p. 132) cites the case of an American company's raising the hourly rate of Mexican employees to encourage them to work longer hours; instead, they worked less, observing that they now had enough money to enjoy life. Some cultures stress heavily the degree of trust that exists in superior-subordinate relationships; others emphasize productivity and performance (Choy 1987).

Obviously, subtle cultural factors lie in wait for corporations involved in technology transfer. Table 6.2 suggests the rich diversity of such factors, which corporations need to consider and assess. It is not surprising, in view of this list, that transferring a corporation's culture and reliability system is much more complex and difficult than transferring its technology or management procedures. In Thailand, for example, Japanese firms have dominated the economy since the 1960s, and Japanese management systems apparently have become quite popular with Thai companies. Nonetheless, transferring the Japanese management system takes longer than transferring the production technology. American-style corporate management systems, for their part, have not become commonplace in Thai corporations, despite

Table 6.2
Potential Impact Areas of Cultural Factors

Management Area	Cultural Value and Attitude Parameters		
Organizational structures	*Social structures:*		
	Hierarchical	<----------->	Egalitarian
	Vertical	<----------->	Horizontal
	Familial	<----------->	Institutional
	High-status differentiation	<---------->	Low-status differentiation
Manager-employee relations	*Societal relationships:*		
	Authoritarian	<----------->	Democratic
	Paternalistic	<----------->	Self-reliant
	Personal	<----------->	Functional
Decision-making	*Decision processes:*		
	Autocratic	<----------->	Participative
	Unilateral	<----------->	Consultative
Group behavior	*Interpersonal orientation:*		
	Collectivism	<---------->	Individualism
	Group welfare	<---------->	Self-interest
	Other-oriented	<---------->	Task-oriented
Communication	*Personal interactions:*		
	Personalized	<----------->	Impersonalized
	Closed	<----------->	Open
	Formal	<----------->	Informal
	Indirect	<----------->	Direct
	Passive	<----------->	Aggressive
Incentives and evaluation	*Motivation:*		
	Economic	<----------->	Noneconomic
	Work	<----------->	Pleasure
	Loyalty	<----------->	Competency
	Role ascription	<----------->	Merit achievement
Control	*Human nature perceptions:*		
	Intrinsic good	<----------->	Intrinsic evil
	Trust	<----------->	Distrust
	Cooperative	<----------->	Conflictive
	Malleable	<----------->	Unchangeable
Time management and planning	*Time perceptions:*		
	Infinite resource	<---------->	Finite resource
	Present-oriented	<---------->	Future-oriented
	Imprecise	<----------->	Precise
	Controllable	<---------->	Uncontrollable
Spatial relationships	*Space perceptions:*		
	Private	<----------->	Public
	Nearness	<----------->	Farness
	Aesthetics	<----------->	Functionality

Source: Austin (1990, p. 355).

the fact that they are more decentralized and individualistic and thus superficially more adapted to Thai cultural values. The reasons for these difficulties are unclear, although public concern about conspicuous consumption is evident in Thailand, as is concern about a loss of cultural identity by Thais working in transnational corporations and about the possibility that Thais are becoming pseudo-Westerners (Patarasuk 1991). Indeed, where Thai managers have been trained in Western management concepts, the result appears to be not the transfer of Western corporate culture and management but a hybrid of Western and Thai norms and cultural behavior patterns (Runglertkrengkrai and Engkaninan 1987).

Gladwin and Terpstra (1978), viewing the wide array of host country cultural variables that impinge upon technology transfer, suggest five cross-cultural factors that all corporations need to address:

Cultural variability—the degree to which conditions within a culture are stable or unstable, and the rate at which they are changing. Variability creates uncertainty and requires a corporation to be highly flexible and adaptive.

Cultural complexity—the extent to which the rules of human behavior are explicit or implicit. In many Western countries, the tendency is for communication to be direct and explicit, whereas in many Asian countries, nonverbal cues and symbolic uses of language are important.

Cultural hostility—the degree of negative reaction in the host country to the in-coming corporation. Such hostility, of course, has deep implications for building corporate values and trust.

Cultural heterogeneity—the degree of sharing of cultural values and meanings between the host country and the country of origin of the parent corporation. Congruence or lack of congruence may set limits as to what is possible in transferring corporate cultures and indicate needed adaptations.

Cultural interdependence—the extent to which developments in other cultures are related, and affect, the host country culture. This variable suggests cultural openness to events or change to external events or development, an important source of uncertainty or ambiguity.

These five factors may then be related to the within-culture and between-culture dimensions shown in Table 6.3.

The plant manager occupies a key position in dealing with the cultural issues attendant on technology transfer. The manager acts as the translator and advocate of corporate culture, the analyst of the host-country environment, and the interpreter of host country culture and subcultures. Because of this role, multinational corporations (including Du Pont) often pursue a strategy of *management indigenization* in which they appoint host-country nationals to key management positions in the local plant. Although this strategy enhances the corporation's knowledge of local circumstances and may help identify opportunities for cultural congruence and adaptation, it also carries the risk that subsidiaries or local plants will substantially modify elements of the onion structure of corporate culture in order to satisfy host-country goals and assumptions.

Corporate and host-country culture operate, then, in a multitiered system in which the parent company, the subsidiary, and the local plant all interact (Figure 6.4). Managers at each level play particularly crucial roles as culture formulators, translators, and interpreters. At each level, the corporation ex-

Table 6.3
Dimensions of the Cultural Environment of International Business

Dimension		Continuum	
		(Low)	(High)
Within cultures	Cultural variability	Low & stable change rate	High & unstable change rate
	Cultural complexity	Simple	Complex
	Cultural hostility	Benevolent	Malevolent
Between cultures	Cultural heterogeneity	Homogeneous	Heterogeneous
	Cultural interdependence	Independent	Interdependent

Source: Gladwin and Terpstra (1978, p. xvii).

ists within the environment of a home country with its own culture, goals, expectations, and constraints. Typically, individuals are recruited from these home-country systems into the corporation or move between levels (and cultures). How these various transactions are managed shapes extensively the performance and outcomes of technology transfer.

From the foregoing conceptual discussion of corporate culture, high-reliability organizations, and cultural issues in technology transfer, the authors next consider one of the three cases treated in this volume, the location of the Du Pont Bangpoo plant in Thailand (see also Chapters 3 and 4). This case provides a rich context for exploring the various ways in which corporate culture enters into technology transfer. In addition, it affords opportunity for interrelating corporate culture and value questions, for Du Pont is widely regarded as a multinational corporation with a strong corporate culture.

THE CORPORATE CULTURE OF DU PONT

In early 1990, *Fortune* carried an article assessing retrospectively the corporate-culture movement of the 1980s, suggesting that, in the midst of all the trendy notions, there was reason to "take heart." "An increasing number of enterprises are at last figuring out how to alter their cultures and more than ever are doing it" (Dumaine 1990, p. 127). The models and illustrations used in this article accorded Du Pont a particularly conspicuous place. This prominence fits closely the self-image of Du Pont's top managers, who energetically embrace the company's corporate culture as a primary vehicle in the success of the corporation and its role in "corporate environmentalism" and industrial health and safety. As Du Pont's chairman and chief operating officer, E. S. Woolard, recently put it, the primary challenge Du Pont faces is to ensure ". . . that we excel in environmental performance and that we enjoy the non-objection—indeed, even the support—of the people and governments in the societies where we operate" (Woolard 1989a, p. 6). This is a tall order in the United States and elsewhere where social trust in corpora-

Figure 6.4
Interactions among Corporate Culture, Organizational Climate, and National Setting in Technology Transfer

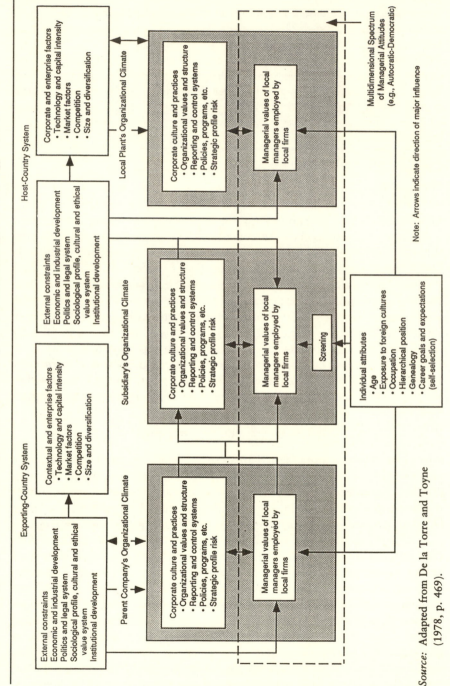

Source: Adapted from De la Torre and Toyne (1978, p. 469).

tions has eroded to very low levels. What are the key components and characteristics of corporate culture at Du Pont, how did this culture arise, how is it maintained, and how does the culture affect Du Pont's operations in the United States and abroad?

Origins and early history can put an enduring stamp on a corporation's culture. Du Pont had its birth in 1802 in explosives. The founding father, Pierre S. du Pont de Nemours, had been a prominent economist and politician in France prior to taking refuge in America during the so-called Reign of Terror attendant on the French Revolution. Originally he planned to establish a colony of balanced agricultural and industrial ventures. When this scheme collapsed, Pierre's son, Eleuthère Irénée, discovered that gunpowder produced in the United States was expensive but poor in quality. With financial backing from France and the United States, he established one of the largest explosives plants in the United States outside of Wilmington, Delaware, on the Brandywine Creek (Taylor and Sudnik 1984).

In these early years, the company operated with a strongly paternal bent that reflected both the need to recruit and retain highly skilled workers and Pierre du Pont's goal to create a harmonious society as well as a productive industrial enterprise. All du Pont family members shared equally in management and profits, and property was held in common and apportioned according to need. Eleuthère du Pont viewed the family as personally responsible for the well-being of its workers; accordingly, the earliest company rules (1811) made it clear that the company was responsible for maintaining safe workplaces. Employees were forbidden to enter a mill before management had first surveyed the mill for hazards and operated the equipment. Although the manufacture of gunpowder at that time typically proceeded in vertical stages on floors of a wooden building, thereby increasing the risk of explosions, the du Ponts set up their works in horizontal stages along the river bank in permanent stone structures (Blanchard 1990). The du Ponts themselves lived on the site of the mills and worked alongside the employees. They also established pensions for families of employees killed on the job and provided company housing for employees. These paternal and safety-oriented traditions were effectively wedded with profits, and by the end of the century Du Pont was the largest explosives producer in the United States.

The early history of family idealism, a productive process associated with high hazards, and a strong paternalism provided a base for a succession of health and safety innovations at Du Pont. In the early 1800s, the first company physician was retained to deal with work-related injuries. In 1915, the company instituted annual physical examinations and hired a full-time medical director. In 1925, Du Pont included x-rays as a routine part of physical exams. A year later, it created a corporate safety and fire-protection division and began to conduct safety audits of its various plants. In 1935, Du Pont established the Haskell Laboratory for Toxicology and Industrial Medicine, one of the first such laboratories in American industry. In 1956, a formal epidemiology program, including a cancer registry, was initiated. In 1979, Du Pont became one of the first corporations to establish a computerized exposure tracking system to document and monitor employee medical histories. The 1980s saw occupational medical program surveys and an alcoholism remediation program for retirees and employee families and survivors (Karrh 1984). Recently, the creation of a health improvement program for employees has addressed a broad range of health issues, including back injuries, nutrition, smoking cessation, blood pressure control, and off-the-job safety. Over its history, in short, Du Pont has been a clear leader in initiating a wide variety of health and safety innovations in the United States (Kasperson et al. 1988).

Even its top managers in health and safety will pointedly tell you that Du Pont "is in business to make money; we do not make decisions that are not sound business decisions" (Du Pont 1990). But it is also clear that this historical record of health and safety innovations has something to do with its early history, its founding values, and its sense of corporate mission.

When Du Pont describes itself as "a company of principles," it does indeed specifically state its intent to adapt well "to rapidly changing conditions in a highly competitive market" (Du Pont 1989, p. 14). But in that highly competitive world, it seeks to maintain a distinctive reputation:

as a company that is committed to the safety of its employees, its neighbors, and its customers; as a company of unquestionable integrity and social responsibility; as a company whose operations are environmentally sound; and as a company whose products and services are consistently of the highest quality (Du Pont 1989, p. 14).

Du Pont officials consistently cite several principles relating to the environment and safety as central to Du Pont's sense of mission:

- There is no privilege without duty. Selling products and employing workers carry key obligations.
- All injuries, occupational illnesses, and (more recently) environmental releases are preventable.
- Du Pont will not sell any product that cannot be manufactured, distributed, used, and eventually disposed of safely.
- All makers and users of Du Pont products must be informed of the attendant risks.
- Management is fundamentally responsible for safety.

So although Du Pont is surely a business that aims to be profitable, it also sees itself as occupying a particular niche in industry. Indeed, these goals are seen as interrelated and mutually reinforcing, not in conflict. Du Pont aims to be an industry leader, an innovator in health and safety programs, and to have one of the safest places to work in the industrial world (Woolard 1989b, p. 2). That means that Du Pont cannot settle for even comparatively favorable safety rates or good grades on its environmental protection performance. Thus when internal statistics record an increase in spills and accidents, Du Pont increases the number of safety-conscious and disciplinarian types in its managerial ranks. The worker who gets to be plant manager needs to know instinctively that if you leave a hose lying across a walkway, sooner or later someone is going to trip. Du Pont must be willing, for example, to spend money for safety on the margins, where other corporations will not. In return, however, Du Pont has emerged as a major marketer of health and safety programs and points with pride to a study of 178 of its clients, which indicates that, as a result of Du Pont expertise, they were able to improve their safety records by an average of 37 percent in the first year and 89 percent by the sixth year (Du Pont 1989, p. 14).

Over the past five years, Du Pont has sought to extend its corporate mission and identity to be an environmental leader as well as a safety innovator (Woolard 1990). In the early 1980s, it became apparent that Du Pont's environmental performance did not match its occupational health and safety performance. A preoccupation with economics and improved labor/management relations had compromised the company's environmental record and the high-volume producer of chemicals found itself at or near the top of lists of major polluters (EPA 1989; Dean, Paje, and Burke 1989; Citizens Fund 1990). In 1986, it committed to a 33 percent reduction in all environmental emissions by the end of the 1990s. It has also adopted an assumption, that of the National Safety Council, that all environmental releases are preventable (which, of course, they are not). Thus, Du Pont has very consciously embarked on a leadership role in *corporate environmentalism,* which it defines as an attitude and a performance commitment that places corporate environmental stewardship fully in line with public desires and expectations (Woolard 1989a, p. 6). This means that Du Pont sees itself as assuming a leadership role in developing an industry-wide environmental agenda over the next decade and will seek opportunities to align itself with the environmental community and to demonstrate that environmental and industrial goals are compatible (Woolard 1989a, p. 6) and even "sustainable" in the long run (Woolard 1992).

Critics label such pronouncements as mere "environmental etiquette of the 1990s" (Doyle 1992, p. 90). Indeed, this is not a matter of altruism; rather, Du Pont sees such leadership as directly in its material self-interest: "The ultimate competitive advantage is to remain in business when your competitors are driven out. In the decades ahead, many companies that have not responded to the environmental imperative will be denied the privilege to operate in important trading nations in key markets" (Woolard 1989c, p. 4). Or, again in Woolard's words:

Industrial companies will ignore the environment only at their peril. Corporations that think they can drag their heels indefinitely on genuine environmental problems should be advised: society won't tolerate it and Du Pont and other companies with real sensitivity and environmental commitment will be there to supply your customers after you're gone (Holcomb 1990, p. 20).

If a strong corporate culture does indeed require both a clear mission and a high degree of consistency, culture building must be omnipresent and effective. Indeed, Du Pont officials will tell you that safety and (now) environmental protection are a condition of employment at Du Pont. "If we have a site manager who does not buy into the Du Pont philosophy, he or she will not be a plant manager long" (personal communication, Du Pont 1990).

But, interestingly, Du Pont does not see recruitment as a key nor does it have a training program radically different from that of most of its competitors. Instead, it works from the top down in instilling attitudes, motivations, and behavior norms through an all-embracing corporate socialization program. We expect all Du Pont employees to have the right attitude, irrespective of job assignment. "We especially expect all managers to constantly convey that attitude. It's from us that the organization learns whether we're serious about safety or whether were just talking a good line" (Woolard 1989b, p. 2). The first-line supervisor plays a particularly critical role with new employees and is expected "to turn around their attitudes" (personal communication, Du Pont 1990). Individual workers, meanwhile, are instilled with the notion that they are responsible not only for their own safety but for that of their co-workers as well, and peer pressure occupies an important socialization and regulatory function.

The reward structure at Du Pont is closely geared to these corporate cultural values and processes. Indeed, chairman Woolard has argued that the best way to create a more trusting corporate environment is to reward the right people: "The first thing people watch is the kind of people you promote. Are you promoting team builders who spend time on relationships, or those who are autocratic?" (Dumaine 1990, p. 131). Accordingly, all Du Pont managers are evaluated on safety and environmental performance as key criteria for promotion and compensation increases.

The cultural values that support Du Pont's mission and identity as a safety and environmental leader are seen as providing broad benefits to the corporation. "Safety is a powerful lever to achieve a whole series of other corporate goals—we learned this long ago," a Du Pont official noted (Du Pont 1990). Safety is viewed as a very effective locus for instilling discipline and building managerial leadership. It is also integrated with other values that support corporate performance. Du Pont specifically espouses a "total person" approach to safety. The company's survivor benefits are extraordinarily high. Fire-hazard, seat-belt usage, and other off-the-job safety information continually goes home with Du Pont employees. Recently, Du Pont instituted "Health Horizons," an employee health improvement program in which more than one-half of its employees worldwide participate (Karrh 1989).

Symbols, rituals, and signals all play an important role in Du Pont's corporate culture. Managers nurture pride in safety and environmental performance through a complex system of awards, flashing green lights, and accolades and awards from top management. The first item of business at all corporate executive board meetings is safety, and any lost-workday cases are discussed specifically. "Near misses" (by which is meant "near mishaps") are major events and receive substantial visibility at top management and through the company. Safety is ubiquitous, almost a mania, in the Du Pont work environment; signs and cues are visible everywhere. Safety is in front of people at all times and built into even the most routine procedures, such as the "tool box" meeting in which safety issues are treated before a work crew undertakes even the most ordinary of maintenance tasks. Workers encounter a constant flow of admonitions to use seat belts even in the back seats of cars, to wear goggles when mowing their lawns, to avoid tilting their chairs while sitting, and always to hold the banister while ascending or descending stairs, at work or away from work.

For all this richness in cues, socialization, symbols, and ritual, Du Pont must struggle to maintain the culture on which it heavily depends. In the midst of economic cutbacks and getting leaner in the mid-1980s, Du Pont found that its safety performance had dropped. Preoccupied with the economic downturn, it discovered that its enunciation of safety principles in various corporate communications had slipped from the top to the bottom of the list. Meanwhile, cutbacks in management had reduced the culture-building and personal relationship between supervisors and subordinates. And so corporate officials found the need to gear up the corporation for a reinvigorated effort if cultural values and behavior norms supporting safety were not to be eroded. And so, lessons were drawn: "We know from experience that when we do stop pumping the safety commitment throughout the company, bad things start to happen" (Woolard 1989b, p. 2).

Clearly, safety is a key ingredient in Du Pont's corporate culture. The foregoing pages have explored at length the nature of that culture, which permeates Du Pont facilities worldwide. Corporate culture sets the context for Du Pont's transfer of technology to its Bangpoo facility in Thailand.

Du Pont Corporate Culture and Technology Transfer

Du Pont, as emphasized in earlier chapters, is a strongly international enterprise. Its 140,000 employees work in 200 manufacturing and processing plants in some 40 countries throughout the world. It also markets in more than 150 countries, and international sales account for more than 40 percent of its revenues [which were expected to increase to 50 percent by the mid-

1990s (Du Pont 1989, p. 2)]. One in four of its employees works in plants outside the United States. During the 1980s, the international character of Du Pont grew substantially, as the company invested more than $10 billion to fund more than 50 major acquisitions and joint ventures with other companies.

Du Pont has a long-standing policy of equivalency in its standards of safety and environmental protection wherever it operates in the world, with, as chairman Woolard bluntly puts it, no exceptions. Equivalency here means something more than the general functional equivalency referred to in Chapter 8. Indeed, Du Pont's central approach to dealing with the myriad of health and safety challenges in locating facilities in developing countries is to transfer not only its safety standards but its entire corporate culture. As one Du Pont official described it,

In Du Pont I think there is only one environmental and safety rule—that is the *E. I. Du Pont Safety and Regulation Rules* apply anywhere that Du Pont operates. If you can't have safety, then you don't acquire that plant. If you can't operate it safely, then you close it down. (Chalat 1989, p. 10).

So when the U.S. Occupational Safety and Health Administration (OSHA) in the mid-1980s required changes of all U.S. companies in their accounting systems for occupational injuries, Du Pont implemented the rule change worldwide, despite objections from its international facility managers about the need for such enlarged bookkeeping changes and dreary record-keeping. The motivation was a sound one—that Du Pont could track and compare all accident statistics across all its facilities on the same database. In other words, once a change is adopted in corporate policies and procedures, all Du Pont facilities must expect to live with it.

But formal rules and procedures are, it is worth recalling, only the outer layer of the onion of corporate culture. More critical is the development of sense of corporate mission and patterns of attitudes and behavior that realize safety goals. In locating plants in other countries, Du Pont officials recognize that the host-country culture necessitates some adaptations. Trophies and cheerleaders don't work in Asia, Du Pont officials informed the authors, nor do financial awards for innovation. So in Asia, Du Pont emphasizes team building, in Germany the plant manager is a strict disciplinarian, and in Taiwan the plant manager is a father figure who seeks a close personal relationship with the workers.

Du Pont attaches great importance to the selection of the plant manager. In Thailand, Du Pont selected an Asian manager from its Singapore facility for that role. A key part of her responsibilities was to understand the local culture, to develop in the plant a specific cultural adaptation that made Du Pont's core values and environmental philosophy work, and to recruit the plant's workers. Specifically, equivalence was sought not only in standards but in employee skills, knowledge, and attitudes, commitment to safety philosophy, and sense of personal stake in the company. The corporation brought the plant manager and production supervisor, both of whom were also part of the Du Pont task force that designed and started up the plant, to the United States for six weeks of advanced training. By the time the first group of workers was hired, the local Du Pont management had received extensive preparation as culture translators.

Much attention in the Bangpoo culture-building centered on the selection and early training of workers. Preference was given to fresh technical school and high school graduates. Job interviews routinely involved a series of questions on personal attitudes toward risk-taking in personal life and a careful evaluation of the candidate's willingness to conform to group norms and practices. Workers received training three times longer than what would have occurred in a comparable U.S. facility. Meticulous observation and evaluation of safety habits at and outside of work occurred over the first six months, and workers' attitudes toward safety were elicited and monitored. Du Pont also developed a system for recruiting and evaluating workers to determine which were most compatible with its corporate culture.

Indeed, the entire Bangpoo operation carries the stamp of Du Pont safety and environmental mission. The site itself could have been adequately developed for $500,000 but was built at a cost of $1.5 million in order to meet Du Pont's own high standards for environmental and occupational health and safety. Safety hats and safety glasses are ubiquitous, doors have outlines on the floor to indicate the direction that they open, and emergency equipment is in place for handling any chlorine release from an accident in the chlorine facility *adjacent* to the Du Pont plant. Confronted by the lack of an adequate local sanitary landfill, Du Pont constructed its own on-site waste incinerator. An engineered dust-control system was installed to avoid the need for uncomfortable face masks. Du Pont also provided special training for the local fire department and hospital to upgrade the local emergency-response infrastructure.

FINAL NOTE

These observations are not intended to suggest that the Bangpoo facility is extraordinarily safe or that Du Pont's transfer of corporate culture to Thailand has been a resounding and unequivocal success. The authors have no independent verification, beyond a brief field visit by colleagues, to permit such findings. But several pertinent observations are possible:

- Du Pont clearly has a well-developed corporate culture in which high safety and environmental performance are a key part of corporate mission and identity.
- In the Bangpoo case the company undertook extraordinary efforts to transfer its corporate culture as intact as possible, making a variety of financial investments

dictated primarily by safety and environmental goals and the needs for culture building.

* The transfer did not simply reproduce a parcel of Du Pont in Thailand. Rather, indigenization of management and some adaptations to local culture were used to realize basic corporate norms and to implement its organizational and rules structure.

* Corporate culture bore most of the burden for safety and environmental performance as Thai environmental monitoring, regulation, and inspection were weak and unintrusive.

Much of this case is reassuring in regard to safety and environmental responsibility, but a down side also exists. Du Pont is centrally committed to its corporate mission and culture wherever its plants are located. The centrality of that commitment reverberates in other value areas. Developing countries sometimes seek as a high priority the transfer of technological capability and the maximization of industrial development. A strong corporate culture like Du Pont's can, perhaps even usually does, interfere with those objectives. For Du Pont's corporate culture to work, full control over operations is essential. Although Du Pont does provide an unquestionably powerful model for a host country to emulate in building risk management and environmental protection regimes, the degree of indigenous rooting of the Du Pont corporate culture is limited. Du Pont, for all its emphasis upon environmental leadership and its worldwide marketing of safety systems, is not about to transfer its productive technology, marketing advantage, or valued patents to other companies or host countries.

REFERENCES

Adler, Nancy J. 1986. *International dimensions of organizational behavior.* Boston: Kent.

Austin, James E. 1990. *Managing in developing countries: Strategic analysis and operating techniques.* New York: Free Press.

Blanchard, E. P., Jr. 1990. Remarks delivered to members of the Norwegian Parliament, Wilmington, DE, February 13.

Blau, Peter M. 1964. *Exchange and power in social life.* New York: Wiley.

Camerer, Colin, and Ari Vepsalainen. 1988. "The economic efficiency of corporate culture." *Strategic Management Journal* 9: 115–126.

Chalat, S. 1989. Transcript of taped interview with Halina S. Brown and Allen V. White, 6 November 1989. Halina S. Brown (Clark University, Worcestor, MA, 01610) provided the authors with a copy of the transcript.

Choy, Chong Li. 1987. "History and managerial culture in Singapore: Pragmatism, openness, and paternalism." *Asia Pacific Journal of Management* 4 (May): 139.

Citizens Fund. 1990. *Manufacturing pollution: A survey of the nation's toxic polluters.* Washington, DC: Citizens Fund.

Deal, Terrence E., and Allen A. Kennedy. 1982. *Corporate cultures: The rites and rituals of corporate life.* Reading, MA: Addison-Wesley.

Dean, Norman L., Jerry Paje, and Randall J. Burke. 1989. *The toxic 500: The 500 largest releases of toxic chemicals in the United States, 1987*. Washington, DC: National Wildlife Federation.

De la Torre, J., and B. Toyne. 1978. "Cross national managerial interaction: A conceptual model." *Academy of Management Review* 3 (July): 462–474.

Denison, Daniel R. 1990. *Corporate culture and organizational effectiveness*. New York: Wiley.

Doyle, Jack. 1992. "Hold the applause: A case study of environmentalism." *The Ecologist* 22 no. 3 (May/June): 84–90.

Dumaine, Brian. 1990. "Creating a new company culture." *Fortune* 121 (January 15): 127–130.

Du Pont. 1989. *This is Du Pont*. Wilmington, DE: Du Pont.

Du Pont. 1990. Personal communication during visit to Clark University, 23 May 1990.

EPA (Environmental Protection Agency). 1989. *The toxics-release inventory: National and local perspectives*. EPA 560/4-89-005. Washington, DC: EPA.

GAO (General Accounting Office). 1990. *Nuclear safety: Concerns about reactor restart and implications for DOE's safety culture*. GAO/RCED-90-104. Washington, DC: GAO.

Geertz, Clifford. 1973. *The interpretation of cultures*. New York: Basic Books.

Giddens, A. 1979. *Central problems in social theory: Action, structure, and contradiction in social analysis*. Berkeley, CA: University of California Press.

Gladwin, Thomas H., and V. Terpstra. 1978. "Introduction." In *The cultural environment of international business*, ed. V. Terpstra, Cincinnati, OH: Southwestern.

Gregory, K. L. 1983. "Native-view paradigms: Multiple cultures and cultural conflicts in organizations." *Administrative Science Quarterly* 28: 359–376.

Hayes, J., and C. W. Allinson. 1988. "Cultural differences in the learning style of managers." *Management International Review* 28 no. 3: 75–80.

Hofstede, Geert. 1980. *Culture's consequences: International differences in work-related values*. Beverly Hills, CA: Sage.

———. 1983. "The cultural relativity of organizational practices and theory." *Journal of International Business Studies* (Fall): 75–89.

Holcomb, John. 1990. "How greens have grown." *Business and Society Review* 75 (Fall): 20–25.

Homans, George C. 1958. "Human behavior as exchange." *American Journal of Sociology* 63: 597–606.

Ingersoll, V. H., and G. B. Adams. 1983. "Beyond organizational boundaries. Exploring the organizational metamyth." Paper presented at the Organizational Folklore Conference, Los Angeles, March.

Isabella, Lynn A. 1986. "Culture, key events, and corporate social responsibility." *Research in Corporate Social Performance and Policy* 8: 175–192.

Jaeger, Alfred M. 1983. "The transfer of organizational culture overseas: An approach to control in the multinational corporation." *Journal of International Business Studies* (Fall): 91–114.

Jaques, Elliot. 1951. *The changing culture of a factory*. New York: Dryden.

Karrh, Bruce W. 1984. "An illustration of voluntary actions to reduce carcinogenic risks in the workplace." In *Reducing the carcinogenic risks in industry*, ed. Paul F. Deisler, Jr., 121–134. New York: Marcel Dekker.

———. 1989. Remarks at the Du Pont International Safety Symposium. Houston, January 16.

Kasperson, Roger E., Jeanne X. Kasperson, Christoph Hohenemser, and Robert W. Kates. 1988. *Corporate management of health and safety hazards: A comparison of current practice.* Boulder, CO: Westview.

Kluckhohn, Clyde. 1951. "The concept of culture." In *The Policy Sciences,* ed. Daniel Lerner and Harold D. Lasswell. Stanford, CA: Stanford University Press.

La Porte, Todd. 1987. *High reliability organizations: The research challenge.* Working paper. Berkeley, CA: University of California, Department of Political Science.

Laurent, André. 1983. "The cultural diversity of Western conceptions of management." *International Studies of Management and Organization* 13 (Spring/Summer): 75–96.

Levi-Strauss, Claude. 1963. *Structural anthropology.* Trans. C. Jacobson and B. Schoeph. New York: Basic Books.

Liedtka, Jeanne. 1988. "Managerial values and corporate decision-making: An empirical analysis of value congruence in two organizations." *Research in Corporate Social Performance and Policy* 11: 55–91.

March, J. G., and H. A. Simon. 1958. *Organizations.* New York: Wiley.

Martin, Joanne. 1982. "Stories and scripts in organizational settings." In *Cognitive social psychology,* ed. A. Hastrof and A. Isen, 155–304. New York: Elsevier-North Holland.

Mitroff, Ian I., Thierry Pauchant, Michael Finney, and Chris Pearson. 1989. "Do (some) organizations cause their own crises?: The cultural profiles of crisis-prone vs. crisis-prepared organizations." *Industrial Crisis Quarterly* 3: 269–283.

Ouchi, William G. 1980. "Markets, bureaucracies, and clans." *Administrative Science Quarterly* 25: 129–141.

Ouchi, William G., and Alan L. Wilkins. 1985. "Organizational culture." *Annual Review of Sociology* 11: 457–483.

Patarasuk, Waranya. 1991. "The role of transnational corporations in Thailand's manufacturing industries." *Regional Development Dialogue* 12 (Spring): 92–114.

Perrow, Charles. 1987. *Normal accidents.* New York: Basic Books.

Peters, T. J. 1978. "Symbols, patterns, and settings: An optimistic case for getting things done." *Organizational Dynamics* 7(2): 3–23.

Pondy, L. R., P. J. Frost, G. Margan, and T. C. Dandridge. 1983. *Organizational symbolism.* Greenwich, CT: JAI.

Roberts, Karlene H. 1989. "New challenges in organizational research: High reliability organizations." *Industrial Crisis Quarterly* 3: 111–125.

Roberts, Karlene H., and Gina Gargano. 1990. "Managing a high-reliability organization: A case for interdependence." In *Managing complexity in high technology organizations,* ed. Mary Ann Glinow and Susan Albers Mohrman, 146–159. New York: Oxford University Press.

Roberts, Karlene H., Todd R. La Porte, and Denise M. Rousseau. 1993 (forthcoming). "The cultures of high reliability." *Journal of High Technology Management.*

Rochlin, G. I. 1989. "Informal organizational networking as a crisis-avoidance strategy: U.S. Naval flight operations as a case study." *Industrial Crisis Quarterly* 3: 159–176.

Ronen, Simcha. 1986. *Comparative and multinational management.* New York: Wiley.

Ronen, Simcha, and O. Shenkar. 1985. "Clustering countries on attitudinal dimensions: A review and synthesis." *Academy of Management Review* 10: 435–454.

Rosen, M. 1985. "Breakfast at Spiro's: The dramaturgy of dominance." *Journal of Management* 11: 31–48.

Rousseau, Denise M. 1989. "The price of success?: Security-oriented cultures and high reliability organizations." *Industrial Crisis Quarterly* 3: 285–302.

Runglertkrengkrai, Somkao, and Suda Engkaninan. 1987. "The pattern of managerial behaviour in Thai culture." *Asia Pacific Journal of Management* 5 (September): 8–15.

Schein, E. H. 1980. *Organizational psychology*. 3rd ed. Englewood Cliffs, NJ: Prentice-Hall.

———. 1985. *Organizational culture and leadership*. San Francisco: Jossey-Bass.

Simon, Herbert. 1951. "A formal theory of the employment relationship." *Econometrics* 9: 293–305.

Smircich, Linda, and Marta B. Calás. 1987. "Organizational culture: A critical assessment." In *Handbook of Organizational Communication,* ed. F. M. Jablin, L. Putnam, K. H. Roberts, and L. W. Porter, 228–263. Newbury Park, CA: Sage.

Taylor, Graham D., and Patricia E. Sudnik. 1984. *Du Pont and the international chemical industry*. Boston: Twayne.

Terpstra, V., ed. 1978. *The cultural environment of international business*. Cincinnati, OH: Southwestern.

Thompson, Michael, Richard Ellis, and Aaron Wildavsky. 1990. *Cultural theory*. Boulder, CO: Westview.

Von Glinow, Mary Ann, and Susan Albers Mohrman, eds. 1989. *Managing complexity in high technology organizations: Systems and people*. New York: Oxford University Press.

Weick, Karl E. 1987. "Organizational culture as a source of high reliability." *California Management Review* 29 (Winter): 112–127.

———. 1989. "Mental models of high-reliability systems." *Industrial Crisis Quarterly* 3: 127–142.

Wilkins, Alan L., and William G. Ouchi. 1983. "Efficient cultures: Exploring the relationship between culture and organizational performance." *Administrative Science Quarterly* 28: 468–481.

Wilkinson, Norman B. 1984. *Lammot du Pont and the American explosives industry, 1850–1884*. Charlottesville, VA: University Press of Virginia.

Woolard, Edgar S. 1989a. "The ethic of environmentalism." *Executive Excellence* (November): 6–7.

———. 1989b. Remarks at the Du Pont International Safety Symposium. Houston, TX, January 16.

———. 1989c. Remarks before the American Chamber of Commerce of Japan. Tokyo, October 6.

———. 1990. "Our commitment to the environment: Du Pont policy must meet public expectations and desires." *Plastics World* (22 April): 20.

———. 1992. "An industry approach to sustainable development." *Issues in Science and Technology* 8 no. 3 (Spring): 29–33.

CHAPTER 7

Business Arrangements
and EH&S

Business arrangements between the parent corporation and its host country affiliate assume a variety of forms, ranging from wholly owned subsidiaries to some degree of shared equity partnerships with regard to marketing, contracting, and licensing agreements. Depending on the arrangements, a variety of constraints may be placed upon the corporation's flexibility and range of options in the facility design and management. The MNC's attitudes toward entering into joint ventures, and toward the ownership and management arrangements at such ventures, reflects the corporate response to these constraints. Similarly, host countries and host enterprises may associate benefits with joint ventures that often do not materialize and lead to disappointing outcomes.

The ultimate structure and details of joint venture agreement is a formal expression of the outcome of negotiations between the venture partners, although informal agreements carry significant weight as well. Both reflect a mix of partners' institutional cultures and business motives operating within the boundaries imposed by host country culture and legal framework. EH&S, in both its hardware dimension (pollution control equipment, worker protective devices) and software dimension (organizational know-how, workers' training, monitoring, reporting, inspection protocols, blueprints, and manuals) is but one among many issues that may be covered in a contractual relationship. These issues stand alongside marketing responsibilities, profit-sharing, risk-sharing, management responsibilities, protection of proprietary technology, and the many other terms and conditions of critical interest to the parent and affiliate.

This chapter explores, through the prism of the Du Pont, Occidental Chemical, and Xerox case studies, the effects that the choice of business arrangements at MNC foreign affiliates may have on EH&S practices and performance. The analysis emphasizes the emergence of EH&S issues during the negotiations between the joint venture partners, the terms of formal and informal joint venture agreements, and the downstream effects of such agreements on the facility's operation.

HISTORICAL CONTEXT

Since the 1950s, parent-affiliate relations have undergone fundamental changes, driven by both the economic reordering and political restructuring of the last four decades. On the political front, beginning in the immediate postwar years and extending into the late 1960s, the surge of independence brought forth new expectations on the part of developing countries in relation to MNCs' operations. Historical patterns of full MNC control of mineral, petroleum, and export agriculture typical of the pre-World War II, colonial period gave way to negotiated agreements in which host governments and local entrepreneurs were granted major roles in both management and ownership of MNC operations. Shedding colonial ties in countries like India, Indonesia, and the nations of central and southern Africa prompted a wave of economic nationalism that manifested itself in tighter controls on ownership and management of MNC operations. A wave of nationalization shifted a majority of basic industries into host country ownership. Efforts to achieve greater participation in MNC enterprises were particularly aggressive in oil and gas exporting countries (e.g., Indonesia, Saudi Arabia, Libya, Nigeria, Venezuela) where postwar economic recovery fueled heavy demand for petroleum products, thereby strengthening the bargaining position of petroleum-producing nations. This may be contrasted to mineral exporters who, though prone to the same nationalization as oil producers, were unable to capitalize on the dependencies of industrial countries for their commodities. Even in those countries where large and rapidly expanding domestic markets attracted MNCs seeking to establish an early market position (such as India and Brazil), MNCs gradually became subject to heavy regulation by host governments seeking to enlarge short- and long-term benefits from MNC operations.

The consequences of nationalization were ambiguous for the host countries, if not counterproductive. MNCs were reluctant to invest in countries with a record of expropriating foreign investments, many developing countries lacked the know-how or the trained personnel to operate the newly acquired facilities, and, due to transitional problems in management and marketing, the nationalized industry lost considerable market shares on the world market. Over the last two decades, most developing countries have changed their policies toward MNCs and adopted a more differentiated approach to foreign investment, ranging from imposing stringent regulations of ownership to adopting a laissez-faire position. This change in policies has been accelerated with the demise of the communist doctrine and its inherent dogma of nationalizing private property.

Concurrent with rapid political changes was the emergence of the manufacturing sector as the dominant growth sector in MNC investment in developing countries. Driven first by import substitution policies and, somewhat later, by export-dominated industrial policies to foster domestic economic growth, host countries created incentives to facilitate establishment of MNC export operations, including special production zones within which hiring, importation, ownership, tariff, and other privileges prevailed. At the same time, controls on production for domestic markets were tightened in an effort to direct the rush of MNC investment toward achieving other social objectives such as protection of indigenous enterprises, retention of foreign currency, balancing growth between urban and rural regions, and building technology development capacity within national enterprises.

As MNC investments shifted from basic, extractive activities to the manufacturing sector, and nationalistic pressures transformed developing countries into more active participants in their industrial growth, parent-affiliate business arrangements became more varied and complex. With few developing countries willing to remain in the role of primary materials exporters for processing at U.S. and European manufacturing sites, MNCs encountered growing demands to build indigenous technology, protect local industries from monopolistic control by MNCs, enlarge equity participation by host governments and entrepreneurs, contribute to local infrastructural improvements, and restrict profits repatriation. At the same time, growth in domestic markets provided developing countries with the leverage needed to bargain with MNCs over the scale, location, profit-sharing and technological content of MNC operations.

None of these trends implies an abrupt shift from economic dependence characteristic of the colonial period or indicates that developing nations' leverage would be applied to realize host country EH&S objectives. Indeed, such objectives rarely appeared in government policy pronouncements or regulations that continued to emphasize developmental goals in regulating MNC activities—import substitution, promotion of indigenous industry, self-reliance, regional development, and job creation.

While developing countries mobilized for a more active role in regulating multinational investments, such initiatives were driven principally by the goal of apportioning a greater share of the profits from resource exploitation for the benefit of indigenous economic development. To achieve this, however, required mechanisms for controlling such investments. These, in turn, necessitated a shift from the dominant mode of MNC wholly owned subsidiaries to alternatives in which equity, production management, marketing, and other functions increasingly would be shared by partners. By the 1980s, a few basic types of such arrangements had emerged, ranging from product-licensing agreements with no equity participation by the local partner to a partnership in which the local participant holds an equal or dominant equity position and management responsibilities. At present, though wholly owned subsidiaries still dominate overseas operations of U.S. firms in terms of total assets and employees, joint ventures have emerged as the dominant parent-partner relationship in new and planned operations (Contractor 1986).

STUDIES OF JOINT VENTURES

Causes and Motives for Joint Ventures

Joint ventures can be of interest to both the MNCs and the host countries. Kogut (1988) reduces joint venture motivations to three:

avoidance of excessive transaction (and therefore total production) costs through joint ownership/control rights and the mutual commitment of resources;

enhancement of competitive/market position; and

creation of a vehicle to transfer so-called tacit knowledge, or know-how that is embedded in the organization itself, in its routines and practices, rather in specific pieces of hardware or software.

Datta (1988, p. 88) provides a more elaborate perspective on the reasons for MNCs to engage in joint ventures, pointing to the following as determinants:

- entering new and potentially profitable markets that would not be available to the MNC without local support by a joint venture partner;
- sharing heightened economic risks in new business ventures;
- satisfying nationalistic demands and reducing risks of expropriation;
- maintaining good relations with host governments;
- pooling organizational know-how to realize synergistic benefits.

From the perspective of a prospective host country business partner, creating a joint venture with an MNC provides several advantages such as access to new technology, use of brand names and trademarks in domestic markets, and entry into new markets in a relatively short time to diversify existing business activities.

A view essentially compatible with Datta's is presented by Contractor (1986), who identifies the following motives:

- joint risk reduction
- economies of scale and/or rationalization of production
- complementary technologies and patents

- co-opting or blocking competition
- overcoming government-mandated trade barriers
- initial international expansion (for medium and small firms)

The extent to which each of these factors affects joint ventures in developing countries varies according to the regulatory structure in host countries. In major markets such as China and India, both of which impose stringent restrictions on foreign investors, MNCs simply cannot operate with a local partner, either government or private, without governmental permission and supervision. The lure of untapped markets positions host governments to bargain for and extract substantial concessions from MNCs in the form of facility location, technology transfer, indigenization of product components, and equity ownership shares. Furthermore, the recognition that the host country's laws, regulations, and political culture cannot be easily learned by expatriates reinforces the propensity of MNCs to seek joint venture arrangements, even when host government policies are less rigid than in China or India (O'Reilly 1988). This is exemplified in the Thai case of Occidental Chemical, where the benefits of preserving links to a savvy local business family proved instrumental is expediting the upgrade and expansion of the chrome products facility acquired during the firm's buy-out of Diamond Shamrock.

Finally, the concept of financial risk reduction cuts across all phases of the firms' operations, including product and process design, materials procurement, production, financing, marketing, and labor relations. For MNCs, operations in developing nations carry additional risks relative to U.S., European, or Japanese locations, such as sudden and disruptive shifts in the treatment of MNC profits and political upheaval or civil strife. Under these conditions, joint ventures provide certain anticipatory and resilient capabilities that wholly owned subsidiaries are less likely to enjoy. The tendency of host governments to target MNCs in times of political and economic unrest, though diminished since the 1960s, remains a compelling incentive to place the overseas enterprise under the protective umbrella of a domestic partner.

Empirical Studies

The theoretical conclusions about the potential benefits of joint ventures are reflected in the empirical studies about joint ventures. Hlakik (1985) has surveyed joint venture activity worldwide during the period 1974–82. He specifically addresses the experiences in developing countries. His sample of 420 joint ventures in manufacturing encompasses those occurring within the manufacturing sector; between a U.S. firm and at least one foreign partner located overseas; and with the U.S. partner holding 10 to 90 percent of equity ownership.

Several trends are noteworthy. First, with the exception of above average activity in 1974, the latter years of the nine-year interval witnessed substantially more activity than the earlier years. Yearly formation of joint ventures approximately doubled during the period, peaking in 1980 with 72 recorded agreements. This confirms our view that joint ventures have become more attractive to MNCs and host countries because of changes in economic policies and world trade patterns.

Second, R&D activity as part of the joint venture agreement was meager. Over the nine-year period, a mere 15 percent of all joint ventures contained some identifiable form of R&D. In relative terms, the 4.8 percent average during the first five years more than doubled to 12.5 percent during the last four years, a significant gain in relative terms but still minimal in absolute terms. Some sectors, namely electric and electronic equipment, instruments, and textiles, showed somewhat higher than average R&D activity (Hlakik 1985, p. 50). Overall, while joint venture activity and, by implication, various forms of technology transfer accelerated overall, the most fundamental and long-term type of technology transfer—the development of indigenous R&D capability—continues to be the exception rather than the rule.

Third, joint ventures with non-majority U.S. ownership totaled slightly over half the sample (55 percent). Over the course of the study period, this figure ranged from 46 to 62 percent, with no obvious difference between the 1970s and early 1980s. These figures, though admittedly not weighted by the dollar values of the enterprises, are a counterpoint to the perception of U.S. domination of overseas joint ventures. Foreign ownership controls imposed by host countries were most prominent in this sample, which may serve as an illustration for the historical shift from both extremes, free investment policies and nationalization.

Finally, the split between developed and developing locations shows a consistent bias against low-income countries (e.g., India, China) to the advantage of high (Europe, Japan) and middle-income (e.g., Brazil, Mexico) countries. Across all joint ventures, a mere 3 percent occurred in the first category, with figures remaining essentially constant (and negligible) over the study period. In contrast, middle-income countries represented 39 percent of all joint ventures, peaking at 48 percent in two of the study years. High income countries accounted for the majority, 55 percent, with figures ranging from 47 to 65 percent. In the 1981–82 U.S. recession period, the preference for high income countries surged, probably a reflection of risk aversion among U.S. MNCs in a period of unstable international prices and politics.

POTENTIAL CONFLICTS BETWEEN JOINT VENTURE PARTNERS

MNCs enter into joint venture partnerships for business reasons, either voluntarily or in response to the host country's pressure. Killing (1983), analyzing a sample of 34 joint ventures, identifies this issue as the primary motive in 57 percent of developing country ventures. In other words, over half the sample formed ventures primarily because doing business in the host country required it. The other key motive was the need for skills—management, technical, financial, marketing—identified by 38 percent of the respondents. Whether cooperation is forced by governmental policies or motivated by business concerns, joint ventures are not only associated with mutual benefits but may also lead to conflicts.

Once the negotiations of the terms of the joint venture agreement commence, at least two forces are at work in producing differing perspectives on how the joint venture ought to be developed and managed (Robinson 1988, p. 192). First, the time value of money typically differs between parent and partner. MNCs normally view their foreign investments as long term, and are willing to live with minimal short-term payoff. Operating losses for three to five years is not uncommon for MNC investments, tolerated as the cost of establishing a market and product profile in a new area. Host country partners, on the other, typically seek to maximize near-term returns with an eye to developing links with other domestic enterprises that they control.

Second, the MNC and domestic partner assign different weights to product diversification. For the MNC, the joint venture is one component of a global network of production. Unlike the domestic partner who emphasizes growth through increased share in one or a few markets (domestic or international) with limited product diversification, the MNC is likely to seek growth through product diversification and geographical diversity. The result is an MNC's propensity to incur longer term risks for new product development and to use the joint venture as a testing ground (and vehicle for risk sharing) in new geographic areas. In contrast, the domestic partner normally prefers proven technologies, markets maximum local value-added, and has less appetite for experimentation in process and product development.

We would expect these various partners' motives to impinge upon the EH&S agenda during negotiations between the MNC and venture partners. First, EH&S know-how and investments—training, hardware, management systems—are by nature long-term investments. They do not directly produce marketable products but instead are part of what might be called the "technology infrastructure" transferred abroad via the joint venture agreement. Because the return on investment and profit horizons of the partner are relatively short and short-term profit maximization is a key driver in the formation of a partnership, it is reasonable to expect initial indifference toward, if not overt disagreement with, the value assigned to EH&S investments during negotiations.

For the MNC, on the other hand, EH&S technologies are likely to be viewed as valued assets, comparable to the types of technological, marketing, and capital assets it brings to the negotiating table. That EH&S investment yields primarily long-term returns in the form of risk reduction, accident prevention, reduced work absenteeism, and lesser plant down time is likely to be valued less highly by the host country partner. Under these circumstances, the effect of divergent planning horizons on the valuation of EH&S assets may occasion disagreements on how the partnership's initial capital resources ought to be apportioned among competing demands.

The MNC and its partner are also likely to have different perspectives on long-term EH&S management decisions. For the MNC, accustomed to operating in a more regulated, monitored, and litigious atmosphere, EH&S compliance is a daily task performed within an elaborate system of internal and external testing, analysis, and reporting of environmental and workplace performance. Shoddy performance has its price in terms of potential penalties, liability claims, and damage to product and corporate image. The short- and long-term repercussions of a major mishap or lawsuit are not limited to the locus of the event, but may well be felt throughout a worldwide network of industrial facilities under control of the MNC. Public image and international reputation have been major drivers for global competitiveness and for gaining access to new markets.

MNCs prefer to have sole or at least major responsibility for all EH&S management decisions in designing and operating the facility. For the MNC, control over EH&S is a way of preserving an asset, a vehicle for accomplishing an efficient and routinized risk management, for ensuring quality control in a facility's operations, and for maintaining a uniform identity among its many international operations. Because effective EH&S management is multifaceted and bound up with corporate culture as much as hardware and management systems, the MNC is likely to resist relinquishing any significant loss of influence over investment decisions and over the day-to-day operations of the facility. Furthermore, when the joint venture agreement does allow for a gradual transition to local responsibility after a specified period of time, as in the Oxychem and Xerox agreements, the MNC is likely to adopt a conservative posture toward terminating its EH&S responsibilities, especially in high hazard industries. A joint venture agreement that assigns the EH&S management to the MNC will assure this.

For a host country partner, however, long-term EH&S management is likely to be a secondary concern. Government pressures on local corporations are usually limited because regulations are uneven and/or enforcement mechanisms are informal and often inadequate (White and Emani 1990). The partner's concern with damages to corporate and product image are likely to be minimal because developing countries generally are characterized by less product competition, disclosure, and media coverage of environmental mishaps; thus the prospect of economic losses caused by tarnished corporate image is less substantiated. Business risk owing to product, personal, and environmental damages is weak in comparison to risks prevailing in the United States and, to a lesser degree, other industrial countries. In addition, host country partners are accustomed to supportive government and public attitudes toward new industrial enterprises and a willingness to ignore or underreport EH&S infractions. Finally, a joint venture partner may be reluctant to give up control over an essential part of the management tasks only because the MNC claims to have superior knowledge of or experience with EH&S policies.

These divergent perspectives of the joint venture partners may result in conflicting preferences in allocating funds for EH&S compared to alternative (more productive) uses and in conflicts over the control of operations that include EH&S management. However, these conflicts may be less pronounced than the abstract arguments imply. First, EH&S investments are normally small compared to overall investment costs. Giving some priority to the MNC in determining EH&S investments and management practices does not compromise the joint venture partners' overall share of responsibilities and equity rights. In pollution-intensive industries such as petroleum refining, chemicals, and leather manufacturing, such investments may represent up to a fifth of initial capital investments and perhaps 10 to 15 percent of operating costs. With internal and external capital resources typically constrained, the host country partner will view skeptically MNC demands to make costly EH&S investments that reduce short-term returns. In technology-based industries, on the other hand, the initial EH&S investments are substantially smaller, typically amounting to well under 5 percent of total capital investment, and therefore unlikely to produce major contention among partners.

Second, host country businesses are usually reluctant to block investments for improving ES&S performance, as they would receive the blame if an accident occurred. Business partners in developing countries may be less vulnerable to international reputation, but may experience domestic problems if they are found to have prevented an MNC from installing additional safety devices. Finally, learning the hardware and management aspects of EH&S is part of technology transfer, integral to the broader question of implanting skills in problem solving over the long term. The host country partner may welcome the MNC's willingness to assume responsibility for day-to-day facility management, including the EH&S aspects of the operations, as in the Oxychem facility in Thailand. In addition, as the Du Pont, Oxychem, and Xerox cases have shown, the cost of altering standardized EH&S systems (equipment, software, training methods, manuals) to which the MNC is accustomed may itself result in longer-term costs that outweigh the more obvious, upfront savings in equipment purchases. For the host country partner, MNC insistence over control of EH&S is therefore likely to emerge as a contentious negotiation point only where substantial capital investments accompany such control.

Turning now to the Oxychem, Xerox, and Du Pont cases, we see that none of the three facilities represents major polluting industries and, not surprisingly, encountered only modest objections to retaining control of EH&S in negotiating their joint venture agreements and to investing in post-start-up EH&S improvements.

THE OUTCOMES

EH&S aspects of joint venture agreements in two case studies, Oxychem and Xerox, may be interpreted in light of the motives, perspectives, and goals of the respective joint venture partners. The analysis focuses on the negotiation process and its outcome, as reflected in formal and informal joint venture agreements. As a counterpoint to these two cases, the Du Pont case provides a portrait of a company in which the business arrangement itself—a wholly owned subsidiary—reflects the corporate philosophy of maximizing ownership and management control, including especially EH&S standards and practices.

Du Pont-Thailand

Du Pont's preference in developing overseas affiliates, from most to least preferred are:

- wholly owned operations,
- contract manufacturing, majority-owned joint ventures (51–80 percent Du Pont),
- equal ownership (50–50),
- minority joint ventures, and
- licensing arrangements.

Where investments of relatively high global strategic locational or marketing value are at stake, a preference for wholly owned operations is particularly strong, allowing Du Pont to retain absolute control over all aspects of the venture: marketing, fiscal, product quality, and EH&S. This preference is matched by reality: Eighty-five percent of all overseas facilities operated by the Agrochemicals Division are wholly owned by Du Pont.

Du Pont's reluctance to enter into joint ventures is both reinforced by, and allows realization of, its corporate EH&S philosophy of faithful replication in all worldwide subsidiaries of its time-tested formula for achieving high EH&S performance. Furthermore, achievement of the company's EH&S standards in the production and application of agrochemicals is closely coupled with a high degree of control over the product life cycle. Given the nature of the product, hazardous exposures may occur in the workplace, in transporting materials, during application by farmers, and at the time of disposal of residuals (materials and packaging), as well as in the postapplication period through contamination of surface and ground water. While the company regards the latter as outside its realm of responsibility, the remaining points of exposure represent multiple opportunities to harm human health and the environment, especially with regard to the large numbers of farmers. Effecting Du Pont's EH&S standards and stewardship objectives under these circumstances is feasible only if the company is directly involved in managing all phases of the product life cycle, from development and production through transport and distribution. The wholly owned subsidiary, though neither a precondition for nor guarantee of achieving this level of EH&S standards, is the business mode most conducive to such goals. In addition, it is DuPont's stated policy to replicate the design of its local facilities and its own management style for any foreign subsidiary. This goal can only be fully accomplished if the company has full control over the design and operation of the facility.

In short, at Du Pont, overseas partnerships are viewed principally as a vehicle for overcoming country-specific constraints that it cannot overcome internally. However, since the corporation is rich in capital, technology, and marketing and management expertise, such constraints are confined to those imposed by host countries in such areas as maximum equity participation limits and minimum use of indigenous materials and suppliers. Outside of these legal/regulatory inducements, what little willingness Du Pont has demonstrated in forming joint ventures has been prompted by specialized, compelling, and relatively infrequent circumstances—for example, a need to market a new, high margin product in a new country. None of these was present in Thailand, a wholly owned and carefully replicated subsidiary.

Thai Occidental Chemical

The somewhat complex ownership history of Oxychem's Thai venture challenged the company along several dimensions relevant to EH&S. By inheriting the facility from a U.S. firm that placed less emphasis on EH&S, the company needed to reshape both management and hardware systems to achieve compatibility with its corporate modus operandi. This would have to occur with the partner's consent, with little turnover in the labor force, and in the face of formidable barriers created by distance from the parent's EH&S operations center in the United States.

We described earlier how a number of the motives of home and host country partners for entering into joint ventures were notably absent in this case, while others were readily identifiable. Not relevant were the motives of government mandates, the need for financial risk spreading, and the requirement of building indigenous technological capabilities. Since Thailand's Board of Investment acts on the principle of incentives (duty-free materials imports, tax exemptions, and employment of foreign nationals—see Chapters 3 and 5) to induce joint venture partnerships, government mandates clearly were not a determinant of Oxychem's decision to retain the arrangement it inherited from the previous owner. Neither did risk management associated with political and legal uncertainties play a significant role since MNCs—including Occidental Chemical—have long viewed Thailand's laissez-faire policies as a stable and predictable setting for overseas operations. Furthermore, Oxychem enjoyed virtual monopoly control over the market for its chromium products. Technology transfer also does not appear as a motivating force in the Oxychem agreement. Neither the partner nor the Thai government itself demonstrated any inclination to make technology transfer a major issue, though Oxychem's use of Thai nationals to both design and manage the facility suggests that local capabilities were upgraded even in the absence of a formal agreement to do so.

Among those motives that appear to have been most compelling in Oxychem's decision to form a partnership was the partner's intimate knowledge of the Thai business climate and practices. In addition, both parties were willing to retain the original joint venture agreement, including, though not decisively, its EH&S provisions. This was true even with the early recognition that certain improvements—installation of a scrubber, diking, and safety gates—may require the Thai partner (according to provisions of the joint venture agreement) to contribute capital if existing resources were not sufficient to cover such improvements. In the same vein, and perhaps most significant, was Oxychem's recognition that continuation of the Thai group's role in developing domestic markets and in providing liaison to the Thai government was an irreplaceable asset essential to the continued vitality of the venture. This was an especially critical asset in the highly personalized environment that characterizes Thai business operations.

For Occidental Chemical, the decision to continue with the existing partner was both a convenience and a complication. By so doing, the personnel at the facility were largely retained, licenses from the industrial estate remained identical, Board of Investment benefits were preserved, and production could continue without major interruption. The challenge, however, was to adjust operations at the site such that Oxychem's EH&S practices and standards were effectively transferred to the facility to improve upon the relatively relaxed standards applied by the former owner. To do this would require, at minimum, the support of the venture partner for elevating EH&S consciousness among managers and workers, as well as agreement to spend approximately 15 percent of the purchase price in upgrading EH&S systems. Furthermore, since the retention of the EH&S responsibilities at the plant by the MNC was a non-negotiable condition, the management arrangements would have to be structured accordingly.

Oxychem's general enthusiasm for overseas joint ventures provided a powerful incentive to make the deal with the Thai group work, though the company was prepared to withdraw from bargaining in the event a satisfactory arrangement could not be reached. The recollections of the company executives and managers from that transition period speak to the careful attempts to probe the Thai partner and the plant managers for their willingness to accept Oxychem's leadership in the EH&S matters and to adopt the company's safety philosophy. Visits by the vice president of Occidental Petroleum (Oxychem's parent company in the United States) for EH&S, and by the

Oxychem's environmental and occupational health and safety specialists focused on personal interactions with key individuals as well as on technical and economic assessment of facility needs. As a result of these visits, short- and long-term plans were produced for upgrading the facility and for education and training of its work force. In addition, the U.S. management was sufficiently assured of the partner's and manager's willingness to cooperate to continue the relationship.

The operative Oxychem–Thai Group joint venture agreement, a replica of an earlier Diamond Shamrock–Thai Group Agreement, is a succinct four-page document that does not fully reflect the nuances of the negotiations that preceded it. It contains the major headings typical of joint venture agreements, but notably little detail or guidance after these major topics appear. After brief statements concerning the organization, capitalization, transfer of shares, board of directors, debt financing, and project description, a single paragraph is devoted to "Environment, Health, and Safety Standards." This comprises of two principal conditions:

1. the facility will be brought up to standards of the U.S. partner as well as applicable Thai laws regulations; and

2. in the event internal funds are inadequate to cover such improvements, the partners will add to the venture's working capital in proportion to their shares (Thai Occidental 1990).

No explicit mention of EH&S management responsibilities appears, though the first item may be interpreted as assigning them to Oxychem. Clearly, the informal understanding between the partners relative to management of EH&S at the Thai Oxychem facility is an important component of the arrangement. Its main strength is a high degree of adaptability to changing circumstances at either corporation or in the host country's business environment. Furthermore, given the Thai partner's minor interest in becoming involved in day-to-day management issues, including EH&S matters, this arrangement gives the MNC significant latitude in implementing its management and EH&S philosophy.

On the other side of the ledger, the arrangement leaves many issues open to interpretation and therefore commits the multinational to long-term involvement in the daily matters of EH&S management. In the Thai Occidental case that involvement includes active oversight by the parent corporation over the facility, including environmental and safety assessments, and visits by the professional and corporate representatives of the parent corporation. The negotiated plan to transfer the key management responsibilities at the enterprise to a representative of the Thai group after the initial years of joint management (the implementation of which was under way at the time of this study) will undoubtedly further test the merits of the flexibility and informality of the joint venture arrangement.

Modi Xerox

In contrast to the Oxychem agreement in which the Thai government was a peripheral player, the Modi Xerox agreement must be viewed against a backdrop of government approvals of virtually every key decision affecting ownership, financing, export allowances, location, and technology transfer. Partnership negotiations, which followed the original Memorandum of Understanding between Xerox and Indian Reproductive Systems (which represented the Modi organization) were characterized by multiple iterations amid governmental rigidity on virtually all key issues. The initial 40 percent ownership cap allowable under Indian law set the stage for the Indian partner to negotiate substantial management and operational authority from the outset of the venture. Though the original division of "technical" responsibilities (engineering, design, construction, installation, product quality) and "business" responsibilities between Rank Xerox and its partner, respectively, was adjusted early in the life of the venture, the host country partner was assured of substantial negotiating leverage by virtue of its ownership share. This, of course, was precisely the intent of mandatory Indian equity position, to ensure that direct foreign investment serves the broader governmental goal of nurturing domestic managerial and technological know-how.

From Rank Xerox's perspective, strengthening its foothold in the potentially enormous (and substantially untapped) Indian market for photocopying equipment represented a powerful incentive to accept a series of government requirements: a limit on equity position; a ceiling on the production scale for the domestic market; a substantial allocation of production for exports; and a gradual indigenization of production materials (see Chapter 4 for more details). Operating under the burden of these requirements did not dissuade Rank Xerox from pursuing the joint venture. Indeed, their potential impact on profit margins and market share was cushioned by links with an Indian organization that could ensure financial stability, a countrywide marketing presence, a long-term vision of the investment compatible with Rank Xerox's, and a shield against risks associated with a politically volatile environment.

Negotiations between the partners devoted little attention to EH&S matters specifically. The reason may be that, because Rank Xerox was supplying virtually all the technical know-how to the venture, it would have been illogical and inefficient to separate the questions of the process, product, and environmental technologies in discussions over the proposed facility. Although EH&S concerns are not explicitly mentioned in the 1983 Technical Agreement (Rank Xerox–Modi Xerox 1983), "know-how" is broadly construed to encompass "secret formulae, processes, technical data, drawings, designs, recipes, product specifications, technical information including information for testing and controlling the quality of Xerographic Machines and all other technical information whether patentable or not . . ."

Further provisions covering the Transfer of Technical Know-How (Article

IV) require Rank Xerox to "provide and impart outside India to Modi Xerox the Rank Xerox Technical Know-How for the design engineering, erection, commissioning, operation and maintenance of the Plant and process equipment for manufacture of the licensed product . . ." and that such know-how shall include: "(a) basic design and engineering including drawing for the Plant; (b) plant lay-out; and (c) specifications of machinery, equipment including those pertaining to construction and fabrication, erection, commissioning, operation and maintenance of the Plant and process equipment."

Although these provisions may be interpreted as effectively, if not formally, assigning the EH&S responsibilities to Rank Xerox, they did not preclude the possibility of disagreements (which, in fact, later materialized) as to the boundary between technologies integral to the production process and those EH&S investments that are desirable, but not essential to, the production process. Neither did they set the philosophical or organizational foundations for addressing and resolving any disagreements that might arise in the future. Thus, similar to the Thai Occidental case, and in spite of the vast differences in the circumstances of the two cases, many details of choosing and implementing EH&S at the facility were left to future interpretation by the joint venture partners.

Another reason for the lack of explicitness in addressing the EH&S issues in the joint venture agreement may have been the perception by the partners that the extensive regulatory requirements already operative in India on the state and federal levels would suffice in assuring an environmentally sound and safe facility and would not leave much freedom in choosing the appropriate response. Such perception would only partially reflect the reality. It is true that many regulations exist in India. Some regulations and standards affecting both workplace and environmental conditions had been in place since the Factories Act of 1948, many more were enacted in the 1960s, 1970s, and 1980s, giving the central government a policy- and standard-setting function, and the state authorities a broad mandate to regulate the domestic and foreign industrial enterprises (White and Emani 1990). In reality, however, deficient enforcement practices (inspection, monitoring, report review) on the part of state officials give most enterprises high flexibility and signify an active, self-policing role for any new enterprise, including Modi Xerox.

All negotiations, agreements, and licenses were consummated months before the Bhopal disaster of December 1984. While it is impossible to articulate precisely how this timing affected the prominence and ultimate resolution of EH&S management responsibilities in negotiations, it is reasonable to speculate that Bhopal had the effect of reinforcing the arrangements ultimately agreed upon. Though the Rampur facility is a comparatively low hazard facility, the post-Bhopal environment is one of increased corporate accountability, disclosure, and heightened awareness of financial risks associated with workplace and community hazards.

During construction and since beginning operations in 1986, the tacit assumption underlying the joint EH&S-related decisions has been to rely on the MNC's expertise and vast experience in that area, and to assign it a leading role. Indeed, the Xerox managers and executives who offered their perspectives on this issue in the course of the study viewed the MNC's leadership as a precondition for a successful long-term partnership, although all stressed the importance of melding Xerox and Modi styles into a Modi Xerox hybrid.

That melding process faced occasional differences in the safety philosophy and practices. During construction, for example, the partners differed on the need for installation of an advanced fire protection system, with Xerox arguing for a company-derived, performance-based system, while the partner favored a lower external standard imposed by the insurer. The incremental capital costs at stake were not enormous, and the Rank Xerox position prevailed after it demonstrated that additional fire protection was in the best long-term economic interest of the facility. However, the episode was an early example of different EH&S philosophies, one driven by meeting the minimum external standards, and the second driven by a corporation's internal safety standard.

The additional stress on this hybrid comes from the modifications in the standard facility blueprints, introduced by Xerox in response to governmental requirement for a full production line within one facility. This requirement shifted the balance in the mix of engineered pollution controls, personal safety devices, and behavior modification of workers away from automation (see Chapters 4 and 5). Under these circumstances, workers' training, the parent company's continuous oversight, and the adoption by the local management of the MNC philosophy, preferably augmented by explicit terms of joint venture agreement, take on an additional significance. Though management in India claims that a singular culture bound by a shared vision has evolved in the Rampur facility, the character and performance of that hybrid over the long-term remains an open question.

BUSINESS ARRANGEMENTS AND EH&S: EMERGING THEMES

Effects of Ownership and MNC Management Style on EH&S

The Du Pont case may be juxtaposed with the Oxychem and Xerox cases to illustrate the contrast between maximum corporate control over EH&S matters, and a solution that requires the MNC to adapt to the constraints introduced by teaming with a venture partner. Whole ownership in general, while by no means assuring high EH&S performance, gives corporations freedom to implement their EH&S system of choice. Such freedom would be particularly valued by corporations like Du Pont, with highly developed corporate culture and EH&S know-how. For those, maximum standardization and replication of both human and hardware aspects of EH&S system from the home country would be the most likely approach.

Du Pont's practice of replication is a key example of a specific style of operating facilities in developing countries. This style is characterized by standardization and centralization. Although this style is more conducive to wholly owned enterprises, it can also be extended to joint ventures if the joint venture partner perceives replication as an advantage for pursuing its own interests. In this standardization-centralization management style, the venture enjoys the benefits of know-how and confidence based on facility performance elsewhere. Adaptation to local culture is minimal under the assumption that *host country workers and managers with sufficient training can bring to the workplace essentially similar behaviors as parent country workers and managers.* This centralized approach, however, has its risks. Because its success depends largely on decisions and solutions originating remotely from the facility, changes in parent country ownership through merger or acquisition, and/or commitment to EH&S owing to financial or other forces, may leave the affiliate without the internal resources and experience to continue EH&S programs at high performance. Such risks occur especially when strong EH&S performance is largely contingent upon the parent's continuous oversight rather than on the adoption by the affiliate of the fundamental philosophy underlying the acquired EH&S behaviors. The Du Pont case underlines the importance of this point as the company has invested considerable time and effort to implant corporate EH&S values at the facility and to internalize its safety culture within its work force. Internalization of standardized EH&S practices reduces the vulnerability of foreign subsidiaries in the absence of direct control from the corporation's headquarters.

At the other end of the corporate spectrum, flexibility and adaptation to country- and site-specific conditions would predominate among MNCs with less commitment to creating a homogeneous worldwide corporate culture, as typified by Occidental Chemical. This flexible-adaptive style has its strengths and weaknesses. On the positive side, dependence on the parent is diminished in comparison to the more centralized arrangement, and the company assigns more confidence in the indigenous capability to troubleshoot and find more locally compatible solutions for environmental and safety problems. These mechanisms would be effective even in the absence of parental oversight. Assignment of EH&S responsibilities is likely to invest local managers and workers in problem solving and, in effect, nurtures indigenous capacity and self-reliance characteristic of the Thai Occidental facility. The limitations derive from uncertainties—uncovered but not fully resolved by the three cases studies—as to how quickly and how effectively parent company practices can be transplanted to developing country affiliates and how effective local practices are in a modern technological environment that often is alien to the traditional cultural means of protecting workers and public health. Workplace practices reflect a wide range of cultural forces that shape workers' and managers' attitudes toward EH&S, and transplanting parent country practices does not take place in isolation from these larger social conditions.

Thus, the decentralized approach brings with it certain tensions between promoting indigenous EH&S management capabilities and the achievement and maintenance of parent country performance standards.

Regardless of the MNC preferences on the continuum bound by the centralized and decentralized management styles, joint ownership introduces a significant additional reduction in the corporate degrees of freedom. These additional constraints may lower the system's buffering capacity such that small changes in the EH&S system may have greater effects on the EH&S performance than in wholly owned enterprises. For example, reliance on individual protective devices instead of automated emission controls in the Rampur facility may increase future risks upon consolidation of management responsibilities in the hands of the host country partner *unless* the partner's commitment to Xerox EH&S principles proves equal to that of the parent corporation.

Under these circumstances, various EH&S management choices—investing in safety and pollution control technology versus less automated systems; aggressive behavior modification of workers to make them indistinguishable from those in the parent country; developing a strong culture at the facility versus relying on the parent's oversight—take on additional significance. Some of these decisions reside well upstream in the negotiation process when the joint venture chooses among alternative technologies and hardware systems. Others appear further downstream after a facility is operating, and EH&S performance is more closely linked to management and worker diligence in following procedures, to the allocation of resources for training and retraining staff, and to ensuring maintenance and repair functions receive adequate management attention and resources. All are heavily influenced by attitudes of the joint venture partner, and all affect the long-term EH&S performance.

Terms of Joint Venture Agreement

The issue of division of EH&S responsibility at the facility, inseparable from that of authority over its daily management, can be viewed as closely linked to the issue of distribution of equity shares among partners, although Killing (1983) and Robinson (1988) have argued that no automatic link between ownership and control should be assumed. Allocating control of various facets of an overseas joint venture (including EH&S) can be, according to these authors, negotiated as part of the joint venture agreement, *independent* of the equity shares among partners. Each can be viewed on a continuum ranging, in the case of management control, from one dominated by either partner to that shared or divided according to the specific provisions of the joint venture, its articles of incorporation, or some other legal instrument used to allocate rights and responsibilities. Any such arrangement, in turn, may occur irrespective of whether equity is split equally or unequally in any proportion among partners.

One of the differences between joint ventures negotiated today and those of early years is that short- and long-term EH&S implications are increasingly penetrating corporate thinking and color the relationship between joint venture partners at all stages of facility life. The Xerox and Oxychem case studies indicate that the EH&S matters were indeed on the corporate agendas from the earliest stages of their interactions with the respective partners. The corporate objectives were also clearly delineated: to implement their respective EH&S standards, to take the leadership and primary responsibility for EH&S throughout the facility's life, and to maintain major influence over its daily management. Given such clarity in agenda, it may be surprising that the actual language of the two joint venture agreements is quite general regarding EH&S matters, and in the Modi Xerox case essentially implicit, leaving much to the informal arrangements among the partners.

The lack of specificity characteristic of the investigated Oxychem and Xerox cases need not be perceived as a weakness in the process, although it certainly makes EH&S performance vulnerable to counter-supportive pressure. Informality allows for flexibility and adaptability to changing circumstances. Some are internal to the host country enterprise, such as transition in management responsibility toward the host country partner. Some are external to the enterprise, such as a merger or acquisition of the parent company. Even the most experienced MNC has imperfect capability to predict future EH&S choices while negotiating the terms of the partnership. Most importantly, such flexible arrangements recognize, if only by implication, the necessity for the foreign affiliate to become an entity wherein managers and workers are equipped and willing to address issues that may arise over a facility's life and to maintain EH&S performance that is consistent with the EH&S values of a socially responsible parent corporation.

Self-sustainable EH&S Systems

The need to create a sustainable EH&S system applies to all MNC foreign subsidiaries, those under extensive control by the parent as well as those enjoying greater autonomy, those wholly owned as well as those partly owned by MNC. The concept of sustainable EH&S systems refers to a management system that assures effective and consistent EH&S performance over time. A system is effective if it accomplishes the desired safety and environmental health objectives with the least monetary and motivational costs; it is consistent if it has institutional means at hand to sustain this performance standard even in the presence of changes in hardware, operations, and management style. From the previous discussion we can assume that the more decentralized, jointly owned enterprises are more capable of implementing an efficient strategy to implement EH&S standards than centralized enterprises. However, the decentralized system is usually more prone to mishaps and pitfalls over time, particularly if a sufficient and technology-compatible safety culture is missing. The current global movement among multinationals toward decentralization, and by developing countries toward greater participation in technology imported by MNCs, adds specific weight to the consistency aspect of sustainability. However, both styles—the standardized-centralized and the decentralized-flexible approach—do not automatically guarantee more or less sustainability. Each style has to develop its own policies and structures to ensure effective and consistent EH&S performance.

How can that be accomplished? Vast corporate experience has accumulated over the past two decades on EH&S management at distant affiliates in developing countries. Although the scope of this book does not include exploration and critical evaluation of that body of experience, one of the major themes emerging from the three case studies is that EH&S performance probably depends as much on successful transplantation and internalization of corporate culture to the subsidiary as on the allocation of management responsibilities, pollution-control and safety-hardware oversight by the parent corporation and on host country regulations and enforcement.

In addition, corporate culture can effectively compensate for the vulnerabilities in other aspects of an EH&S system that are attributable to business arrangements. Its importance therefore grows in proportion to the extent of such vulnerabilities. For example, a distant parent's difficulty in enforcing individual safety behaviors at the facility, differences in commitment to EH&S among the partners, acquisition of the parent or partner companies, or risks potentially associated with transition of management from the MNC to host country partner can be significantly offset by local management and workers who share the parent corporation's values, beliefs, and norms. No formal agreement, no matter how finely structured, offers a viable substitute for this unity of mission and vision.

REFERENCES

Contractor, Farok J. "International Business: An Alternative View." *International Marketing Review* (Spring 1986): 74–85.

Datta, Deepak K. "International Joint Ventures: A Framework for Analysis." *Journal of General Management* 14:2(1988): 78–91.

Diamond Shamrock Chemicals Company. *Joint Venture Agreement.* November 4, 1984.

Hlakik, Karen. *International Joint Ventures: An Economic Analysis of U.S.–Foreign Business Partnerships.* Lexington, MA: Lexington Books, 1985.

Killing, J. Peter. *Strategies for Joint Venture Success.* New York: Praeger, 1983.

Kogut, Bruce. "Joint Ventures: Theoretical and Empirical Perspectives." *Strategic Management Journal* 9(1988): 319–332.

Leonard, H. Jeffrey. *Are Environmental Regulations Driving U.S. Industry Overseas?* Washington, DC: Conservation Foundation, 1987.

Mowry, David C. "Collaborative Ventures between U.S. and Foreign Manufacturing Firms." *Research Policy* 18(1989): 19–32.

O'Reilly, Anthony J. F. "Establishing Successful Joint Ventures in Developing Nations: A CEO's Perspective." *Columbia Journal of World Business* 23:1(1988): 65–71.

Rank Xerox–Modi Xerox. *Technical Agreement.* October 27, 1983.

Robinson, Richard D. *The International Transfer of Technology: Theory, Issues, and Practice.* Cambridge, MA: Ballinger, 1988.

Sanger, David E. "Behind the Thai Boom: The Japanese." *New York Times* (May 10, 1990): B1.

Thailand Ministry of Industry. *Factory License Granted to Thai Occidental Chemical Ltd.* June 28, 1989.

Thai Occidental, Joint Venture Agreement between Diamond Shamrock Chemical Company and Thai Group, November 4, 1985. Provided by Thai Occidental in January 1990.

White, Allen L., and Srinivas Emani. *Environmental Regulations in Developing Countries: Case Studies of India, Thailand and Venezuela and Recommendations for Capacity-Building Programs.* Report prepared by Tellus Institute, Boston, for The Center for Environmental Management, Tufts University, 1990.

CHAPTER 8

Synthesis: Value Conflicts and Implications for International Technology Transfer

The facility-siting process is dynamic and interactive. The host country's institutions, the multinational corporation, and the joint venture partner are its principal participants. Each enters the process with a set of objectives and expectations that it is empowered to pursue by means of a variety of policy tools.

The objectives of the key actors are deeply rooted in their values. Chapter 2 identified two clusters of values most likely to explain the behavior of the principal participants in the course of facility-siting: environment, health and safety values, development, equity, and independence values. The first group includes values related to human well-being as well as those related to protection of natural resources. DE&I values include those related to economic growth, such as national prosperity, corporate profitability, standard of living, or productive capacity, as well as those related to national, political, and social goals, such as equitable sharing of the fruits of growth, social justice, self-determination, and international reputation. Collectively, the values, objectives, and expectations of the key actors guide their interactions and ultimately shape facility design and performance in relation to environment, health, and safety.

The explanation of the siting process and facility characteristics observed in the case studies began in Chapter 4 with identifying three factors that constrain the range of options available to the key actors that indirectly influence EH&S outcomes: corporate safety culture, host country development policies, and business arrangements at foreign affiliates. Each factor was explored in depth. The theme of Chapter 5 was that the pursuit of development objectives by host countries via policies toward multinational corporations may indirectly affect environmental, occupational, and safety performance of facilities. The analysis in Chapter 6 focused on the key role of corporate culture in facility negotiations and performance. Chapter 7 focused on the effects of two elements of the business arrangements—the nature of facility ownership and the management arrangement between joint venture partners—on EH&S outcomes.

The purpose of this final chapter is to consolidate the key findings of the study, distinguishing between those that appear specific to the three cases and those that may be generalizable. The analysis concentrates on the entry of EH&S considerations into the facility development process, the roles played by the key actors in shaping the environmental and occupational aspects of MNC facilities in developing countries, and the nature of interactions among the two groups of values, including both conflicts and trade-offs.

CONCEPTUAL MODELING OF FACILITY SITING PROCESS

Facility-siting may be conceptualized as a sequence of events that starts with a contact between the corporation and the government of the host country and ends with an operational facility. In Chapter 2, four stages of that process were identified: negotiations, construction, start-up, and sustained operations. The key types of decisions and events within each stage also were discussed.

This study has focused primarily on the first two stages of facility transfer. The analysis of the subsequent two stages has been conducted only to the extent necessary to (1) understand the effects of the first two stages on the management and performance of EH&S in the three facilities, and (2) to understand the policies of the three corporations relative to EH&S management at their foreign affiliates. Quantitative and qualitative evaluation criteria were used to analyze the stages of the facility's life cycle. The qualitative criteria included an inquiry into the corporate policies on foreign affiliates, evaluation of management systems for implementing EH&S at the foreign affiliates, and specific manifestations of commitment to EH&S goals. These were supplemented with quantitative performance indicators such as standardized incidence rates, compliance with corporate standards (for Xerox), and, for Oxychem, environmental assessment scores. Furthermore, since it was not the purpose of the study to compare the performance of the three facilities with each other or to draw inferences about performance of multinational corporations in general, the analysis of data was limited largely to comparisons of facilities within each corporation. We examined to the extent possible whether the EH&S management practices at the overseas affiliate approximates that of a similar facility in the United States; what the nature and extent of any differences are; whether any differences from the parent country's facility are likely to increase or decrease EH&S risks; how the

U.S.-based facilities of the company compare in performance with its foreign-based facilities; and how the choice of engineered controls, management systems, training, and personal protective devices evolved. As shown later in this chapter, the analysis of the third and fourth stages of the life of each facility was not only crucial for achieving the objectives of this chapter, but also introduced important dimensions to the concepts of functional equivalency and corporate environmentalism.

The chronological model introduced in Chapter 2 is primarily operational: It identifies the decisions and events typical of the various stages of facility development without characterizing the contributions made to these decisions and events by the principal participants or to the EH&S outcomes at the facility level. Now, however, the case studies conducted in the preceding three chapters can be used to illuminate (1) the key forces at work at each stage, and (2) their entry into the process. These are summarized in the input/output model shown in Figure 8.1.

Input and *output* are descriptive terms denoting the categories of variables that shape the interactions among participants at each stage of facility development and contribute to the facility-level outcomes. Two types of inputs can be distinguished: those that characterize the principal participants — their values, policies, and practices — and termed *key variables,* and those that represent the decisions made during a particular stage and that affect the events of the following stage, termed *intervening variables.* Collectively, both types of inputs represent the constraints on, as well as opportunities for, each key actor at each stage of the process.

Although the input/output model contains greater explanatory power than the operational model introduced earlier, it nevertheless remains highly simplified and linear, reducing the complex interactions and feedback loops to a unidirectional flow. Moreover, to maintain consistency with the focus of this study, only those inputs that are related to EH&S outcomes are included. Nonetheless, the model serves as a helpful tool in synthesizing the major findings of the study into a generalized framework applicable to other corporations and host countries.

THE KEY FINDINGS

The Corporations

Multinational corporations as initiators of EH&S dialogue and negotiation. Throughout the facility-siting process, the three corporations displayed leadership in most matters related to EH&S. They entered the process with well-articulated policies, explicit occupational standards, and time-tested procedures for achieving high levels of EH&S performance in the overseas affiliates, often implemented in advance of, or in place of, the host country's practices. For example, the corporations chose to rely on their own occupa-

Figure 8.1
Input/Output Model of Facility Siting

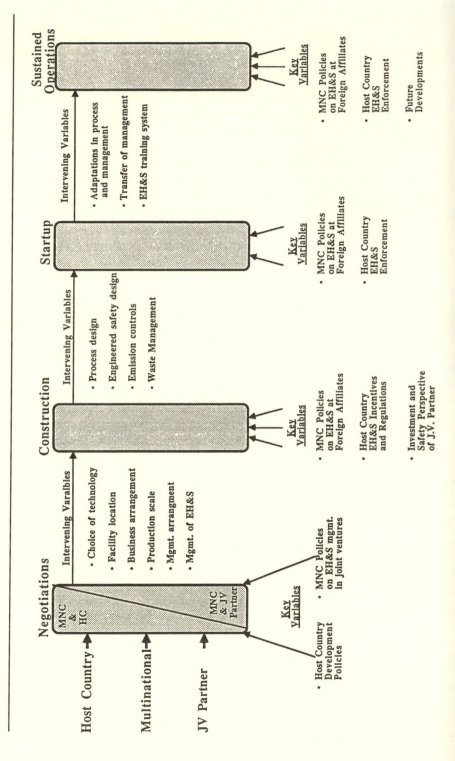

tional standards rather than those of the host countries, and for products with significant downstream hazards (pesticides and leather-tanning agents) took an active interest in managing those hazards. In the absence of adequate local regulations covering hazardous waste disposal, the corporations also assumed primary responsibility in that area: both companies with facilities in Thailand chose on-site treatment of hazardous waste instead of an off-site landfill.

The two companies engaged in jointly owned enterprises also put significant emphasis on maintaining control over the management of EH&S in their respective facilities. The nonnegotiable corporate goal in each case was to create the conditions favorable for implementing the corporate formula for achieving safe and environmentally sound conditions at the forthcoming foreign affiliate: a special mix of technology, training, management, and enforcement. In the Occidental Chemical case, such conditions were partly accomplished through a written agreement that specified the Oxychem standards be adopted at the facility. In the Xerox case, the joint venture agreement was less explicit, relying instead on informal agreements outside the agreement. Equally important in each case was the achievement of understanding between the partners of shared safety and environmental philosophy, cooperation, and the undisputed leadership by the multinational corporation in designing and implementing EH&S systems at each facility.

The corporate leadership in the EH&S area is attributable to several factors. A commitment to establishing environmentally sound and safe facilities, regardless of locations and of local regulations, is clearly one. Such a commitment would motivate a company to ensure control over the decisions that may affect future EH&S outcomes. Hence, the propensity to take charge. It is noteworthy, of course, that the three corporations represent one end of the corporate spectrum in terms of size and resources available for EH&S management and, therefore, are not representative of the industry as a whole. In addition, the ventures examined are recent, the oldest (Du Pont) dating to 1982. The companies and their choice of case-study facilities undoubtedly shift the balance toward the more desirable EH&S outcomes.

Another factor that explains the corporate initiative in the EH&S matters derives from their unchallenged leadership in the matters of technological design and quality control—their primary contribution to the host country— namely, the fundamental link between product quality and EH&S performance. The corporate representatives interviewed for this study consistently perceived high product quality and high EH&S performance as coupled results of a well-managed enterprise. A faithful replication—in its design, management system, and training practices—of an existing facility in a parent country, typically is the most cost-effective method of assuring that the locally manufactured product is identical to that manufactured in the parent country. The Occidental and Modi Xerox cases illustrate this perspective. Many process and material changes in the Thai Occidental facility simultaneously increased cost effectiveness, improved safety, and improved quality of the product, a major reason for the business failure of the previous owner. In the India case, the corporation introduced numerous modifications in the facility's safety and process design in response to the host country's policies, including some that reduced the degree of automated safety, but carefully avoided any modifications that could affect the quality of the product.

Corporate confidence in their technology and management capabilities also played a role in the corporate quest for EH&S leadership. For the three companies, EH&S expertise formed part of the technology package—a set of tested and proved skills, knowledge, and hardware—brought to the host country. Both host countries and joint venture partners welcomed and encouraged this transfer of EH&S know-how.

Corporations as responsible players. The study produced consistent evidence of the companies' serious commitment to sound environmental and occupational management. Some manifestations of that commitment already were mentioned, such as downstream hazard management, explicit articulation of corporate policies, and control over EH&S management in jointly owned enterprises. The three corporations also apply uniform worldwide performance standards at the facilities for occupational accidents and exposures and showed a consistent drop in accident rates over the past decade. Although limited, the database available on compliance with the corporate standards at the three facilities showed no significant departures from company averages. A broader comparison of the safety performance between the U.S.-based facilities and the international facilities of each company, measured by standardized incidence rate, showed that the international facilities have over the years performed in each case as well as, or better than, their domestic counterparts. Because of the uncertainty in practices of reporting incidents leading to lost work days, such findings warrant caution.

One of the limitations of the data collected through this study is the superficial evaluation of the actual performance of the three facilities. This is partly because of a primary focus on negotiations, construction, and, to a lesser extent, on start-up, and sustained operations. Moreover, at the time of this study the three facilities were still relatively new, thereby disallowing the performance tracking over a 5- to 10-year period necessary for more reliable performance measurement. Within these limitations, the study uncovered no evidence of major shortcomings in the facilities' performances. All three appeared to comply with corporate standards, and all have been subject to consistent oversight by the parent EH&S managers.

While these findings are no doubt slanted by the self-selection of corporations and facilities, they depart from the view that facilities of even leading corporations in developing countries are likely to under perform in relation to the parent country counterparts, owing to the lax regulatory climate of such countries (Ives 1985, Castleman 1987, Flaherty and Rappaport 1991,

Rappaport and Flaherty 1991). Most challenges to that notion of "double standard" have traditionally come from the industry itself, primarily through emphasizing the importance of reputation, liability costs, and moral responsibility as the motivating factors (Winter 1988, Anderson and Leal 1991, Bergen Conference 1990) and have therefore been viewed with skepticism. Although independent reports to the contrary have been made as well (Royston 1985), little supporting empirical data have been available until now.

In the limited sample of firms we analyzed, the interviews with the managers and executives of the three corporations pointed to liability, global reputation, and moral responsibility as powerful inducements to responsible corporate conduct. In addition, the three case studies indicate that the effects of pursuing quality control and cost-effectiveness are equally important.

The presence of direct economic and technological components among the factors favoring responsible corporate EH&S conduct is likely to be characteristic of a wide range of technologies and corporations, including those with lesser resources and corporate commitment of the EH&S values than the three participants here.

Notwithstanding the apparent commitment to sound EH&S performance, the three corporations exhibited a surprisingly modest interest in retrospective and interregional evaluation of the actual performance of their many facilities, as discussed in Chapter 3. Indeed, most of the comparative performance analyses presented earlier in this book, both interfacility and time trends, were produced in response to specific requests that developed over the course of the research. It appears that the primary corporate use of the quantitative performance indicators is to set internal goals for each facility, to motivate local personnel to improve facility performance, and to spot significant departures from company averages. Other potential uses of the quantitative performance indicators—for example, as an analytical tool for testing the double standard hypothesis—does not appear to hold intrinsic interest for the firms. This finding is particularly significant considering that the three corporations represent the leading end of the corporate spectrum in terms of size, resources, and commitment to EH&S.

The corporate commitment to EH&S revealed in this study does not necessarily equate with long-term guarantees of strong performance. EH&S performance is tightly coupled with the culture of the parent company and with the effective transplanting to the foreign subsidiary. Corporate culture is, however, a dynamic phenomenon, continuously in need of reinforcement and feedback, and highly sensitive to future internal and external changes in economic circumstances, corporate leadership, shifts in management arrangements, relaxation of parent corporation's oversight, and changes in the ownership arrangements. Thus, the future performance of the three facilities will only be answerable through monitoring over a period well beyond the time of this study.

The Process

Environment, health, and safety considerations during negotiations. The case studies show that while the environmental and occupational matters were notably absent from negotiations between the corporations and the host countries, they were prominent during negotiations between the corporations and their respective joint venture partners. This is to be expected since many issues commonly included in formal joint venture agreements — division of management responsibilities, hiring authority, equity participation, liability — are integrally related to EH&S control.

In the two cases, the joint venture agreements gave the MNCs principal authority for EH&S management and, at least during the initial years of the facilities operation, the major role in overall management. However, these EH&S arrangements were formalized only in the most general language in the written documents. The tasks of defining the implementation tools and principles, and of resolving any future disagreements, were left largely to the partners and to the managers of each facility, to be worked out informally over time.

It is not clear whether the informality in the EH&S arrangements between partners was intended by the MNCs or was simply an outcome of negotiations that primarily focused on other matters. In any event, its major consequence was that of assuring a commitment to corporate EH&S philosophy by the host country partner and a willingness to do whatever was necessary to achieve that goal. The chronologies of the two jointly owned ventures indicate early and systematic attempts by the MNC to secure such a commitment. Occidental Chemical was even willing to forgo the business deal in the event it could not secure control of EH&S at the Bangpoo facility. In both cases, it appears that the joint venture partners were essentially receptive to the idea that safety is a good business investment or, as an Occidental Chemical executive phrased it, "pay now or pay later."

Beyond these general agreements, however, several questions remain unanswered, due in part to the design of the study and in part to our inability to gain access to the joint venture partners. These include the depth of the long-term commitment by the host country venture partner to investing in engineered safety infrastructure; the depth of the long-term commitment by the MNC to continuous reinforcement of its EH&S philosophy and, if necessary, to overriding the partner in disagreements; the future effects of shifts in top management responsibility to the host country partner; and the long-term effects of local conditions on the MNC's success in maintaining the safety culture at its foreign affiliate. In short, relationships between the joint venture partners in Stage 4 — sustained operations — remains unchartered territory.

In contrast to the joint venture partners' negotiations, those between the corporations and the host countries largely consisted of economic, technical, locational, and ownership-related aspects of the proposed facility. In each case, the host country, which greatly influenced the agenda, actively pursued its development objectives. India viewed the Modi Xerox application as an opportunity to pursue multiple economic, social, and technological objectives. The remote location of the facility reflects the policy of regional development; the full integration of the xerographic technology in Rampur reflects the country's pursuit of advanced foreign technologies; the ceiling on domestic production serves as a preventive measure against market domination by multinationals; and the ceiling on MNC equity participation is aimed at limiting the MNC's power and promoting domestic industrial development. The protracted and inflexible (from the MNC's perspective) negotiations were consistent with India's regulatory style, which is characterized by active and far-reaching government involvement through extensive use of direct controls.

In Thailand, where economic growth receives decidedly more weight than in India, expedient and mostly indirect administrative procedures took the place of direct negotiations. Whereas the Board of Investment was clearly interested in the matters of location, equity participation, and the size and nature of technology, its mode of influencing the companies was indirect, via incentives, which preserves corporate choice in final decisions.

In the three cases, the host countries' authorities most directly engaged in negotiations with the MNCs delegated EH&S matters to local authorities and, for the most part, to the later stages in the facility-siting process. Thus, in Thailand the major (though not exclusive) regulatory responsibility fell to the industrial estate, whereas in India it rested with the local and state authorities.

In India, the minor role of EH&S considerations during negotiations may be traced to the system of environmental and locational regulations for manufacturing facilities. Environmental issues become significant to the central government when the potential impacts of the proposed facility are a dominant, rather than incidental, feature of a proposed facility and when such impacts are geographically sensitive. This is the case with highly polluting, resource-intensive industries such as metal processing, paper manufacturing, mining, or energy generation. In those cases, environmental concerns tend to emerge early and prominently as part of negotiations over facility location. For less polluting industries, such as the Modi Xerox facility, the environmental impacts are viewed as a routine matter best handled by state authorities during the design, construction, and operational stages of the facility-siting process. That this was the case in the Rampur facility is evident from the industrial license issued by the Ministry of Industry after two years of negotiations; the license is conditioned upon compliance with all applicable state environmental regulations.

In the two Thai cases, the delegation of the EH&S matters largely to the industrial estate authorities is consistent with the country's administrative structure, with the relatively minor projected environmental impacts of the two facilities, and with Thailand's laissez-faire posture vis-à-vis multinationals. However, the dominant developmental mission of the Industrial Estate Authority in Thailand, as compared with state pollution control boards in India, together with weak enforcement, creates the preconditions for minimal sustained government oversight. Our findings and prognoses are consistent with the results of a survey conducted by the United Nations among multinational investors in facilities in Thailand: inclusion of environmental conditions in formal documents was uncommon; the great majority of those interviewed admitted to meeting only the minimum EH&S requirements of the host country; and a majority believe that a double standard was widely practiced by multinationals in Thailand (United Nations Economic and Social Commission for Asia and the Pacific 1988 and 1990).

Based on analysis of negotiations between host country and MNC investors in highly polluting or resource-intensive technologies in Ireland, Mexico, Spain, and Rumania, Leonard (1985, 1988) also notes the low visibility of EH&S matters. When EH&S negotiations did occur, it was on a case-by-case basis rather that in response to formal host country or corporate policies and usually in response to local public pressure or the initiative of a concerned local official. Among the factors identified by Leonard as contributing to the absence of EH&S negotiations were:

1. procedural factors—general bargaining that tends to proceed in stages, with each stage centering on a different level of government and different aspects of the enterprise. That increases the likelihood that the EH&S matters will fall between the cracks, especially when the connection—often indirect—between the early decisions and their EH&S implications are not perceived at any one stage by the parties involved.

2. institutional factors—environmental policies often developed and implemented by local and regional authorities, whereas the licensing process and the accompanying negotiations are led by central authorities. Furthermore, it is not uncommon for the central authorities to have few means of ensuring that the EH&S conditions they would like to impose on the MNC will in fact be endorsed and enforced by regional and local authorities.

3. conceptual/historical factors—host country institutions that often suffer from lack of experience, poor access to technical information, short planning horizons, narrowly defined missions, and lack of vision.

Conditions contributing to low EH&S profile during the negotiations in our case studies can be found in the list. Yet the similar practices of delegating most EH&S responsibilities to local authorities demonstrated by two countries as different as India and Thailand suggest that relatively nonpolluting industries are handled in similar fashion in other countries, regardless of the political and socioeconomic context.

Our cases also suggest that many procedural and institutional factors listed by Leonard, and operative in our cases, are linked to the dominant development philosophy of the host country. Thailand, where the institutional missions, responsibilities, and procedures bearing on the EH&S directly reflect the country's overriding commitment to development values, serves as a particularly telling example.

Environment, health, and safety considerations during construction and downstream stages. This is the stage when the multinational, as the owner of the technology, is expected to assume a leading role, although that leadership is constrained by three sets of factors: various host country constraints previously solidified through negotiations and exerted indirectly through the conditions of industrial license; the need to account for the joint venture partner's views; and the necessity to respond to the host country's environmental and occupational regulations.

Relative to the negotiations, EH&S was a pervasive theme during the construction stage, although manifestations were highly case-specific. The three case studies show that the MNCs responded to the constraints created during the negotiations in a manner consistent with their respective safety philosophies and past experiences with foreign affiliates. Du Pont, having achieved the greatest flexibility of the three (owing to whole ownership and the limited role of the Thai government), proceeded to design a facility practically identical to any Du Pont formulation/packaging plant anywhere in the world. Blueprints for facility design and construction were developed at the U.S. headquarters. This was to be another Du Pont facility that happened to be in Thailand, with only minor modifications to a standard design. At this stage, for example, the company installed a vacuum system for dust control in order to eliminate the need for face masks, a particularly cumbersome device in the Thai climate.

For Occidental and Xerox, the construction stage necessitated adaptation to constraints introduced by the joint venture partners, the host country, and, in the case of Occidental, the history of the facility itself. These included scaling down and redesigning the India facility; upgrading and significantly modifying the Thai facility; and, in both India and Thailand, introducing workers and management to the corporate safety philosophy and policies. Also during construction the host countries began implementing their respective environmental and safety regulations. True to its philosophy vis-à-vis multinationals, the Thai government showed only modest interest in the design of the safety and environmental features of the facilities. India, in contrast, exercised considerable oversight over the environmental design aspects, such as waste water and hazardous waste treatment technology. For the MNCs, the prominence of EH&S considerations during construction is most likely a general phenomenon for firms with strong commitments in that area, since design decisions are integral to long-term EH&S performance.

Our limited analysis of the downstream stages of the three facilities suggests that EH&S played a significant role in the interactions of the key actors during start-up and sustained operations, both in the highly regulated India and the more open Thai settings. This took the form of EH&S training, adaptations in process and management, inspections by host country officials, and oversight by the parent corporation. From the corporate perspective, these activities are typical for hazardous technologies and likely to occur to some degree at all foreign affiliates.

In summary, the case studies suggest that the EH&S considerations enter the facility-siting process in a predictable manner, conceptualized in Figure 8.1. For relatively nonpolluting technologies, their entry during the first two stages is initiated primarily by the MNC. In wholly owned ventures EH&S matters play a minor role during the host country/corporation negotiations, followed by high visibility during construction. In joint ventures, the EH&S matters are prominent during the negotiations between the partners, again primarily due to the MNC initiative. During the downstream stages, the EH&S matters are a recurrent theme in the interactions of all principal participants.

Downstream EH&S consequences of upstream business decisions. The relatively minor role of EH&S during negotiations between the host country and the corporation does not imply that EH&S outcomes are unrelated to such negotiations. To the contrary. One of our major findings is that the decisions made jointly during the negotiations by a host country and a corporation, which appear remote from the safety matters, nevertheless had significant though delayed effects on the EH&S outcomes. Moreover, these effects created in some instances a strain between host country development and EH&S objectives, created inadvertently by the vigorous pursuit a development agenda.

The specific workings of the Thai industrial estates illustrate that phenomenon. The estates successfully serve as magnets for foreign investors because of their superior infrastructures and relief from congestion in Bangkok. However, they also allow, or even induce, the concentration of large numbers of hazardous facilities in close proximity to each other and to the neighboring community.

The multiple functions of the Industrial Estate Authority of Thailand, which manages the industrial estates—to help foreign corporations obtain necessary permits, to manage the infrastructure of the industrial estates, to coexist productively with the joint venture partner, to set and enforce environmental standards, and to oversee the safety of the resident facilities—illustrate even more strikingly the effects of the Thai pursuit of efficiency. They produce a weakened, conflict-averse agency with strong preference for negotiated rather than imposed solutions to any conflicts. This gives multinationals substantial flexibility to implement the EH&S systems of their choice, good and bad, without measurable input from the authorities.

Would the safety and environmental outcomes of negotiations be more favorable if efficiency played a secondary role to government-initiated direct influence on the activities of multinational corporations? The India case shows that such a system may create a different set of trade-offs. In this case the combination of the antimonopoly and technology transfer policies of India imposed on the company two contradictory requirements: to "backward integrate" the technology, and to keep domestic production low. These requirements led the corporation to choose a scaled down and highly integrated facility and, in pursuit of cost-effective solutions, to opt for a manual rather than an engineered safety system. Although the adjustment was clearly adequate to meet the corporate occupational standard, it nevertheless put to test the corporate safety policy of using engineered safety systems as the primary method of controlling employee exposure to hazardous agents.

To ensure maintenance of EH&S standards under these conditions will require of Modi Xerox a persistent and focused corporate commitment to safety on the part of both Rank-Xerox and Modi Xerox management. Its success will also depend on the effectiveness of transfer of corporate philosophy to the joint venture partner and to a work force that will outlast the initial intense oversight by the parent company and serve as the principal players for addressing future EH&S problems. We observed the beginnings of such an effort at the case study corporations, but clearly continuation cannot be assumed. As analyses of the Bhopal accident have shown, accumulation of unfavorable external economic, regulatory, locational, and management conditions, in conjunction with inadequate corporate commitment to safety, can lead to gradual deterioration of standards with potentially disastrous consequences (Bowonder, Kasperson, and Kasperson 1985, Gladwin 1987a, Shrivastava 1987, Weir 1987).

Summary of variables. Based on the foregoing discussion, the key variables introduced in the conceptual model in Figure 8.1 may now summarized. The case studies also suggest that these inputs may be generalized to other cases where conditions are comparable: a host country with a well-articulated development agenda and a multinational corporation with strong commitment to environment, health, and safety.

During the first stage, host country development policies are a key independent variable. In addition, the company's policies relative to EH&S at international affiliates play an important role by shaping its attitudes toward joint ventures, and toward negotiating with venture partners. The outputs of the first stage, manifested in an industrial license and joint venture agreement, represent de facto a comprehensive blueprint of the facility before the engineer's blueprints are produced.

During the second stage, which is dominated by the technology owner, the MNC's policies on EH&S continue to play a major role. The host country's presence, secondary to that of the MNC, is manifested primarily through various EH&S permits. The perspective of the joint venture partner on EH&S matters may also affect the design of the facility, including its environmental and occupational features.

During the third and fourth stages, corporate policies relative to their foreign affiliates, including training, enforcement, oversight, and reporting, clearly play an important role. Similarly, host country enforcement plays a significant part at both stages. In addition, the long-term EH&S performance at the MNC facilities will depend on the extent to which the corporate safety culture is transplanted to the foreign affiliate. This will be partly reflected in the training system implemented during the start-up stage. Other elements of that culture are, however, less tangible, as discussed in Chapter 6.

The management arrangements in jointly owned ventures are also important in the last two stages, primarily in cases where partners differ in their EH&S objectives and where the joint venture agreement provides for gradual transition of management from the shared arrangement to one dominated by the host country partner. The significance of this factor in maintaining safety at MNC facilities has been raised by several authors (Ashford and Ayers 1985, Gladwin and Walter 1976, United Nations Centre on Transnational Corporations 1988, p. 233). Finally, a variety of external circumstances has affected the long-term facility performance, as the Bhopal case dramatically illustrates. These are the key variables of future developments.

Figure 8.1 highlights the importance of corporate culture in determining the facility-level EH&S outcomes. In its different forms, such as corporate policies on international EH&S management and on joint ventures, corporate culture affects all stages of the process. It also illustrates the large array of constraints on the principal participants as they progressively address various issues over the course of the transaction. These constraints rapidly increase in number at the conclusion of negotiations and remain numerous. Once the negotiations are completed, the flexibility of the principal participants, including the corporations, is severely limited.

As proposed earlier, the case studies suggest that the types and timing of the inputs shown in the conceptual model — the key variables and intervening variables — are common to other cases of facility siting. That is not to say, however, that similar starting ingredients (type of technology, type of corporation, type of host country regulations) will yield similar products in a form of facility management and performance. At the heart of this generic model is a complex chemistry of interactions of policies related to environment, health, and safety values and those related to development, equity, and independence values. Outcomes are difficult to predict. When these interactions lead to tension among mutually desirable but competing objectives, corporate culture may become a crucial determinant in how that tension is resolved.

Lessons Learned

Hidden trade-offs. How clearly do the host countries and multinational corporations perceive the linkages between the negotiations and their downstream consequences? How clearly do they perceive the connections between values and specific implementation policies? How explicitly are trade-offs made? The answers vary and depend on case-specific circumstances. The limited scope of this study allows for tentative but instructive observations at best, based on a mix of evidence and inferences.

In the case of Thailand, the increasingly urgent concerns voiced during recent years over the environmental effects of rapid industrialization of the country suggest that the trade-offs highlighted by two of the case studies are not new discoveries. (Christensen 1990, Hirsh and Lohmann 1989, Ruyabhorn and Phantumvanit 1988). The types of trade-offs illustrated by the Xerox case, however, were different. They were indirect and incremental and arose in response to early decisions not apparently related to EH&S matters. Such trade-offs were less likely to be foreseen during negotiations. This is for several reasons.

First, a substantial interval (usually several years) normally separates the negotiation stage and the construction and operation phases. In India, that interval was close to four years. Even in the expedient Thai system of industrial licensing, the interval would have likely approached a year or more.

Second, the complexity of the linkages between the independent variables and the EH&S outcomes at the facility level further complicates the predictive ability of both corporation and host country. It favors making decisions, including any trade-offs, incrementally and in a fragmented manner. In the Modi Xerox case, for example, the EH&S managers were not included in the decision to implement a fully integrated small-scale plant. Similarly, the safety technology was chosen incrementally at the facility, partially by trial and error.

Third, the division of responsibilities for regulating multinational corporations among several host country institutions is a significant obstacle to formulating a comprehensive view of the ongoing interactions. Each institution is committed to its particular mission, shaped by its historical context and by select values, which it pursues through narrowly conceived policies and objectives. This is particularly vivid in the Thai system where the mission of the Board of Investments is distinctly different from that of the National Environmental Board and where the administrative process does not envision a platform that forces both institutions to jointly consider the economic, geographic, health, environmental, and other aspects of a proposed facility. Although in India the process attempts to create common ground in the form of the technical committee assembled within the Ministry of Industry, the scope of the committee's deliberations may not be all-inclusive. Consequently, the agencies most likely to bring up the matters of environment, health, and safety, such as state pollution control boards or the state inspector of factories, were excluded from the first stage of the process.

Finally, it is unlikely that government officials, whose primary responsibilities are to see that the specific development policies are implemented and objectives achieved, would know, or want to know, about the potential effects of their efforts on the safety systems in the facilities.

The practical meaning of functional equivalency. Among the dimensions of the debate on the norms of conduct for multinational corporations in developing countries, two questions have been particularly prominent: Should the MNCs apply uniform worldwide standards, even if that means inconsistency with local regulations (when such are less protective than their own)? Should the EH&S objective be to install systems at foreign facilities identical to those in their domestic counterparts, or should the functional equivalency be sought instead?

A decade ago, Shue (1981) conceptualized the first question as a conflict between EH&S values and economic values and used the principle of an individual's right to no harm to argue in favor of equality in protection among MNC domestic and foreign facilities, regardless of the host country's regulations. That question has also underlined the recurrent accusations that MNCs apply double standards in the operations of their home and developing countries facilities (Ives 1985, Castleman 1987), counteracted by claims that MNCs operate according to high standards (Royston 1979, 1985). From a normative perspective several governmental and nongovernmental organizations and trade associations, leading multinationals, and various consensus-seeking groups (Renn et al. 1991) have become vocal proponents of uniform standards as well as functional equivalency. The Tripartite Declaration of Principles Concerning Multinational Enterprises and Social Policy by the International Labor Organization (1977) called for "the highest standards of safety and health." More recently, the World Commission on Environment and Development called for the "highest safety and health protection standards practicable" (1987), while the OECD Ministerial Declaration (1989) stated that "affiliates of enterprises which are based in OECD countries should operate those facilities at equivalent levels of safety." The UN Commission on Transnational Corporations echoed these sentiments (1991) by stressing in its report to the secretary general the need for uniform worldwide standards.

The arguments presented by the three companies in support of uniform worldwide standards are compelling. In addition to moral obligations, the corporations cited economic arguments: It is more cost-effective to have a single implementation and enforcement system worldwide; it is also more cost-effective to install engineered safety during facility construction instead of retrofitting later, an increasingly likely scenario as developing countries catch up and mimic industrialized countries in their environmental and occupational regulations.

Friedman (1991) defines functional equivalency as maintaining the same level of protection of human health and environment among facilities by employing site-specific methods for achieving it. For example, different technologies may be employed among facilities to achieve compliance with a uniform worldwide occupational standard; or a company may substitute a best-available-technology method, legally mandated in the United States, with an environmental standard in order to protect the natural resources from effects of pollutants. So defined, functional equivalency is distinct from faithful replication of the EH&S system of an equivalent facility elsewhere, both in terms of hardware and management.

Three arguments in favor of functional equivalency (rather than exact replication) are that it favors adaptation to local conditions, usually necessary to implement the manufacturing process and often actually a source of improved performance; it circumvents certain parent country requirements that may be motivated by social or legal reasons, and not be directly related to improved performance; it is the closest approximation of the cost-effective reproduction of an equivalent domestic facility, which, as discussed earlier in this chapter, may be favored on the economic grounds.

The difficulty with Friedman's definition is its lack of specificity on how the equality in the level of protection should be measured and ascertained. The simplest approach would consist of compliance with uniform worldwide corporate occupational and environmental standards. That definition is very useful because it allows for relatively objective evaluation of compliance with that EH&S objective.

Applying that definition of functional equivalency to the three case studies (while acknowledging its limitations) shows that the three corporations indeed adopted functional equivalency as their objective and that each interpreted the concept according to the case-specific circumstances and to its own tradition. Du Pont, which has the longest accumulated experience with occupational safety and whose corporate culture accords high value to tradition, consistency, predictability, and foresight, was least likely to experiment with time-tested design and implementation systems. Furthermore, the simplicity of the Du Pont technology, the existence of a similar facility elsewhere, and the wide-ranging flexibility the company had in the Thai environment further reinforced reliance on a well-tested model. Not surprisingly, Du Pont attempted to replicate as faithfully as possible all the components of its EH&S system, using equivalent Du Pont domestic facilities as templates and making some additional local adaptations.

In the cases of Modi Xerox and Occidental Chemical, the companies relied on their respective accumulated experience, but did not attempt to replicate their equivalent facilities elsewhere by installing identical safety and pollution control systems. Instead, they chose the engineering safety and pollution control systems during facility design and construction, and later relied on performance indicators, such as compliance with corporate standards and recordable incidence records, to verify the functional equivalency of the facilities. The difference can be attributed partly to the fact that Modi Xerox and Oxychem facilities were more complex and represented substantial departures from their closest equivalents in other countries.

The three case studies suggest that the terms of the debate have been generally miscast in relation to EH&S leaders within the industrial sector. Uniform standards and functional equivalency are the most sensible and workable principles for such corporations to adopt. Therefore, the question should be *not whether functional equivalency ought to be the objective, but how to interpret that principle.* The case studies also indicate that corporations retain a substantial flexibility in that interpretation and therefore the outcome is consistent with general corporate philosophy on business development and EH&S.

The flexibility in implementation of the uniform standards and equivalency principles clearly represents a window of opportunity for some companies, but for others it is a loophole for compromise. The individual interpretation will no doubt be determined by the depth of the corporate commitment to the fundamental environmental and safety values.

Value conflicts and trade-offs. Most observers believe that national and corporate development goals must be harmonized with EH&S values. This consensus rests upon two assumptions.

First, for the most part, this literature takes for granted that view that the several distinct social, individual, and environmental values included in the EH&S cluster are in fact mutually compatible. We share this view, and it is easy to sketch some of the arguments that might support it: Environmental protection promotes public health; facility design and management choices that limit toxic environmental discharges are consistent with design and management choices to limit workers' exposure; and a strong safety culture is prerequisite to an environmentally responsible corporation.

Second, with only a few exceptions, it is assumed that multinational corporations and developing countries have sufficiently strong and similar commitments to EH&S values to permit constructive and collaborative pursuit of shared goals. Our conclusions are generally consistent with this view. None of the key actors whom we have studied can be fairly represented as having an overriding interest in a single value (e.g., economic growth, corporate profit, or national self-determination).

With regard to the two countries we have studied, India is the stronger case in point. A strong national commitment to development is modulated by commitments to self-reliance and to independence and to environmental, health, and safety values. But Thailand's decision to adopt a development path driven by the view that "wealthier is healthier" should not be taken as evidence of a unidimensional national commitment to this one value. On the contrary, it should be taken as evidence of a different understanding of the relationships between different values in specific economic and historical circumstances. Thai policy has given priority to the pursuit of economic development goals, not because it devalues equity or ignores EH&S concerns, but because it was based on a particular understanding, which construes economic development as the instrumental precondition for fulfilling other values. As Thailand's economic and political situation has evolved, so has the sequential viewpoint of the relationship between development and

EH&S policies. One sees today that increasing attention to the environmental, social, and cultural aspects of economic development.

With regard to the three corporations, it is equally clear that each company is concerned with multiple values. To be sure, each company's initial decision to build in Thailand or India was motivated by corporate development values: profit, market share, and market access. Nevertheless, each step taken to implement that initial decision was clearly conditioned by respect for the host countries' development policies and by local socioeconomic realities. All three corporations made design, investment, and management decisions with an eye toward *better* EH&S performance than host country regulations require. Our research suggests that these decisions are grounded in a complex set of ethical, cultural, economic, and technical considerations—not in a simplistic devotion to any single overriding value.

It is now widely understood that in order to provide for the well-being of future generations, it is necessary to treat the Earth's natural resources as a precious and irreplaceable endowment. In a similar way, many large and visible multinational corporations now understand that their own prosperity and survival is tightly linked to their EH&S attitudes and reputation. This understanding is evident not only in new corporate structures and policies, but even in such slogans as "Safety pays." Since both of these understandings are widely shared by the important players in international technology transfer, it is not surprising that our research—focused on good corporate actors and sophisticated host nations—found all the key actors to be concerned with multiple values.

In particular transactions, it can be difficult to perceive this commitment to the multiple goods included in the DE&I and EH&S value sets. But this is an issue of perspective; for, in the same way, it is impossible to appreciate the harmonious interplay of multiple colors and shapes in a painting if one focuses only on particular brushstrokes. As the aesthetic coherence of the picture emerges only when all the individual strokes are taken in their interrelated aggregate, so the value coherence of a particular facility siting or technology transfer may emerge only when all the particular decisions and transactions (regarding business arrangements, facility design, management, etc.) are taken in their interrelated aggregate.

Although it is clear that all the major actors studied in this research were guided by a substantial set of shared values, the specific decisions investigated in the case studies represent, for the most part, the brushstrokes rather than the painting. And at this level, one cannot expect unbroken harmony. On the contrary, there is considerable competition and conflict between the various values and goods, which (on a larger scale) are sought by all participants.

Most of the value conflicts noted in the case studies were experienced internally by the key actors. For example, key Thai actors were acutely aware of the evolving tensions between economic growth and EH&S protection. India officials struggled to balance a long list of worthy social and national goals, knowing that each goal has a significant economic price. And in at least one of the corporate cases, there was a clear internal tension between the company's development and business values and its EH&S values.

Perhaps the most obvious conflicts between actors in the case studies centered on discussions between the MNC and the local venture partner regarding the level of capital and managerial investment in EH&S performance.

Reviewing all the value conflicts noted in the case studies, several observations emerge. First, the most difficult conflicts appear to be internal conflicts experienced by the host countries. Because these conflicts are deeply rooted in each country's history and national identity, and may only be resolvable by significant policy and institutional shifts, their resolution will be a challenging task for any government. By comparison, the internal value conflicts experienced by the corporate players, which were typically resolvable by modest allocations of additional resources, seem almost trivially simple.

Second, value conflicts may not be identified by key actors until the siting process is far advanced (or even completed). In part, this is because there are so many other issues to be dealt with and so many institutions and individuals involved. In part, it is due to the incremental nature of the decision process itself. In the India case, for example, the host country's unwillingness to make trade-offs between its multiple development objectives was simply internalized by the MNC and became an internal economics versus EH&S problem for the corporation. The failure to recognize and explicitly consider value trade-offs earlier in the process has serious costs: Choices may be made without a clear perception of their indirect or long-term implications for the central value trade-offs, and the key actors may miss opportunities to negotiate or devise solutions that produce more optimal results for all concerned.

Third, the value conflicts uncovered by our case studies are almost all of the "weak" variety—meaning that the policy and implementation options that would best advance some value competed for scarce attention and resources with the policy and implementation options that would best advance other values, but that there is no inherent conflict between the values themselves. Moreover, all these conflicts could have been significantly ameliorated (though not eliminated) by creative institutional and policy changes, by greater foresight and flexibility in the negotiating process, or by an increased allocation of national or corporate resources.

For example, in Thailand, a more balanced distribution of power between the agencies dedicated to economic growth and those dedicated to EH&S objectives, coupled with some decentralization of the government's EH&S regulatory and enforcement network, might substantially improve EH&S outcomes without reducing the pace of direct foreign investments. In this regard, India offers a model of development regulation that Thailand might emulate. At the same time, Thailand's strategic use of its menu of investment incentives offers India a model that could substantially increase corporate investment without compromising national social goals or international prestige.

Ongoing value conflicts between the MNC and the joint venture partner can be alleviated by the MNC holding a majority or complete ownership (as in two of the cases) or by explicit management agreements that give the MNC control over facility design and EH&S management. In the India case, these conflicts could have been dealt with more easily if the host country had shown greater flexibility in its policy implementation and if the full costs of EH&S management had been put on the table early in the negotiation stage.[1]

In conclusion, this study does not support the commonly accepted belief that strong conflicts between DE&I and EH&S values are an inevitable feature of international technology transfers. Nor does it support the belief that, when value conflicts do arise, they will typically be of the inter-actor type, between the host country and the MNC—and, more particularly, that they will center on conflicts between corporate business values and host country EH&S values. Three explanations for this finding are possible.

First, the self-selected actors involved in these three case studies may represent only a small and atypical minority of the actors involved in technology transfer worldwide. On this hypothesis, the old stereotype may still be true for most actors, but some socially responsible MNCs have shown that it *need not remain true.*

Second, the study may reflect recent but fundamental changes in the attitudes and relationships of developing countries and multinational corporations. As corporations and countries struggle to implement a new vision of sustainable development, they are more likely to deal cooperatively with the multitude of competing goals, values, and constraints. On this view, changing attitudes and circumstances have made the old stereotypes obsolete.

Third, as ideologically driven rhetoric gradually gives way to pragmatism and flexibility, business and DE&I and EH&S values may be naturally moving toward a new and very different equilibrium. From this perspective, the old stereotypes—replete with severe conflicts and evil actors—may have run their course.

Corporate environmentalism. Throughout this volume, repeated references have been made to the changing relationship of the multinational corporations and society, especially concerning the EH&S and international development. More recently, the concept of corporate environmentalism has taken root among the progressive corporations to give voice to that general philosophy (Woolard 1989, Winter 1988).

What is corporate environmentalism in relation to MNC overseas facilities and, more pointedly, how can it be achieved at these facilities? The case

[1]In fact, in 1992, immediately following the completion of the Rampur case study, India embarked on such a liberalization policy toward multinational corporations, which includes lifting the restrictions on majority ownership by MNCs of their foreign affiliates.

studies suggest that the *corporate view* of that concept can be operationally defined through the following principles of conduct:

- The corporation needs to maintain major influence over the design and management of the facility, regardless of the ownership arrangements.

- The corporation needs to assume leadership in many decisions concerned with EH&S, regardless of the degree of host country regulations and enforcement.

- Foreign facilities should be, at minimum, functionally equivalent to those at domestic facilities.

- Transfer of home country EH&S systems to developing countries requires site-specific adaptations to accommodate local natural environment, infrastructure, nature of the work force, and social arrangements, as well as cultural, historical, and religious circumstances. These adaptations determine the ultimate mix of four EH&S implementation tools for achieving functional equivalence: engineering controls, management system, education and training, and personal safety devices.

- Transfer of corporate commitment and policies to the foreign affiliates, combined with clever local adaptations, realistic planning horizons, and district implementation, assures the equivalence in EH&S performance.

In short, the three case studies suggest that the corporate concept of environmentalism in overseas facilities derives from a fundamental confidence in the power of technology and good management, capacity to innovate, value of parent company's experience, and the force of corporate accountability. It is also premised on the assumed relative corporate freedom in implementing these principles of conduct by the corporation. This confidence appears to be shared by other organizations and individuals, as illustrated by policy statements calling for corporate contribution to sustainable development (International Chamber of Commerce 1989, United Nations Centre on Transnational Corporations 1988, United Nations Environmental Programme 1989).

The case studies indicate that the corporate freedom can be significantly constrained by the host country's pursuit of development objectives, the nature of the relationship with a joint venture partner, and by its own tradition and culture. Whereas it is unlikely that such constraints would result in major compromise in EH&S performance among socially responsible corporations, other subtle trade-offs may occur, especially when the connection between the upstream decisions and downstream facility outcomes are not perceived early in the process. In light of these findings, the concept of corporate environmentalism may need careful and repeated reevaluation.

RECOMMENDATIONS

Our chronicle of three facilities suggests that sound EH&S performance at the MNC overseas facilities requires more than the know-how and resources and a commitment by the key actors to do the right thing (Renn, Brown, and White 1991). Specific procedural and structural changes may be necessary if the trade-offs between the EH&S and DE&I values at work during facility development are to be satisfactorily reconciled. Based on the study results, we recommend three such changes, addressed specifically to host countries and MNCs committed to responsible EH&S management.

1. Include environment, health, and safety in the agenda for negotiations between the host country and the MNC. For technologies not perceived as highly polluting, acutely hazardous, or resource-intensive, EH&S issues are likely to be introduced into the development process after the main features of the facility have been settled. Without a concerted effort to alter the current modus operandi, both sides will continue with their current patterns: a reactive corporate attitude of "do not bring it up unless asked to do so" and a host country focused primarily on social, economic, and political priorities.

   Shifting EH&S issues into the earlier part of the process would have several benefits. First, it would give the key players a clearer vision of the links between non-EH&S decisions and their downstream, indirect EH&S consequences. Second, the key players would be more likely to recognize when a competitive relationship exists between EH&S objectives and DE&I objectives, and to seek solutions that do not unduly burden one or the other of these desirable objectives. Third, it would facilitate inclusion of EH&S into the overall cost calculus, from both an internal corporate perspective and a social, host country perspective, of various alternatives for the design, location, ownership, and management of the facility.

   In a world in which EH&S issues were treated openly as shared responsibilities of the MNC and the host country, the arguments in favor of this proposal might encounter little resistance. However, the reality of the negotiations, as traditionally practiced, provides the key players with little incentive to openly discuss their own internal value conflicts, much less include them in efforts to reconcile them. This is particularly, though by no means exclusively, true of MNCs suspected of trading off EH&S for financial gain. Furthermore, as enumerated in the earlier sections of this chapter, there are on both sides formidable institutional, procedural, and cultural barriers to inclusion of EH&S in the negotiations.

   Despite these obstacles, in our view, the ultimate benefits outweigh the costs. This would seem particularly true for the host country, which would more likely attract more responsible foreign investors. From the MNC perspective, considering the EH&S aspects of the facility in the context of multiple host country requirements regarding ownership, location, scale, and technology may be more cost effective than if EH&S continues to be treated as a discrete objective in facility planning. Furthermore, the costs of complying with certain host country requirements may become a bargaining chip for a corporation arguing for relaxation of some restrictions.

2. Define facility-specific criteria and performance indicators of functional equivalency, and implement an explicit program for monitoring and implementation. Concensus seems to be emerging at all levels of corporate management that functional equivalency is a workable EH&S norm. The three cases indicate, however, that operationalization of that principle is decidedly case-specific. It also appears

that this operationalization is often accomplished implicitly and incrementally, and over multiple stages of facility developments by various individuals responsible for its design and management.

Several advantages would accrue if the functional equivalency were explicitly defined by MNC and accompanied by an appropriately designed monitoring program. First, the host country would have an opportunity to participate in setting standards to a degree not too commonly seen otherwise, owing to the lack of generally recognized performance indicators, its limited knowledge of technology, and inadequate resources. Second, an explicit facility-specific definition of functional equivalency would reduce the risk of adverse effects owing to future changes in management, the work force, or the corporate or host country commitment to EH&S principles. Third, it would at least partially immunize the corporation from accusations of cutting corners and applying lower EH&S standards at the foreign facilities. With an emphasis on outcomes rather than methods, official oversight and public scrutiny would be properly focused on the EH&S bottom line.

3. Specify the EH&S goals and objectives in the formal joint venture agreement. It appears that informal arrangements between joint venture partners play no lesser, and perhaps a greater, role in specifying the division of responsibilities in managing EH&S. We earlier argued that this may actually be a strength, as it gives the affiliate and the partners the flexibility necessary to adapt to changing circumstances and the freedom to develop a sustainable EH&S culture at the affiliate. However, such informality may also become a weakness, especially when there are strong differences in EH&S philosophy and commitment between the partners or when the management arrangements undergo major changes. These weaknesses may be minimized by explicit recognition of the EH&S principles in the formal joint venture agreement, while stopping short introducing a rigid prescription for managing EH&S. For example, an agreement may openly state the principle of functional equivalency at the affiliate and define its criteria, or it may specifically address which environmental and occupational standards would be used and under what circumstances (including those when there are no applicable standards).

We recognize that in some cases such terms and conditions may not be appropriate in a joint venture agreement, and that, once specified, they may have limited usefulness. Nevertheless, the process of articulating the goals and objectives of EH&S management at the facility during the negotiations is likely to benefit both parties in the long run, by setting forth expectations established through a process of shared development and consent. In short, such process may be a significant first step toward creating a strong culture at the new enterprise and toward building a sustainable EH&S system.

REFERENCES

Anderson, Terry L., and Donals R. Leal. *Free Market Environmentalism*. San Francisco: Pacific Research Institute for Public Policy, 1991.

Ashford, Nicholas A., and Christine Ayers. "Policy Issues for Consideration in Transferring Technology to Developing Countries." *Ecology Law Quarterly* 12:4 (1985): 871–905.

Ayres, Robert U., and Pradeep K. Rohatgi. "Bhopal: Lessons for Technological Decision-Makers." *Technology in Society* 9 (1987): 19–45.

Bowonder, B. "The Bhopal Accident." *Technological Forcasting and Social Change* 32 (1987): 169–182.

Bowonder, B., Jeanne X. Kasperson, and Roger E. Kasperson. "Avoiding Future Bhopals." *Environment* 27 (1985): 6–13, 31–37.

Bowonder, B., and H. A. Linstone. "Notes on the Bhopal Accident: Risk Analysis and Multiple Perspectives." *Technological Forcasting and Social Change* 32 (1987): 183–202.

Castleman, Barry. "Double Standards: Asbestos in India." *New Scientist* 89 (1981): 522–523.

——. "The Double Standard in Industrial Hazards." Pages 60–89 in Jane Ives (ed.), *The Export of Hazard: Transnational Corporations and Environmental Control Issues.* Boston: Routledge and Kegan Paul, 1985.

——. "Workplace Health in Developing Countries." Pages 149–172 in Charles S. Pearson (ed.), *Multinational Corporations, Environment, and Third World: Business Matters.* Durham, NC: Duke University Press, 1987.

Castleman, Barry, and Purkavastha Prabir. "The Bhopal Disaster as a Case Study in Double Standards." Pages 213–222 in Jane Ives (ed.), *The Export of Hazard: Transnational Corporations and Environmental Control Issues.* Boston: Routledge and Kegan Paul, 1985.

Christensen, Scott R. "Thailand in 1989: Consensus at Bay." *Asian Survey* 30: 178–186 (1990).

Flaherty, M., and Ann Rappaport. *Multinational Corporations and the Environment: A Survey of Global Practices.* Medford, MA: Tufts University Center for Environmental Management, 1991.

Friedman, Frank. *A Practical Guide to Environmental Management.* Washington, DC: Environmental Law Institute, 1991. Second Edition.

Gladwin, Thomas N. "A Case Study of the Bhopal Tragedy." Pages 221–239 in Charles S. Pearson (ed.), *Multinational Corporations, Environment, and Third World: Business Matters.* Durham, NC: Duke University Press, 1987.

Gladwin, Thomas N., and Ingo Walter. "Multinational Enterprise, Social Responsiveness, and Pollution Control." *Journal of International Business Studies* 7 (Fall-Winter, 1976): 57–74.

Granger, John Van Nuys. *Technology & International Relations.* San Francisco: W. H. Freeman, 1979.

Hirsch, Philip, and Larry Lohmann. "Contemporary Politics of Environment in Thailand." *Asian Survey* 29:4 (1989): 439–451.

International Chamber of Commerce. *Sustainable Development, The Business Approach.* Washington, DC: Publication 210/330, 1989.

International Chamber of Commerce. Papers presented at the Industry Forum on Environment: A Meeting for Industry Leaders in Connection with the 1990 Berger Conference "Action for a Common Future." Bergen, Norway, 8–16, May 1990.

International Labor Organization. *Tripartite Declaration of Principles Concerning Multinational Enterprises and Social Policy.* Geneva: International Labor Organization, 1977.

Ives, Jane, H. (ed.). *The Export of Hazard: Transnational Corporations and Envi-*

ronmental Control Issues. Boston: Routledge and Kegan Paul, 1985.

Kasperson, Roger E., Jeanne X. Kasperson, Christoph Hohenemser, and Robert W. Kates. *Corporate Management of Health and Safety Hazards: A Comparison of Current Practice.* Boulder, CO: Westview Press, 1988.

Leonard, H. Jeffrey. "Confronting Industrial Pollution in Rapidly Industrializing Countries: Myths, Pitfalls, and Opportunities." *Ecology Law Quarterly* 12 (1985): 779–816.

——. *Pollution and the Struggle for World Product.* Cambridge, UK: Cambridge University Press, 1988.

Lepkowski, Wil. "Chemical Safety in Developing Countries: The Lessons of Bhopal." *Chemical and Engineering News* 63:14 (1985): 9–13.

Organization for Economic Cooperation and Development. *Ministerial Declaration on the Avoidance of Accidents Involving Hazardous Substances.* Paris: OECD, 1989.

Rappaport, Ann, and Margaret Flaherty. "Multinational Corporations and the Environment: Context and Challenges." *International Environment Reporter* 14:9 (1991): 261–267.

Renn, Ortwin, Halina Brown, and Allen White. "Doing the Right Thing in Exporting Hazardous Technologies." *Environment, Science and Technology* 25 (1991): 1965–1970.

Royston, Michael G. "Control by Multinational Corporations: The Environmental Case for Scenario 4." *Ambio* 8:2/3 (1979): 84–89.

——. "Local and Multinational Corporations: Reappraising Environmental Management." *Environment* 27:1 (1985): 12–20, 39–43.

Ruyabhorn, Pravit, and Dhira Phantumvanit. "Coastal and Marine Resources of Thailand: Emerging Issues Facing an Industrializing Country." *Ambio* 17:3 (1988): 230–232.

Shrivastava, Paul. *Bhopal: Anatomy of a Crisis.* Cambridge, MA: Ballinger, 1987.

Shue, Henry. Exporting Hazards. *Ethics* (July 1981): 579–606.

Snidvongs, Kasem, and Kosit Panpiemras. "Environment and Development Planning in Thailand." Pages 347–360 in UNEP (ed.), *Environment and Development in Asia and the Pacific: Experiences and Prospects.* Nairobi: UNEP Reports and Proceedings Series 6, 1982.

Tuntawiroon, Nart. "The Environmental Impact of Industrialization in Thailand." *Ecologist* 15:4 (1985): 161–164.

United Nations Centre on Transnational Corporations. *Transnational Corporations in World Development: Trends and Prospects.* New York: United Nations, 1988.

United Nations Economic and Social Commission for Asia and the Pacific/United Nations Center on Transnational Corporations Joint Unit on Transnational Corporations. *Transnational Corporations and Environmental Management in Selected Asian and Pacific Developing Countries,* pages 288–331. Bangkok: United Nations, 1988.

United Nations Economic and Social Commission for Asia and the Pacific/United Nations Center on Transnational Corporations Joint Unit on Transnational Corporations. *Environmental Aspects of Transnational Corporation Activities in Pollution-Intensive Industries in Selected Asian and Pacific Developing Countries,* pages 320–374. Bangkok: United Nations, 1990.

United Nations Economic and Social Council, Commission on Transnational Corporations. *Transnational Corporations and Issues Relating to the Environment: The Contribution of the Commission and UNCTC to the Work of the Preparatory Committee for the United Nations Conference on Environment and Development.* New York: United Nations Document E/C.10/1991/1, 1991.

United Nations Environmental Program. "Sustainable Industrial Development Journal." *Industry and Environment* 12:3–4 (1989): 1–69.

Weir, David. *The Bhopal Syndrome: Pesticides, Environment, and Health.* San Francisco: Sierra Club, 1987.

Winter, George. *Business and the Environment.* New York: McGraw Hill, 1988.

Woolard, Edgar S. "The Ethic of Environmentalism." *Executive Excellence* X (November, 1989) pp. 6–7.

World Commission on Environment and Development. *Our Common Future.* Oxford: Oxford University Press, 1987.

Xerox Corporation. *Environmental Health and Safety Manual: Materials Safety Assessment Standard.* CEHS STD No. 2.3.0, 1983.

Bibliography

Abdullah, Maisom. 1988. *Transfer of Industrial Technology of the Manufacturing Sector: The Case of Malaysia.* ISU–TSCP.

Adams, Bill. 1990. *Green Development: Environment & Sustainability in the Third World.* New York: Routledge, Chapman, and Hall.

Agmon, Tamir, and Mary A. Von Glinow. 1991. *Technology Transfer in International Business.* New York: Oxford University Press.

Akinsanya, Adeoye. 1984. *Multinationals in a Changing Environment: A Study of Business & Government Relations in the Third World.* Westport, CT: Greenwood.

Ali, Abbas, Mohammed Al-Shkhis, and Somanathan Nataraj. 1991. "Work Centrality and Individualism: A Cross-National Perspective." *International Journal of Manpower* 12(1): 30–38.

Al-Moneef, Ibrahim A. 1980. *Technology to Developing Nations: The Role of Multinational Oil Firms in Saudi Arabia.* Salem, NH: Ayer.

——. 1980. *Transfer of Management Technology to Developing Nations: The Role of Multinational Oil Firms in Saudi Arabia.* Edited by S. Brouchey. Salem, NH: Ayer.

American Conference of Governmental Industrial Hygienists. 1989. *Hazard Assessment and Control Technology in Semiconductor Manufacturing.* Chelsea, MI: Lewis Publishers.

Amsalem, Michel A. 1984. "Technology Crossing Borders: The Choice, Transfer, and Management of International Technology Flows." *Finance & Development* 21(December): 49.

Anand, R. P. 1980. "Industrialization of the Developing Countries and the Problem of Environmental Protection." *Mazingira* 4: 10–25.

Asfahl, C. Ray. 1990. *Industrial Safety & Health Management.* Englewood Cliffs, NJ: Prentice-Hall.

Ashford, Nicholas A., and Christine Ayers. 1985. "Policy Issues for Consideration in Transferring Technology to Developing Countries." *Ecology Law Quarterly* 12: 871–905.

Austin, James E. 1990. *Managing in Developing Countries: Strategic Analysis & Operating Techniques.* New York: Free Press.

Balassa, B. 1988. "The Lessons of East Asian Development: An Overview." *Economic Development and Cultural Change* 36(3): S274–9–290.

Balasubramanayam, V. 1973. *International Transfer of Technology to India.* New York: Praeger.

——. 1973. *International Transfer of Technology to India.* New York: Irvington.

Ball, George W. 1975. *Global Companies: The Political Economy of World Business.* Englewood Cliffs, NJ: Prentice-Hall.

Baram, Michael S., and Daniel G. Partan. 1990. *Corporate Disclosure of Environmental Risks: U.S. & European Law.* Austin, TX: Butterworth Legal Publishers.

Baranson, Jack. 1970. "Technology Transfer through the International Firm." *American Economic Review* 60: 435–440.

Barnet, R. S., and R. E. Muller. 1974. *Global Reach: The Power of Multinational Corporations.* New York: Simon and Schuster.

Bartelmus, P. 1986. *Environment and Development.* Boston: Allen & Unwin.

Bartlett, Christopher A., and Sumantra Ghoshal. 1991. *Managing across Borders: The Transnational Solution.* Boston: Harvard Business School Press.

Behrman, Jack N., and Robert E. Grosse. 1990. *International Business & Governments: Issues & Institutions.* Columbia, SC: University of South Carolina Press.

Berle, Adolf A., and Gardiner C. Means. 1932. *The Modern Corporation and Private Property.* New York: Macmillan Publishing Company.

Berle, Gustav. 1991. *The Green Entrepreneur: Business Opportunities that Can Save the Earth & Make You Money.* Salt Lake City, UT: Liberty Bell Press.

Biersteker, T. J. 1978. *Distortion or Development?: Contending Perspectives on the Multinational Corporation.* Cambridge, MA: MIT Press.

Blackburn, Anne M. 1986. *Pieces of the Global Puzzle: International Approaches to Environmental Concerns.* Golden, CO: Fulcrum.

Blumenfeld, Mark. 1989. *Conducting an Environmental Audit (Environmental Audit Handbook Ser.: Vol. 2).* New York: Executive Enterprise.

Bonerjee, B. N. 1987. *Environmental Pollution & Bhopal Killings.* New Delhi: Gyan Publishing House India.

Bornschier, Volker, and Christopher Chase-Dunn. 1985. *Multinational Corporations & Underdevelopment.* Westport, CT: Greenwood.

Bowonder, B. 1981. "Environmental Risk Assessment Issues in the Third World." *Technological Forecasting and Social Change* 19: 99–127.

——. 1987. "The Bhopal Accident." *Technological Forecasting and Social Change* 32: 169–182.

——. 1987. "Management of Environment in Developing Countries." *The Environmentalist* 7: 111–122.

Bowonder, B., J. X. Kasperson, and R. E. Kasperson. 1985. "Avoiding Future Bhopals." *Environment* 27(September): 6–13, 31–37.

Bowonder, B., and H. A. Linstone. 1987. "Notes on the Bhopal Accident: Risk

Analysis and Multiple Perspectives." *Technological Forecasting and Social Change* 32: 183–202.

Boylston, Raymond P. 1990. *Managing Safety & Health Programs*. New York: Van Nostrand Reinhold.

Bradshaw, Thornton, and David Vogel. 1981. *Corporations and Their Critics: Issues and Answers to the Problems of Corporate Social Responsibility*. New York: McGraw-Hill.

Brown, Lester R. 1991. *On Global Environmental Issues*. New York: N. W. Norton.

Buckley, Peter J. 1987. *The Theory of the Multinational Enterprise*. Sweden: Coronet Books.

———. 1989. *The Multinational Enterprise: Theory & Application*. New York: Macmillan Publishing Company (UK).

Buckley, Peter J., and Jeremy Clegg, (eds.). 1991. *Multinational Enterprises in Less Developed Countries*. New York: St. Martin's Press.

Buller, Paul F., John J. Kohls, and Kenneth S. Anderson. 1991. "The Challenge of Global Ethics. *Journal of Business Ethics* 10(October): 767–775.

Cable, V., and B. Persaud. 1987. *Development with the Multinational Corporation*. London: Commonwealth Secretariat and Croom Helm.

Caldwell, L. K. 1984. "Political Aspects of Ecologically Sustainable Development. *Environmental Conservation* 11: 299–308.

Casson, M. C. 1990. *Multinational Corporations*. Brookfield, CT: Gower.

Castleman, Barry. 1978. "How We Export Dangerous Industries." *Business and Society Review* (Fall): 7–14.

———. 1978. "The Export of Hazardous Factories to Developing Nations." *Congressional Record* (June 29): 19763–19770.

———. 1979. "The Export of Hazardous Factories to Developing Countries." *International Journal of Health Services* 9: 569–606.

———. 1981. "Double Standards: Asbestos in India." *New Scientist* (February): 522–523.

———. 1983. "The Double Standard in Industrial Hazards." *International Journal of Health Services* 13(1): 5–14.

Castleman, Barry I., and V. Navarro. 1987. "International Mobility of Hazardous Products, Industries, and Wastes." *Annual Review of Public Health* 8: 1–19.

Castleman, Barry I., and Purkavastha Prabir. 1985. "The Bhopal Disaster as a Case Study in Double Standards." In *The Export of Hazard: Transnational Corporations and Environmental Control Issues*. Edited by J. H. Ives. Boston: Routledge, Kegan Paul.

Castleman, Barry I., and Manual J. Vera. 1980. "Impending Proliferation of Asbestos." *International Journal of Health Services* 10: 389–403.

Chanaron, J. J., and J. Perrin. 1987. "The Transfer of Research, Development and Design to Developing Countries: Analysis and Proposals." *Futures* (UK) 19(5): 503–512.

Chand, Attar. 1989. *Industrial Safety, Environmental Pollution, Health Hazards & Nuclear Accidents: A Global Survey*. New Delhi: Mittal.

Chapman, Peter. 1984. "Mexico's Catalogue of Gas Disaster." *New Scientist* 92 (November 29): 3–4.

Chaudhuri, Adhip. 1988. "Multinational Corporations in Less-Developed Countries:

What Is in Store?" *Columbia Journal of World Business* 23(1): 57–63.

Cheremisinoff, Paul N. 1984. *Management of Hazardous Occupational Environments.* Lancaster, PA: Technomic.

Chissick, Seymour S., and R. Derricott. 1981. *Occupational Health & Safety Management.* Properties of Materials Safety & Environmental Factors Series. Chichester, NY: J. Wiley.

Chittmittrapap, Weerawong. 1990. "Joint Ventures in Thailand–Part I: Business Forms, Incentives, Taxes." *East Asian Executive Reports* 12(12): 8, 21–26.

———. 1991. "Joint Ventures in Thailand–Part II: Choosing the Right Business Form." *East Asian Executive Reports* 13(2): 8, 20–24.

Christiansson, C., and J. Ashuvud. 1985. "Heavy Industry in a Rural Tropical Ecosystem." *Ambio* 14: 122–33.

Cody, John. 1980. *Policies for Industrial Progress in Developing Countries.* World Bank Research Publications Series. New York: Oxford University Press.

Colling, David. 1990. *Industrial Safety.* Englewood Cliffs, NJ: Prentice-Hall.

Commission, Brandt. 1980. *A Programme for Survival.* London: Pan Books.

Connolly, Seamus G. 1987. *Finding, Entering & Succeeding in a Foreign Market.* Englewood Cliffs, NJ: Prentice-Hall.

Contractor, Farok J. 1985. *Licensing in International Strategy: A Guide for Planning & Negotiations.* Westport, CT: Greenwood.

———. 1990. "Ownership Patterns of U.S. Joint Ventures Abroad and the Liberalization of Foreign Government Regulations in the 1980s: Evidence from the Benchmark Surveys." *Journal of International Business Studies* 21(1): 55–73.

Contractor, Farok J., and T. Sagafi-Nejad. 1981. "International Technology Transfer: Major Issues and Policy Responses." *Journal of International Business Studies* (Fall): 113–135.

Corbett, William J. 1986. "The Communication Tools Inherent in Corporate Culture." *Personnel Journal* 65(4): 71–72, 74.

Costanza, R. 1989. "What Is Ecological Economics?" *Ecological Economics* 1(1): 1–8.

Coughlin, Cletus C. 1983. "The Relationship between Foreign Ownership and Technology Transfer." *Journal of Comparative Economics* 7: 400–414.

Cowling, Keith, and Roger Sugden. 1987. *Transnational Monopoly Capitalism.* New York: St. Martin's Press.

Cralley, Lewis. 1985. *Industrial Hygiene Aspects of Plant Operations: Engineering Considerations in Equipment Selection, Layout, and Building Design.* Melbourne, FL: Krieger.

Crist, Joseph B. 1989. *Disclosure Requirements for an Environmental Audit (Environmental Audit Handbook Ser.: Vol. 2).* New York: Executive Enterprise.

Cumo, Maurizio, and Antonio Naviglio. 1989. *Safety Design Criteria for Industrial Plants.* Boca Raton, FL: CRC Press.

Czinkota, Michael R., Pietra Rivoli, and Ilkka A. Ronkainen (eds.). 1992. *International Business.* (2nd ed.). Fort Worth, TX: Dryden Press.

Daly, H. 1991. "Sustainable Development: From Concept and Theory towards Operational Principles." In *Steady-state Economics: 2nd Edition with New Essays.* Edited by H. E. Daly. Washington, DC: Island Press.

Daniels, J. D., and L. H. Radebaugh. 1986. *International Business: Environment and Operations.* (4th ed.). Reading, MA: Addison-Wesley.

Dassbach, Carl H. 1990. *Global Enterprises & the World Economy; Ford, General Motors, & IBM, the Emergence of the Transnational Enterprise (Studies in Entrepreneurship)*. New York: Garland.

Davidar, David. 1985. "Beyond Bhopal: The Toxic Waste Hazard in India." *Ambio* 14: 112–116.

Davidson, William. 1983. "Structure and Performance in International Technology Transfer." *Journal of Management Studies* 20(4): 453–465.

Davidson, William, and D. G. McFetridge. 1984. "International Technology Transactions and the Theory of the Firm." *Journal of Industrial Economics* 34: 253–264.

Davies, Howard. 1977. "Technology Transfer through Commercial Transactions and the Theory of the Firm." *Journal of Industrial Economics* 26: 161–175.

Dawson, Leslie M. 1987. "Transferring Industrial Technology to Less Developed Countries." *Industrial Marketing Management* 16(4): 265–271.

De Grazia, Alfred. 1985. *A Cloud over Bhopal—Causes, Consequences*. Calcutta, India: Asia Publishing.

Deo, Som. 1986. *Multinational Corporations & the Third World*. New Delhi: Ashish.

Desai, A. V. 1984. "India's Technological Capability: An Analysis of Its Achievements and Limits." *Research Policy* 13: 303–310.

Dixon, C. J., D. W. Drakakis-Smith, and H. D. Watts. 1986. *Multinational Corporations & the Third World*. Boulder, CO: Westview Press.

Djeflat, Abdelkader. 1988. "The Management of Technology Transfer: Views and Experiences of Developing Countries." *International Journal of Technology Management* (Switzerland) 3(1–2): 149–165.

Dobkin, James A., (ed.). 1988. *International Technology Joint Ventures in the Countries of the Pacific Rim*. Austin, TX: Butterworth Legal Publishers.

———. 1988. "Structuring an International Technology Joint Venture." *International Financial Law Review* (UK) 7(9): 20–23.

Dobson, John. 1990. "The Role of Ethics in Global Corporate Culture." *Journal of Business Ethics* 9(June): 481–488.

Dohrs, L. S. 1987. "Thailand: Good Times Mean More Bickering." *Southeast Asia Business* 13(Spring): 20–22.

Dowling, Peter, and Randall S. Schuler. 1990. *International Dimensions of Human Resource Management*. Boston: PWS-Kent Publishers.

Duerksen, Christopher J. 1983. *Environmental Regulation of Industrial Plant Siting: How to Make It Work Better*. Washington, DC: Conservation Foundation.

Duerksen, Christopher, and H. Jeffrey Leonard. 1980. "Environmental Regulations and the Location of Industries: An International Perspective." *Columbia Journal of World Business* (Summer): 52–58.

Duncan, Cynthia J. 1982. *Business and Environment: Some Case Studies*.

Dunning, John H. 1981. *International Production and the Multinational Enterprise*. Boston: Allen and Unwin.

———. 1988. *Explaining International Production*. Winchester, MA: Unwin-Hyman.

Edwards, John D., and Brian H. Kleiner. 1988. "Transforming Organizational Values and Culture Effectively." *Leadership and Organization Development Journal* 9(1): 13–16.

Ekholm, E. L. 1988. "Transferring Technology to Developing Nations." *Engineering Management International* (Netherlands) 5(1): 45–52.

Ekins, P. 1986. *The Living Economy: A New Economics in the Making.* New York: Routledge, Chapman, and Hall.

Elfstrom, Gerard. 1991. *Moral Issues & Multinational Corporations.* New York: St. Martin's Press.

Encarnation, Dennis J. 1989. *Dislodging Multinationals: India's Strategy in Comparative Perspective.* Ithaca, NY: Cornell University Press.

Enderle, George. 1990. *People in Corporations: Ethical Responsibilities & Corporate Effectiveness.* Boston: Kluwer Academic.

"Environmental Management in the Private Sector." 1991. *Public Management* 73 (May): 23–24.

Ernest, Robert C. 1985. "Corporate Cultures and Effective Planning." *Personnel Administrator* 30(3): 49–60.

Etmad, Hamid, and Louise S. Dulude. 1986. *Managing the Multinational Subsidiary.* New York: St. Martin's Press.

Evans, Don A. 1991. *The Cultural & Political Environment of International Business: A Guide for Business Professionals.* London: McFarland & Company.

Ferraro, Gary. 1990. *The Cultural Dimension of International Business.* Englewood Cliffs, NJ: Prentice-Hall.

Finlayson, Jock A., and Mark W. Zacher. 1988. *Managing International Markets: Developing Countries & the Commodity Trade Regime.* New York: Columbia University Press.

Fisher, Glen. 1982. *International Negotiation: A Cross Cultural Perspective.* Yarmouth, ME: Intercultural Press.

Fitzgerald, Thomas H. 1988. "Can Change in Organizational Culture Really Be Managed?" *Organizational-Dynamics* 17(2): 5–15.

Forsyth, David J. 1990. Technology Policy for Small Developing Countries. Boston: St. Martin's Press.

Frame, J. Davidson. 1983. *International Business & Global Technology.* New York: Free Press.

Francis, Rebecca S. 1983. "Attitudes toward Industrial Pollution, Strategies for Protecting the Environment, and Environmental Economic Trade-offs." *Journal of Applied Social Psychology* 13(July/August): 310–327.

Fransman, Martin. 1986. *Technology and Economic Development.* Boulder, CO: Westview Press.

Freedman, Audrey. 1981. *Industry Response to Health Risk: A Research Report from the Conference Board.* Report Series No. 811. New York: Conference Board.

Galbraith, Craig S. 1990. "Transferring Core Manufacturing Technologies in High-Technology Firms." *California Management Review* 32(4): 56–70.

Garell, Dale C., and Solomon H. Snyder. 1989. *Occupational Health.* Medical Issues Series. New York: Chelsea House.

Garrett, Jack T. 1988. *Industrial Hygiene Management.* New York: Wiley.

Geller, Peter B. 1985. *Technology Transfer & Human Values: Concepts, Applications, Cases.* Washington, DC: University Press of America.

Gentry, Bradford S. 1990. *Global Environmental Issues & International Business: A Manager's Guide to Trends, Risks & Opportunities.* Washington, DC: Bureau of National Affairs.

Ghauri, P. N. 1983. *Negotiating International Package Deals: Swedish Firms and Developing Countries.* Stockholm: Almqvist & Wiksell.

——. 1986. "Guidelines for International Business Negotiations." *International Marketing Review* 3(3): 72–82.

Ghosh, Pradip K. 1984. *Multi-National Corporations & Third World Development.* Westport, CT: Greenwood.

Ghoshal, Sumantra, and Christopher A. Bartlett. 1988. "Creation, Adoption, and Diffusion of Innovations by Subsidiaries of Multinational Corporations." *Journal of International Business Studies* 19(3): 365–388.

Girling, Robert H. 1985. *Multinational Institutions & the Third World.* New York: Praeger.

Gladwin, Thomas N. 1977. *Environment, Planning & the Multinational Corporation.* Greenwich, CT: Jai Press.

——. 1977. "Planning & the Multinational Corporation." In *Contemporary Studies in Economic & Financial Analysis.* Edited by E. I. Altman and I. Walter. Greenwich, CT: Jai Press.

Gladwin, Thomas N., and Ingo Walter. 1980. *Multinationals under Fire: Lessons in the Management of Conflict.* New York: Wiley.

Glaeser, B. 1984. *Ecodevelopment: Concepts, Projects, Strategies.* Elmsford, NY: Pergamon.

Godkin, Lynn. 1988. "Problems and Practicalities of Technology Transfer: A Survey of the Literature." *International Journal of Technology Management* 3(5): 587–603.

Gold, David. 1991. "The Determinants of FDI and Their Implications for Host Developing Countries." *CTC Reporter* (31): 21–24.

Goldenberg, Susan. 1988. *Hands across the Ocean: Managing Joint Ventures with a Spotlight on China & Japan.* Boston: Harvard Business School Press.

Goodland, R., and G. Ledec. 1987. "Neoclassical Economics and Principles of Sustainable Development." *Ecological Monitoring* 38: 19–46.

Goulet, Denis. 1989. *The Uncertain Promise: Value Conflicts in Technology Transfer.* New York: New Horizons.

Graham, John. 1988. *International Business Negotiations: John Wayne Style.* New York: Wiley.

Graham, J. L. 1985. "The Influence of Culture on the Process of Business Negotiations: An Exploratory Study." *Journal of International Business Studies* (Spring): 81–96.

Graves, Desmond. 1986. *Corporate Culture-Diagnosis and Change: Auditing and Changing the Culture of Organizations.* New York: St. Martin's Press.

Grosse, Christine, and Robert Grosse. 1988. *Case Studies in International Business.* Englewood Cliffs, NJ: Prentice-Hall.

Grosse, Robert, and Duane Hujawa. 1988. *International Business: Theory & Managerial Applications.* Springfield, IL: Irwin.

Gutknecht, Douglas B., and David M. Gutknecht. 1990. *Building Productive Organizations through Health & Wellness Programs.* Washington, DC: University Press of America.

Hall, Edward T., and Mildred Hall. 1990. *Understanding Cultural Differences: Germans, French & Americans.* Yarmouth, ME: Intercultural Press.

Hall, Patricia H., and William Gudykunst B. 1989. "The Relationship of Perceived Ethnocentrism in Corporate Cultures to the Selection, Training, and Success of International Employees." *International Journal of Intercultural Relations* 13(2): 183–201.

Harvey, Michael G. 1984. "Application of Technology Life Cycles to Technology Transfers." *The Journal of Business Strategy* (Fall): 51–58.

Heiba, F. I. 1984. "International Business Negotiations: A Strategic Planning Model." *International Marketing Review* 1(4): 5–16.

Hennart, Jean-Francois. 1982. *A Theory of Multinational Enterprise*. Ann Arbor, MI: University of Michigan Press.

Hofstede, G. 1984. "Cultural Dimensions in Management and Planning." *Asian Pacific Journal of Management* 1(2): 81–89.

Hoover, Reynold L. 1989. *Health, Safety, & Environmental Control*. New York: Van Nostrand Reinhold.

Hughes, Helen. 1988. *Achieving Industrialization in East Asia*. New York: Cambridge University Press.

International Labour Office. 1985. *Employment Effects of Multinational Enterprises in Developing Countries*. (2nd ed.). Geneva: International Labour Office.

——. 1986. *Safety & Health Practices of Multinational Enterprises*. (2nd ed.). Geneva: International Labour Office.

——. 1988. *Safety, Health, & Working Conditions in the Transfer of Technology to Developing Countries*. Geneva: International Labour Office.

Ives, Jane H. 1981. *International Occupational Safety & Health Resource Catalogue*. Westport, CT: Greenwood.

Jacobs, Peter, and David A. Munro. 1987. *Conservation with Equity: Strategies for Sustainable Development*. Gland, Switzerland: International Union for Conservation of Nature and Natural Resources.

Jones, Stanley E. 1989. *Occupational Hygiene Management Guide*. Chelsea, MI: Lewis.

Kapoor, A. 1970. *International Business Negotiations—A Study in India*. Pennington, NY: Darwin Press.

Kasperson, Roger E., Jeanne X. Kasperson, Christoph Hohenemser, and Robert W. Kates. 1988. *Corporate Management of Health & Safety Hazards: A Comparison of Current Practice*. Boulder, CO: Westview Press.

Kedia, Ben L., and Rabi S. Bhagat. 1988. "Cultural Constraints on Transfer of Technology across Nations: Implications for Research in International and Comparative Management." *Academy of Management Review* 13(4): 559–571.

Keller, Robert T., and Ravi R. Chinta. 1990. "International Technology Transfer: Strategies for Success." *Academy of Management Executive* 4(2): 33–43.

Kennedy, G. 1985. *Doing Business Abroad*. New York: Simon and Schuster.

Kiggundu, Moses N. 1989. *Managing Organizations in Developing Countries: An Operation & Strategic Approach*. West Hartford, CT: Kumarian.

Killing, J. Peter. 1983. *Strategies for Joint Venture Success*. Westport, CT: Greenwood.

Kizer, William M. 1987. *The Healthy Workplace: A Blueprint for Corporate Action*. Albany, NY: Delmar.

Kolde, J. E. 1982. *Environment of International Business*. Kent, OH: Kent State University Press.

Kolland, Franz. 1990. "National Cultures and Technology Transfer: The Influence of the Mexican Life Style on Technology Adaptation." *International Journal of Intercultural Relations* 14(3): 319–336.

Konz, Leo E. 1980. *The International Transfer of Commercial Technology: The Role of the Multinational Corporation*. Edited by S. Bruchey. Salem, NH: Ayer.

Kormondy, Edward J. (ed.). 1989. *International Handbook of Pollution Control.* Westport, CT: Greenwood.

Kumar, Nagesh. 1990. *Multinational Enterprises in India: Industrial Distribution.* New York: Routledge, Chapman, and Hall.

Kumar, R. 1987. *Environmental Pollution & Health Hazards in India.* New Delhi: Ashish.

Lagadee, Patrick. 1987. "From Seveso to Mexico and Bhopal: Learning to Cope with Crisis." In *Insuring and Managing Hazardous Risks: From Seveso to Bhopal and Beyond.* Edited by P. K. and H. Kunreuther. Berlin: Springer-Verlag.

Lake, Arthur W. 1979. "Technology Creation and Technology Transfer by Multinational Firms." *Research in International Business and Finance* 1: 137–177.

Lall, Sanjaya. 1977. "Medicines and Multinationals: Problems in the Transfer of Pharmaceutical Technology to the Third World." *Monthly Review* 28: 19–30.

———. 1978. "Transnationals, Domestic Enterprises and Industrial Structure in Host LDC's: A Survey." *Oxford Economic Papers* (July): 217–248.

Lall, S., and P. Streeten. 1977. *Foreign Investment, Transnationals and Developing Countries.* Boulder, CO: Westview.

Lall, Sanjaya, and P. Streeten. 1977. *Foreign Investment, Transnationals and Developing Countries.* New York: Macmillan.

Lee, Joon Koo, and Gill Chin Lim. 1983. "Environmental Policies in Developing Countries: A Case of International Movements of Polluting Industries." *Journal of Development Economics* 13(August/October): 159–173.

Lehman, Cheryl R. 1991. *Multinational Culture: Social Impacts of a Global Economy (Contributions in Economics & Economic History Ser.: No. 122).* Westport, CT: Greenwood.

Leonard, H. Jeffrey. 1984. *Pollution and Multinational Corporations in Rapidly Industrializing Nations.* Washington, DC: Conservation Foundation.

———. 1985. "Industrial Flight: Myth or Reality." *EPA Journal* 11(1): 10.

———. 1988. *Pollution & the Struggle for the World Product: Multinational Corporations, Environment, & International Comparative Advantage.* Cambridge, MA: Cambridge University Press.

———. 1991. *Pollution & the Struggle for the World Product: Multinational Corporations, Environment & International Comparative Advantage.* Cambridge, MA: Cambridge University Press.

Leonard, H. Jeffrey, and Christopher J. Duerksen. 1980. "Environmental Regulation and the Location of Industry: An International-Perspective." *Columbia Journal of World Business* 15: 55–68.

Leonard, H. Jeffrey, and D. Morrell. 1985. "The Emergence of Environmental Concern in Developing Countries: A Political Perspective." *Stanford Journal of Environmental Law* 17: 281–313.

Leonard, J. Jeffrey. 1985. "Confronting Industrial Pollution in Rapidly Industrializing Countries: Myths, Pitfalls, and Opportunities." *Ecology Law Quarterly* 12: 779–816.

Lester, Mark. (ed.). 1989. *Technology Transfer in Export Processing Zones the Semiconductor Industry in Malaysia (Contemporary Studies in Economic & Financial Analysis Vol. 47).* Greenwich, CT: Jai Press.

Lewis, Jordan D. 1990. *Partnership for Profit: Structuring & Managing Strategic Alliances.* New York: Free Press.

Liedtka, Jeanne. 1991. "Organizational Value Contention and Managerial Mindsets." *Journal of Business Ethics* 10(July): 543–557.

Lunenberger, T. (ed.). 1991. *From Technology Transfer to Technology Management in China*. New York: Springer-Verlag.

Lyles, Marjorie A. 1987. "Common Mistakes of Joint Venture Experienced Firms." *Columbia Journal of World Business* 22(2): 79–85.

Madeuf, Bernadette. 1984. "International Technology Transfers and International Technology Payments: Definitions, Measurement and Firms' Behavior." *Research Policy* 13: 125–140.

Madu, Christian N. 1989. "Transferring Technology to Developing Countries — Critical Factors for Success." *Long Range Planning* (UK) 22(4): 115–124.

Mahini, Amir. 1988. *Making Decisions in Multinational Corporations: Managing Relations with Sovereign Governments*. New York: Wiley.

Malgavkar, P. D. 1989. *High Technology: Managerial Considerations*. Calcutta: Asia.

Mansfield, Edwin. 1975. "International Technology Transfer: Forms, Resource Requirements, and Policies." *American Economic Review* 65: 372–376.

Mansfield, Edwin, and Anthony Romeo. 1980. "Technology Transfer to Overseas Subsidiaries by U.S.-Based Firms." *Quarterly Journal of Economics* (December): 737–750.

Marginson, Paul. 1988. *Beyond the Workplace: Managing Industrial Relations in the Multi-Plant Enterprise*. Warwick Studies in Industrial Relations. Cambridge, MA: Basil Blackwell.

Martinussen, John. 1988. *Transnational Corporations in a Developing Country: The Indian Experience*. Newbury Park, CA: Sage.

Marton, Katherin. 1986. *Multinationals, Technology, & Industrialization: Implications & Impact in Third World Countries*. New York: Free Press.

———. 1986. "Technology Transfer to Developing Countries via Multinationals." *World Economy* (December): 409–426.

———. 1987. *Multinationals, Technology & Industrialization: A Study of the Implications & Impact in Third World Countries (Contemporary Studies in Economic & Financial Analysis*. Greenwich, CT: Jai Press.

Mascarenhas, Oswald A. 1980. *Measuring the Technological Impact of Multinational Corporations in the Less Developed Countries*. Edited by S. Bruchey. Salem, NH: Ayer.

Mascarenhas, R. C. 1982. *Technology Transfer & Development: India's Hindustan Machine Tools Company*. Boulder, CO: Westview Press.

Mason, R. H. 1973. "Some Observations on the Choice of Technology by Multinational Firms in Developing Countries." *Review of Economics and Statistics* 55(3): 349–355.

Mason, R. Hal, R. R. Miller, and D. R. Ewigel. 1981. *International Business*. (2nd ed.). New York: Wiley.

Matkin, Gary. 1990. *Technology Transfer & the University*. New York: ACE.

Mattelart, Armand. 1985. *Transnationals & the Third World: The Struggle for Culture*. Westport, CT: Greenwood.

Mattila, Olavi J. 1986. "Transferring Technology across Borders — From the Point of View of a Neutral Country." *International Journal of Technology Management* (Switzerland) 1(1, 2): 13–21.

Mayda, Jaro. 1985. "Environmental Legislation in Developing Countries: Some Parameters and Constraints." *Ecology Quarterly* 12: 997–1024.

McCall, J. B., and M. B. Warrington. 1984. *Marketing by Agreement—A Cross-Cultural Approach to Business Negotiations.* Chichester, UK: Wiley.

McCoy, Charles S. 1985. *Management of Values: The Ethical Difference in Corporate Policy and Performance.* Boston, MA: Pitman.

McCulloch, Rachel. 1981. "Technology Transfer to Developing Countries: Implications of International Regulation." *Annals of the American Academy of Political and Social Science* 458: 110–122.

McCulloch, Rachel, and Janet L. Yellen. 1982. "Technology Transfer and the National Interest." *International Economic Review* (June): 421–428.

McIntyre, John R., and Daniel S. Papp. (eds.). 1986. *The Political Economy of International Technology Transfer.* Westport, CT: Quorum.

McRobert, D. 1988. "Questionable Faith." *Probe Post* 11(1): 24–29.

Mehrotra, Santosh K. 1991. *India & the Soviet Union: Trade & Technology Transfer.* New York: Cambridge University Press.

Moran, Theodore H. 1974. *Multinational Corporations & the Politics of Dependence: Copper in Chile.* Princeton, NJ: Princeton University Press.

——. (ed.). 1985. *Multinational Corporations: The Political Economy of Foreign Direct Investment.* New York: Free Press.

Morell, David, and Joanna Poznanski. 1985. "Rhetoric and Reality: Environmental-Politics and Environmental Administration in Developing Countries." In *Diverting Nature's Capital: The Political Economy of Environmental Abuse in the Third World.* Edited by H. J. Leonard. Portsmouth, NH: Holmes and Meier.

Moritani, Masanori. 1987. "Technology Transfer Management." *Management Japan* (Japan) 20(1): 18–24.

Mowery, David C. 1989. "Collaborative Ventures between U.S. and Foreign Manufacturing Firms." *Research Policy* (Netherlands) 18(1): 19–32.

Multinational Enterprises, Technology, & Competitiveness. 1988. Winchester, MA: Unwin Hyman, Inc.

Mukerjee, Dilip, and R. C. Murthy. 1990. "India: Economic Realities Forbid Sweeping Changes in Policy: Deregulation Will Stay with Vigour." *Asian Finance* (Hong Kong) 16(4): 78–84.

Neale, Bill, and Chris Pass. 1990. "Foreign Direct Investment: Potential Costs and Benefits for Host and Source Countries." *Management Accounting* (UK) 68(2): 32–34, 49.

Nilakant, V. 1991. "Dynamics of Middle Managerial Roles: A Study in Four Indian Organizations." *Journal of Managerial Psychology* 6(1): 17–24.

Norgaard, R. B. 1987. "Economics as Mechanics and the Demise of Biological Diversity." *Ecological Modelling* 38: 107–121.

Nvstrom, Paul C. 1990. "Differences in Moral Values between Corporations." *Journal of Business Ethics* 9(December): 971–979.

O'Riordan, T. 1985. "Future Directions in Environmental Policy." *Journal of Environment and Planning* 17: 1431–1446.

Oppenheimer, Michael F., and Donna M. Tuths. 1987. *Nontariff Barriers: The Effects on Corporate Strategy in High-Technology Sectors.* Boulder, CO: Westview Press.

Ouchi, William G., and Alan L. Wilkins. 1985. "Organizational Culture." *Annual Review of Sociology* 11: 457–483.

Pandia, Rajeev M. 1989. "Transfer of Technology: Techniques for Chemical and

Pharmaceutical Projects." *Project Management Journal* 20(3): 39–45.

Parry, Thomas G. 1988. "The Multinational Enterprise and Restrictive Conditions in International Technology Transfer: Some New Australian Evidence." *Journal of Industrial Economics* (UK) 36(3): 359–365.

Pearce, Fred. 1985. "Who Remembered Ixhuatepec?" *New Scientist* 93(July 18): 22–23.

Pearson, Charles. 1976. *Implications for the Trade and Investment of Developing Countries of United States Environmental Controls*. New York: United Nations.

———. 1987. *Multinational Corporations, Environment, & the Third World: Business Matters*. Durham, NC: Duke University Press-Policy Studies.

Pearson, Charles S. 1985. *Down to Business: Multinational Corporations, the Environment & Development*. Washington, DC: World Resources Institute.

Pennsylvania Bar Institute. 1988. *International Business Deals*. Philadelphia: Pennsylvania Bar Institute.

Perkins, Jimmy L., and Vernon E. Rose. 1987. *Case Studies in Industrial Hygiene*. New York: Wiley.

Plossl, George. 1967. *Managing in the New World of Manufacturing: How Companies Can Improve Operations to Compete Globally*. Englewood Cliffs, NJ: Prentice-Hall.

Porritt, Jonathon. 1985. *Seeing Green: The Politics of Ecology Explained*. Cambridge, MA: Basil Blackwell.

Poynter, Thomas. 1985. *Multinational Enterprises & Government Intervention*. New York: St. Martin's Press.

Prahalad, C. K., and Y. L. Doz. 1987. *The Multinational Mission*. New York: Free Press.

Prasad, S. Benjamin. 1967. *Management in International Perspective*. New York: Irvington.

———. 1986. "Technology Transfer: The Approach of a Dutch Multinational." *Technovation* 4: 3–15.

Pratt, Cornelius B. 1991. "Multinational Corporate Social Policy Process for Ethical Responsibility in Sub-Saharan Africa." *Journal of Business Ethics* 10(7): 527–541.

Pye, L. 1982. *Chinese Commercial Negotiating Style*. Cambridge, MA: Oelgeschlager, Gunn, & Hain.

Quaeyhaegens, John. 1988. "Technology Transfer to Korea." *International Journal of Technology Management* (Switzerland) 3(1–2): 211–217.

Quinn, James B. 1969. "Technology Transfer by Multinational Companies." *Harvard Business Review* (November-December): 147–161.

Rafii, Farchad. 1984. *Joint Ventures and Transfer of Technology: The Case of Iran*. In *Technology Crossing Borders*. Edited by Stobaugh and Wells. pp. 203–243. Boston, MA: Harvard Business School Press.

Rainforest Action Network. 1987. *Financing Ecological Destruction: The World Bank and the International Monetary Fund*. San Francisco: Rainforest Action Network.

Ramanadham, V. V. 1980. *Joint Ventures & Public Enterprises in Developing Countries*. West Hartford, CT: Kumarian.

Ranis, Gustav. 1979. "Appropriate Technology: Obstacles and Opportunities." In

Technology and Economic Development. Edited by S. M. Rosenblatt. Boulder, CO: Westview Press.

Rastogi, P. N. 1986. *Productivity, Innovation, Management & Development: A Study in the Productivity Cultures of Nations & System Renewal.* Newbury Park, CA: Sage.

Redclift, M. 1987. *Sustainable Development: Exploring the Contradictions.* New York: Methuen.

Reddy, N. Mohan, and Liming Zhao. 1990. "International Technology Transfer: A Review." *Research Policy* (Netherlands) 19(4): 285–307.

Rees, Joseph. 1988. *Reforming the Workplace: A Study of Self-Regulation in Occupational Safety.* Law in Social Context Series. Philadelphia: University of Pennsylvania Press.

Reilly, Bernard J., and Joseph A. DiAngelo. 1990. "Communication: A Cultural System of Meaning and Value." *Human Relations* 43(February): 129–140.

Reilly, David J. 1989. "Technology Transfer: Successful Only if Process Is Managed." *Manufacturing Systems* 6(4): 62–64.

Reuber, G. I., H. Crookell, M. Emerson, and G. Gallais-Hamonno. 1973. *Private Foreign Investment in Development.* Oxford, UK: Clarendon.

Ricks, David A., Brian Toyne, and Zaida Martinez. 1990. "Recent Developments in International Management Research." *Journal of Management* 16(2): 219–253.

Riddell, Robert. 1981. *Ecodevelopment.* New York: St. Martin's Press.

Roben, Donald, P. Reidenbach, and R. Eric. 1989. *Business Ethics: Where Profits Meet Value Systems.* Englewood Cliffs, NJ: Prentice-Hall.

Robinson, R. 1988. *The International Transfer of Technology.* Cambridge, MA: Ballinger.

Robinson, Richard D. 1988. *The International Transfer of Technology: Theory, Issues, and Practice.* Cambridge, MA: Ballinger.

Ronen, Simcha. 1986. *Comparative and Multinational Management.* New York: Wiley.

Rosenburg, Nathan, and Clausio Frischtak. (eds.). 1985. *International Technology Transfer: Concepts, Measures, & Comparisons.* New York: Praeger.

Royston, M. B. 1985. "Local and Multinational Corporations: Reappraising Environmental Management." *Environment* 27(January/February): 12–20, 39–43.

Royston, Michael G. 1980. "Making Pollution Prevention Pay." *The Harvard Business Review* (November-December): 6–27.

Rugman, Alan M. 1983. *Multinationals & Technology Transfer: The Canadian Experience.* Westport, CT: Greenwood.

Ruttenberg, Ruth, and Randall Hudgins. 1981. *Occupational Safety & Health in the Chemical Industry.* (2nd ed.). New York: Council for Economic Priorities.

Safarian, A. E., and Gilles Y. Bertin. 1987. *Multinationals, Governments & International Technology Transfer.* New York: St. Martin's Press.

Samli, A. C. 1985. "Technology Transfer: The General Model." In *Technology Transfer: Geographic, Economic, Cultural, and Technical Dimensions.* Edited by A. C. Samli. Westport, CT: Quorum.

Samli, A. Coskun. (ed.). 1985. *Technology Transfer: Geographic, Economic, Cultural & Technical Dimensions.* Westport, CT: Quorum.

Sathe, Vijay. 1983. "Implications of Corporate Culture: A Manager's Guide to Action." *Organizational Dynamics* 12(2): 5–23.

Satomons, W., and U. Forstner. 1988. *Environmental Management of Solid Waste.* New York: Springer-Verlag.

Savery, Lawson K., and Pamela A. Swain. 1985. "Leadership Style: Differences between Expatriates and Locals." *Leadership and Organization Development Journal* 6(4): 8–11.

Sen, Falguni, and William G. Egelhoff. 1991. "Six Years and Counting: Learning from Crisis Management at Bhopal." *Public Relations Review* 17(1): 69–83.

Seth, Vijay K. 1988. *Industrialization in India: Spatial Perspective.* New York: Advent.

Sethi, S. Prakash. 1987. "The Multinational Challenge." *New Management* 4(4): 53–55.

Shaikh, Rashid A. 1986. "The Dilemmas of Advanced Technology for the Third World." *Technology Review* 89(April): 57–64.

Shapiro, James E., et al. 1991. *Direct Investment & Joint Ventures in China: A Handbook for Corporate Negotiations.* Westport, CT: Greenwood.

Sharma, Basu. 1984. "Multinational Corporations and Industrialization in Southeast and East Asia." *Contemporary Southeast Asia* 6(2): 159–171.

Shibagaki, Kazuo, and Malcolm Trevor. 1989. *Japanese & European Management: Their International Adaptability.* New York: Columbia University Press.

Shrivastava, Paul. 1987. *Bhopal: Anatomy of a Crisis.* Cambridge, MA: Ballinger.

Shue, Henry. 1981. "Exporting Hazards." In *Boundaries: National Autonomy and Its Limits.* Edited by P. G. Brown and H. Shue. Savage, MD: Rowman and Littlefield.

Siemsen, Peter D. 1988. "Technology Transfer and Licensing in Brazil." *International Journal of Technology Management* (Switzerland) 3(1–2): 143–147.

Simai, Mihaly. 1990. *Global Power Structures: Technology & the World Economy in the Late 20th Century.* New York: Columbia University Press.

Singh, Chaitram. 1989. *Multinationals, the State, & the Management of Economic Nationalism: The Case of Trinidad.* New York: Praeger.

Singh, Joginder P., and Geert Hofstede. 1990. "Managerial Culture and Work-Related Values in India: Reply and Comment." *Organization Studies* 11(1): 75–106.

Singh, Rana K. D. N., and Premila Nazareth. 1990. "Perspectives on Foreign Investment in India: New Delhi Round Table on FDI and Technology Transfer." *CTC Reporter* (30): 17–21, 23–24, 33.

Skorpen, Erling. 1991. "Images of the Environment in Corporate America." *Journal of Business Ethics* 10(September): 687–697.

Slotkin, Richard. 1986. *The Fatal Environment: The Myth of the Frontier in the Age of Industrialization 1800–1890.* Hanover, NH: University Press of New England.

Smircich, Linda. 1983. "Concepts of Culture and Organizational Analysis." *Administrative Science Quarterly* 28(3): 339–358.

Smith, Ann C., and William A. Yodis. 1989. *Environmental Auditing Quality Management (Environmental Audit Handbook Ser.: Vol. 3).* New York: Executive Enterprise.

Smith, D. N., and L. T. Wells. 1975. *Negotiating Third World Mineral Agreements.* Cambridge, MA: Ballinger.

Smith, Glenn R., and Brian H. Kleiner. 1987. "Differences in Corporate Cultures and Their Relationship to Organizational Effectiveness." *Leadership and Organization Development Journal* 8(5): 3–9.

Sombke, Larry. 1991. *The Solution to Pollution in the Workplace*. New York: Master Media.

Southgate, Douglas D., and John F. Disinger. (eds.). 1987. *Sustainable Resource Development in the Third World (Special Studies in Natural Resources & Energy Management)*. Boulder, CO: Westview Press.

Stacey, Gary S., and W. Bradford Ashton. 1990. "A Structured Approach to Corporate Technology Strategy." *International Journal of Technology Management* (Switzerland) 5(4): 389–407.

Stewart, Charles T. 1987. *Technology Transfer & Human Factors*. New York: Free Press.

Stewart, Frances. 1979. *International Technology Transfer: Issues and Policy Options*. Washington, DC: World Bank.

Stewart, Frances, and Jeffrey James. 1982. *The Economics of New Technology in Developing Countries*. London and Boulder, CO: Frances Printer and Westview Press.

Stobaugh, Robert B. 1971. *The International Transfer of Technology in the Establishment of the Petrochemical Industry in Developing Countries*. New York: United Nations.

Stocker, Frederick. (ed.). 1987. *The Role of Executives in Controlling Pollution*. Franklin Lakes, NJ: Lincoln Spring Press.

Stockholm Group for Studies on Natural Resources Management. 1988. *Perspectives of Sustainable Development: Some Critical Issues Related to the Brundtland Report*. Stockholm: Stockholm Group for Studies on Natural Resources Management.

Stoever, William A. 1989. "Foreign Collaborations Policy in India: A Review." *Journal of Developing Areas* 23(4): 485–504.

Streeten, P. P. 1973. "The Multinational Enterprise and the Theory of Development Policy." *World Development* 1(10): 1–14.

Succar, Patricia. 1987. "International Technology Transfer: A Model of Endogenous Technological Assimilation." *Journal of Development Economics* (Netherlands) 26(2): 375–395.

Sufrin, Sidney C. 1985. *Bhopal: Its Setting, Responsibility & Challenge*. Calcutta: Asia.

Swierczek, Fredric William. 1990. "Culture and Negotiation in the Asian Context: Key Issues in the Marketing of Technology." *Journal of Managerial Psychology* (UK) 5(5): 17–24.

Tavis, Lee A. 1988. *Multinational Managers & Host Government Interactions*. South Bend, IN: University of Notre Dame.

Thakur, S. Y. 1985. *Rural Industrialization in India*. New Delhi: Sterling.

Thiry, James R. 1988. *Critical Issues in Facilities Management: Personnel Management & Development*. Alexandria, VA: Association of Physical Plant Administrators.

Tolba, M. K. 1987. *Sustainable Development: Constraints and Opportunities*. Austin, TX: Butterworth Legal Publishers.

Tomlinson, J. W. C. 1970. *The Joint Venture Process in International Business: India and Pakistan.* Cambridge, MA: MIT Press.

Travis, Lee. (ed.). 1984. *Multinational Managers & Poverty in the Third World.* South Bend, IN: University of Notre Dame.

Trotter, R., R. Clayton, Susan G. Day, and Amy E. Love. 1989. "Bhopal, India and Union Carbide: The Second Tragedy." *Journal of Business Ethics* (Netherlands) 8(6): 439–454.

Tuma, Elias H. 1987. "Technology Transfer and Economic Development: Lessons of History." *Journal of Developing Areas* 21(4): 403–427.

Turner, Barry A. 1986. "Sociological Aspects of Organizational Symbolism." *Organization Studies* 7 (2 Special Issue: Organizational Symbolism): 101–115.

Turner, R. Kerry. 1988. *Sustainable Environmental Management: Principles & Practice.* Boulder, CO: Westview Press.

United Nations Centre on Transnational Corporations. 1986. *The United Nations Code of Conduct on Transnational Corporations (UNCTC Current Studies A: No. 4).* New York: United Nations.

——. 1987. *Arrangements between Joint Venture Partners in Developing Countries.* New York: United Nations.

——. 1987. *Arrangements with Transnational Corporations: Selected Industrial Case Studies in Thailand.* Technology Acquisition under Alternative Arrangements. New York: United Nations.

——. 1987. *Transnational Corporations & Technology Transfer: Effects & Policy Issues.* New York: United Nations.

——. 1987. *Transnational Corporations in World Development, Trends & Prospects.* New York: United Nations.

United Nations Environment Program. 1984. *Industry and Environment.* Narobi: United Nations Environment Programme.

Vaghefi, M. Reza, Steven Paulson, and William Tomlinson. 1991. *International Business: Theory & Practice.* New York: Taylor & Fr..ncis.

Valenti, Michael. 1991. "Appropriate Technology: Designing to Fit Local Culture." *Mechanical Engineering* 113(6): 64–69.

Vernon, Raymond. 1971. *Sovereignty at Bay: The Multinational Spread of U.S. Enterprises.* New York: Basic.

——. 1975. *Multinational Enterprise in Developing Countries: Analysis of National Policies.* New York: United Nations Industrial Development Organization.

Viljoen, John. 1987. "Successful Post Merger Management and Corporate Culture." *Management and Labour Studies* 12(2): 63–69.

Villamil, J. J. 1979. *Transnational Capitalism and National Development.* Atlantic Highlands, NJ: Humanities Press.

Walter, I., and J. L. Ugelow. 1979. "Environmental Problems in Developing Countries." *Ambio* 8: 102–109.

Wang, Charleston C. 1988. *How to Manage Workplace Derived Hazards & Avoid Liability.* Park Ridge, NJ: Noyes.

Watkins, William M. 1990. *Business Aspects of Technology Transfer: Marketing & Acquisition.* Park Ridge, NJ: Noyes.

Weir, David. 1987. *The Bhopal Syndrome: Pesticides, Environment, and Health.* San Francisco: Sierra Club.

Weiss, Bernard, and Thomas W. Clarkson. 1986. "Toxic Chemical Disasters and the Implications of Bhopal for Technology Transfer." *The Milbank Quarterly* 64: 216–240.

Weiss, Joseph, and Andre Delbecq. 1987. "High Technology Cultures and Management: Silicon Valley and Route 128." *Group and Organization Studies* 12(1): 39–54.

World Bank. 1984. *Environment and Development.* Washington, DC: World Bank.

——. 1987. *Environment, Growth and Development.* Washington, DC: World Bank.

——. 1987. *Conable Announces New Steps to Protect Environment in Developing Countries.* Washington, DC: World Bank.

——. 1989. *Striking a Balance: The Environmental Challenge of Development.* Washington, DC: World Bank.

World Commission on Environment and Development. 1987. *Our Common Future.* New York: Oxford University Press.

Index

ABOUT THE AUTHORS

HALINA SZEJNWALD BROWN is an Associate Professor at Clark University and is associated with the Center for Technology, Environment, and Development.

PATRICK DERR holds a Ph.D. from Notre Dame University.

ORTWIN RENN holds a Ph.D. from the University of Colon.

ALLEN L. WHITE is Director, Risk Analysis Group, Tellus Institute, Boston, and Senior Research Associate at CENTED.

JEANNE X. KASPERSON is Research Librarian for the George Perkins Marsh Institute at Clark University and Senior Research Associate at the World Hunger Program at Brown University.

ROGER E. KASPERSON is Professor of Government and Geography and Senior Researcher at the George Perkins Marsh Institute at Clark University.